Practical Planning Law

Practical Planning Law

A Handbook for Planners, Architects and Surveyors

J.F. Garner

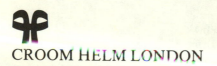
CROOM HELM LONDON

© 1981 J.F. Garner
Croom Helm Ltd, 2-10 St John's Road, London SW11

British Library Cataloguing in Publication Data

Garner, J.F.
   Practical Planning Law.
    1. Regional planning — law and legislation — England
    2. Zoning Law — England
    3. City planning and redevelopment law — England
   I. Title
   344.2064'5   KD1125

ISBN 0-7099-1106-8
ISBN 0-7099-1107-6 Pbk

Printed and bound in Great Britain by
Biddles Ltd, Guildford and King's Lynn

Contents

Preface

This book is not intended to be a detailed exposition of all the many finer points of English land use law.[1] It is intended as a guide for practising and student planners, architects and surveyors and therefore some explanation of our legal system and of planning administration has been included in the early chapters. The emphasis is perforce on the Town and Country Planning Act 1971 and its subsequent amendments (including the Local Government, Land and Planning Act 1980), and it has been necessary to deal with many of the sections of that Act in some detail. Relevant case law, especially on such subjects as the meaning of 'development' is also considered and so are the theories of land use planning, its ideologies (to borrow Professor McAuslan's term) and the problems of land value as affected by planning legislation. The niceties of more abstruse legal problems are only touched on and no attempt has been made at more than a summary treatment of public health and housing controls.

The author therefore makes no apology for the appearance of a new book on planning law; it is hoped that this volume will be seen as a new approach to what has become an established subject of great practical importance, which is also worthy of serious academic study. The book is based on lectures the author has given in the Institute of Planning Studies at the University of Nottingham over nearly 20 years, and he has been greatly encouraged by the enthusiasm for the subject shown by students from various disciplines and differing cultures. He would also like to express his thanks to Professor G.B. Dix, Lever Professor of Civic Design in the University of Liverpool, who was largely responsible for the text seeing the light of day.

It is intended that the law should be stated as it stood on 1 April 1981, but it is assumed that the Wildlife and Countryside Bill 1981 has come into force.

J.F. Garner
Nottingham

Note

1. For this, refer to the *Encyclopaedia of Planning Law and Practice;* see Bibliography, p.241.

Abbreviations

Act of 1947) Act of 1962) Act of 1968) Act of 1971)	The Town and Country Planning Acts of these dates
Act of 1980	The Local Government Land and Planning Act 1980
JPL	Journal of Planning and Environment Law
LGA	The Local Government Act (of 1972 or 1974, as the case may be)
DoE	Department of the Environment
GDO	The Town and Country Planning General Development Order, 1977 (SI 1977 No. 289) as amended by SI 1980 No. 1946 and SI 1981 No. 245
Secretary of State	The Secretary of State for the Environment *or* for Wales (as appropriate), unless otherwise indicated
Sched.	Schedule [of a statute]

Practical Planning Law

I Introduction: the Need for Law

1. General Observations

Law is a piece of social machinery; it exists to be used by those persons who are concerned with changing or preserving our physical and social environment, such as the planners, the surveyors, the architects and the highway engineers. Without law no amount of work at the drawing board could ever achieve anything in reality. The machinery of the law has to be put in motion so as to enable a local authority or a government department to hire staff, to purchase premises, or to acquire land. Planning authorities in pursuit of their objectives also have to interfere in many different ways with private land ownership. A development plan outlining the optimum use of land for the future is meaningless if there is no machinery available that will enable public authorities to implement the plan and to control development that might otherwise take place contrary to the proposals of the plan. It is the law that provides this machinery, that requires planning permission to be obtained before development takes place, and that lays down sanctions (eventually even of imprisonment) if its procedures and dictates are not obeyed.

In England and Wales[1] the law consists of a series of rules recognised and applied by the courts as law, emanating principally from Parliament. Parliament[2] in our legal system is supreme; it can do anything. It can change the succession to the throne,[3] change the religion of the country,[4] and even change its own mind.[5] Everything that Parliament declares to be law will be recognised by the courts as law, however sensible or however absurd; but of course it is for the courts to tell us what statutes — Acts of Parliament — mean, and how they are to be applied to particular situations.[6]

As Parliament is supreme, so no other body or authority in the country is or could be supreme. A Minister of the Crown can advise lesser authorities, but he, like they, is subject to the law and he cannot change the law (or even explain it in any authoritative manner). Therefore if he makes regulations under powers given to him by Parliament,[7] he must not overstep those powers. If regulations made

11

by a Minister — under statutory powers — in some manner exceed the powers given by Parliament, they will be *ultra vires*[8], and therefore of no effect in law. Local authorities also are restricted by the same principle. When they are given power by Parliament (Section 29(1) of the Act of 1971) to grant or refuse planning permission for some proposed development, they must make their decision on planning grounds and on planning grounds alone, because Parliament has entrusted them to make such a decision in a planning Act, to be exercised in a planning context.[9]

However, in spite of what has already been said, the courts also have a part to play; in strict theory they cannot make law (that is exclusively, as we have said, a matter for Parliament), but they can declare what the law is. In a field where Parliament has not yet spoken, the courts must declare the law in certain and precise terms. The courts also every day are required in cases brought before them to apply the words of statute law to particular situations. Thus, the exact meaning of the definition of 'development' contained in Section 22(1) of the Act of 1971 has been the subject of many cases in the courts, and as a consequence we know a great deal more about the definition and its application in practice, than has been told us precisely by Parliament.[10] This is because of the doctrine of precedent. Once a superior court has ruled on a question of law, this may become a precedent, which should be followed when the *same* question arises in a subsequent case before another court of the same or a lower status.[11]

How then is the law administered? Made by the legislature (Parliament), interpreted and applied by the judiciary (the courts), it is put into operation by the executive; at the central level, by the Ministers and the cabinet, at the local level, by local authorities. It is therefore now appropriate to outline the organs and functions of the executive, first at the central level and then at the local level.

2. Central Government

The principal Minister of the Crown in the planning and land use field is the Secretary of State for the Environment. In Wales his functions are performed by the Secretary of State for Wales.[12] He exercises the following functions, mainly of a supervisory character over the functions of local authorities:

(1) consideration and approval of development plans made by local authorities;

(2) confirmation of compulsory purchase orders submitted by local authorities; when the order is opposed by a land owner or other interested body, this will involve the holding of a local inquiry;

(3) determining appeals against refusal or conditions imposed in, planning permission and enforcement notices etc., made or served by local authorities (again involving the holding of a local inquiry);

(4) making of grants to local authorities in respect of particular planning projects, such as the reclamation of derelict land;[13]

(5) making regulations or orders, etc.,[14] prescribing detailed legal provisions, where he has been authorised so to act by statute.

These functions are all conferred on the Secretary of State by Act of Parliament (the list is not complete; only the most important in practice have been mentioned). In addition, the Secretary of State is the member of the Government responsible for introducing new legislation in Parliament, as and when this may be considered necessary. He will also from time to time give advice to local authorities in the form of Circulars (or perhaps by individual letters), advising them of the effect of new legislation or regulations, and assisting them on details of administration, in particular as to central government policy (for example, he may give guidance as to the manner in which an application for a government grant in aid of some project should be submitted). None of these Circulars or other forms of advice can, however, have any legal effect, except in so far as they may have been issued in pursuance of some express authority contained in a statute. Nevertheless, advice of this kind is generally heeded by local authorities, unless there may be some difference of political party affiliation as between the centre and the local authority.

Circulars giving guidance on planning (as distinct from legal) matters may be of considerable significance, as giving an indication as to how the Secretary of State is likely to decide a matter arising on an appeal to him against a refusal of planning permission. For example, a former Minister has advised that the number of petrol filling stations on main roads should be restricted, that where possible one on either side of a main road should be encouraged, and that the brand or brands of petrol offered for sale at a particular station is not a relevant planning consideration. Advice of this kind is obviously of great importance to prospective developers. Advice is also given from time to time about the consultation that a planning authority should undertake when considering development applications with other relevant bodies, such as the Department of Transport or other highway authority, or the water authority. When considering whether to declare conservation areas, the local authority has been advised to consult widely with appropriate local pressure groups, such as a civic or other amenity society.

3. Local Government

Land use planning in England and Wales is, however, primarily a local function. This does not mean that, as in the United States, each local authority formulates its own planning law and master plan, with little co-ordination between authorities. The law in this country is uniform and contained principally in a single statute, the Act of 1971, which is of universal application. Nevertheless, the initiative, within this legal framework set by Parliament, and subject to a certain measure of supervision from the Secretary of State,[15] rests with the local authorities that prepare the development plans, which are designed to outline the optimum land use for the future of their areas. It is also the local authorities that exercise the detailed functions of development control, acting again within the framework of the law, and having regard to the provisions of the development plan and other material considerations. Planning authorities grant or refuse planning permission, decide to take enforcement action in appropriate cases, and administer subsidiary controls over buildings of historic or architectural interest, over trees and woodlands, over the display of advertisements, and over the control of waste land.[16]

It is therefore the *local* authorities, at both county and district level,[17] that exercise the essential part of the executive function in land use planning. The Land Commission Act of 1967, which was repealed in 1970, had introduced a third type of agency, the Land Commission, which was given powers of compulsory purchase for planning purposes. This concept was repeated in the Community Land Act 1975, in Wales alone, where some of the land acquisition powers elsewhere exercisable by local authorities, were vested in a special public corporation known as the Land Authority for Wales. The Community Land Act also has now been repealed, but the Land Authority for Wales has been re-constituted with somewhat different powers; this body is discussed further in Chapter 4.

4. Geographical Extent

The English common law, and the statutes that we shall have to consider in this book (and the Town and Country Planning Act 1971 and subsequent amendments in particular) apply only to England and Wales, to the exclusion of Scotland,[18] Northern Ireland, the Isle of Man and the Channel Islands. England and Wales is for most purposes in the eyes of the law a single jurisdiction, where the law and the court system is the same throughout, although there are a few variants in respect of Wales (for example, 'parishes' are known as 'communities' in Wales). The Act of 1971 applies to the Isles of Scilly with minor modifications made by the Secretary of State under section 269 of that Act.[19]

The administration of the Act of 1971 is also modified somewhat in relation to the area of Greater London, but this will not be discussed in detail.

5. Conclusion

In this book we are concerned with the law relating to land use. This highly specialised and complicated piece of machinery has a vitally important part to play under modern conditions. Land is a finite resource, and we cannot afford to waste it or to despoil it with avoidable pollution. The law is the most valuable tool available to prevent waste and pollution; our land use controls highly complex as they are, must be understood so that they may be used effectively to secure the environment against the ravages of man, for future generations. Land use controls can anticipate and prevent waste and pollution if they are used with care and forethought. When they fail or are used improperly we must turn to the law again and attempt to stop further harm to our rivers, our atmosphere, and our land.

Notes

1. This book is not concerned with the law of Scotland. Basic principles of the law in Scotland are not always the same as they are in England, as Scots law has a close relationship in origin with continental law. The Act of 1971 does not apply to Scotland, although that country has its own Town and Country Planning Acts which are very similar to the English Acts.

2. I.e. Her Majesty the Queen, the House of Lords and the House of Commons, acting in concert.

3. A recent example of this was HM Act of Abdication Act 1936, whereby any children of His Majesty King Edward VIII were, on his abdication, excluded from the succession to the throne.

4. Act of Supremacy 1558.

5. See *Ellen Street Estates Ltd* v. *Minister of Health* [1934] 1 KB 590.

6. *See* Chapter 2, p.25.

7. For example, to make a Use Classes Order, expanding the statutory definition of 'development': 1971 Act, section 22(2) (f).

8. 'Beyond the powers'. This is a very important fundamental principle of the law, flowing naturally from the doctrine of Parliamentary sovereignty.

9. This is discussed further in Chapter 2, p.27.

10. Chapter 8, p.96.

11. Chapter 2, p.19.

12. Before 1970 the Secretary of State for the Environment was known as the Minister of Housing and Local Government; before 1950 as the Minister of Health, and before 1919 such central government functions as then existed, were carried out by the Local Government Board.

13. Under s.9 of the Local Government Act 1966, as amended by the Act of 1980, s.117.

14. For example, the Town and Country Planning (Use Classes) Order 1972, made under s.22(2) (f) of the Act of 1971.

15. Exercised through the functions of the Secretary of State as described above.

16. See Chapter 15, p.163.

17. Further explained in Chapter 4, p.43.

18. As to Scotland, see note 1, above.

19. Town and Country Planning (Isles of Scilly) Order 1973, SI 1973 No. 239.

2　The Nature of Law

1. What is Law?

This is a difficult question to answer; it may perhaps be said that law in a given society consists of a series of rules for the ordering of that society, and in that sense law must be distinguished from the rules of nature such as the 'law' of gravity or 'Boyle's law'. In the English system law consists of two principal kinds; the common law and statute law. Common law is the law that has existed in this country from time immemorial; it has been developed through innumerable decisions of the courts. The common law has never been written down in an authoritative or orderly form; it is sometimes said to exist only *in gremio judicis,* in the bosom of the judge.

When a case comes before a court the judge must decide it. He first finds what are the correct facts, and then applies the existing rules of law to those facts; as the situation may never have arisen before precisely in that form, he must then for the first time declare what the law is in that particular factual situation. He will first look for any law contained in an Act of Parliament; if there is none relevant to the case before him he must look for a decision in a previous similar case. His decision in effect, makes new law (although it is always claimed that he is *declaring* what the law is, not *making* it), and that decision will in turn (subject to what is said below) become a *precedent,* or rule of law to be followed in future cases. In this way, many of our fundamental principles of law have been developed, including such elementary everyday rules as the law relating to the making of a contract, or the civil wrongs ('torts') of nuisance and of negligence, and even the definition of serious crimes such as murder and rape. Of course these rules developed through the common law by the system of precedent, are subject to any new or additional law made by Parliament. This is because, as we have seen in Chapter 1, Parliament is supreme and Parliament can always change the law and override decisions of the court. Although the common law defines murder, statute law has abolished the death penalty, and the common law knows nothing of aeroplanes or motor cars, or of town and country planning (although it is pefectly well acquainted with the basic rights and duties of a landowner, as we shall see) nor is the common law aware of all the

ramifications of the modern Welfare State. Law on these subjects —
and many others — has become the concern of Parliament. But even
here the common law cannot be totally excluded. The courts have to
solve problems arising from the application of Acts of Parliament; the
courts must tell us what the words of a statute mean, and how they are
to be applied in particular factual situations (often situations not
thought of in advance by the Parliament draftsman). So rules of
statutory interpretation enacted by Parliament have been developed
by the courts and these rules become encrusted on top of a statute.
Although 'development' for the purposes of the 1971 Act is defined by
s.22(1) to include *(inter alia)*, the 'making of a material change of use' of
land, we did not really know what was meant by 'development' until
the courts had applied and explained for us what was a 'material'
change of use of the land. For example, is it a material change of use to
bring an egg-vending machine on to a petrol filling station forecourt?[1]

2. What is the Purpose of Planning Law?

In his interesting book *The Ideologies of Planning Law*, Professor
McAuslan examines the underlying objectives of the planning
legislation. He identifies three ideologies which are at times in conflict.
These are the protection of the private interests of landowners, the
protection of the public interest, and the furtherance of the cause of
public participation in decision-making. Certainly the common law,
'private', controls over land use discussed in Chapter 3, are exclusively
concerned with the protection of private interests, while the later
legislation is primarily concerned with the public interest as expressed
by the decisions of the elected members of local planning authority and
at central (and final) level, of the Secretary of State, responsible to
Parliament. As explained in Chapter 12, the law does go some way to
ensure a measure of public participation by requiring consultation and
publication of advertisements in some contexts, and also by the
maintenance of the planning register. Sir Desmond Heap has argued[2]
that there is public participation in every decision, as the elected
representatives of 'the people' are responsible for every decision taken
by or on behalf of the local planning authority. Moreover, although
private interests may and sometimes must, be overridden in the public
interest, the planning authority are liable to be criticised by the
Commissioner for Local Administration if they ride roughshod over
private interests. The rules of natural justice that must be observed at

an inquiry are rules of the common law, designed to protect the interests of the individual.

These three ideologies of Professor McAuslan therefore can be seen to react upon one another: whichever is considered to be the most significant, it is clear that these three can be accepted as the principal motives behind the legal machinery. But it remains true that without the law — and under modern conditions this really means legislation — the objectives of the 'planners' — elected representatives, the professionally qualified officials, and the various pressure groups and environmentalists — would all be futile. Without planning law, planning becomes the exclusive toy of the private landowner, exercised in a state of anarchy.

We ought to ask ourselves another question; what is the 'public interest'? To preserve the environment, to make roads for the motorist, to safeguard employment, to plan schools and open spaces, to reserve national parks? Many of these objectives again may conflict.

Planning control in England and Wales is all-embracing; unlike the law of most European countries it applies to changes of use, and not only to the development of open land. It is also uniformly administered throughout the country; there are only minor variations (the Special Development Orders for Limestone areas for example, and a few variations for London) and the 1971 Act applies everywhere.

Having considered in outline the nature and purpose of law, we must consider in some detail the two branches of the law in the English system, the common law and statute law.

3. The Constituents of the Law: The Common Law

When does a decision of a court become a precedent — when does a decision enunciate or declare a principle of law that must be followed in future cases? The answer to this question depends on two separate factors, (1) the nature of the decision itself, and (2) the status of the two courts concerned; the court making the decision, and the court applying that decision in a subsequent case.

The Nature of the Decision

The binding effect of a decision — the 'precedent' — is confined to the law applied to the particular situation before the court making the initial decision. The precedent consists of the principle of law that was the deciding or principal factor in the case, but it will be binding for future cases only when the facts that were treated by the court as being *material,* are also material in the second case. By 'material' here is meant essential to the particular situation.

Thus, in *Coleshill*[3] the court was asked to determine whether the demolition of blast walls round a former explosives factory situated in the green belt near Birmingham, was a 'building, mining, engineering or other operation' within the definition of 'development' in s.22(1) of the 1971 Act. Having discounted the argument that 'other operations' should be construed restrictively,[4] the court (the House of Lords on appeal) decided that, as this operation would affect the amenities of the neighbourhood, there was development. The fact that the site was in the green belt, and was near Birmingham and that there had previously been an explosives factory, were all facts in the case, but none of these was material for the decision. What was material to the decision was the fact that the blast walls had become grown over with grass and had come to look attractive. The proposed demolition would spoil the amenities of the site. Therefore the case becomes a precedent and must be followed whenever in a future case some feature is to be removed from the landscape in circumstances where that removal would seriously affect the amenities of the neighbourhood. In those circumstances, there is development. The binding effect of the case is closely confined to the material facts essential to the original decision.

Again, when a young man took his girlfriend out one summer day in 1931, they stopped at a café and he bought her some ginger beer in an opaque earthenware bottle.[5] She poured some of the liquid into a glass and drank it with apparent enjoyment. Then she poured out the remainder of the liquid and out came the remains of a decomposed snail. She became ill as a consequence, and sued the manufacturer for damages. She did not sue the proprietor of the café because he could not have known anything about the snail. The manufacturer was held to be liable. How far was this decision a precedent? What were the material facts?

It was clearly not material that the liquid was ginger beer and not lemonade, or that the foreign object was a decomposed snail, or that the plaintiff was a young lady and not an elderly man. It was, however, material that there had been no opportunity of examining this sealed opaque bottle from the time it left the manufacturer's premises until it was opened for the plaintiff. Therefore the case established the principle that a manufacturer will be liable for his act of negligence if that act causes harm to some plaintiff whom he ought reasonably to have had in contemplation (here the eventual consumer of the ginger beer) in circumstances where there is no opportunity for the article in question to be examined.

Subsequently this same principle has been extended in later cases. Thus, in *Malfroot* v. *Noxall*[6] it was held that the fact that the defendant was a manufacturer was not material to the decision in the ginger beer case; the principle would apply equally if the defendant was a repairer. And so, for example, the repairer of a motor cycle and side-car was liable when one wheel came off while the plaintiff passenger was being driven away from the defendant's garage. Subsequently, the principle has even been applied to false or misleading statements made by a defendant on which a plaintiff relies, to his disadvantage.[7] Thus, suppose a prospective developer of land asks a local planning officer whether planning permission is required for development of that land, and he is informed that permission is not necessary. Relying on that statement the developer buys the land. Then he finds that the statement was untrue, and that he cannot obtain planning permission. Provided he can prove that the planning officer was negligent in making the statement, the developer will be able to sue him (and his employer, the local authority) in damages — on the basis of the precedent in the ginger beer case.

The Status of the Court

Only decisions of the higher courts can form precedents for future cases. Although a bench of magistrates may — and usually will — wish to follow a consistent line in making their decisions, they are not legally obliged to do so, nor is a county court judge bound to follow his own previous decisions, or the decisions of another county court judge. The decisions of the higher courts are however, in the sense explained above, binding on the courts below them.

Thus, in the following table of courts each level in the hierarchy is bound by decisions of the court of a higher level. High Court judges are bound by the decisions of other High Court judges in previous cases, and the Court of Appeal is bound by its own previous decisions. The House of Lords similarly is normally bound by its own previous decisions, but it is entitled to depart from an earlier decision which it is now satisfied was clearly wrong in principle;[8] but the House would do this only in an exceptional case.

But in all these instances, it is only the *ratio decidendi* (the reason for the decision) that is binding on the inferior subsequent court, when the material facts are the same, or rather when the second court finds that the material facts in the second case are the same as the facts that were treated as being material by the court in the earlier case. This leaves plenty of room in argument for the second court to *distinguish* their case from the facts in the earlier case. Also, the second court may find that some remarks about the law made in the earlier case were not relevant for the purposes of that decision; these remarks are known as *obiter dicta* (remarks made by the way), and they will not be part of the *ratio decidendi,* and so not be binding as a precedent on the second court.

This complex but highly logical system gives certainty to the law, and also flexibility; as an infinity of new facts and circumstances may arise, so the existing law can be adapted and applied to suit new situations. The law of liability for accidents on the highway, developed by the courts for the horse and buggy age of the eighteenth and nineteenth centuries were suitably adjusted by judicial decision to meet the age of the motor car and the jet plane. The criminal offence of driving furiously, developed in the 1840s can be applied to bicycles, which were not invented until some 50 years later.

(A) THE HIERARCHY OF CIVIL COURTS a

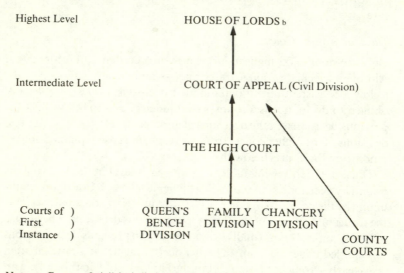

Highest Level   HOUSE OF LORDS b

Intermediate Level   COURT OF APPEAL (Civil Division)

                                 THE HIGH COURT

Courts of)   QUEEN'S   FAMILY   CHANCERY
First   )   BENCH   DIVISION DIVISION
Instance   )   DIVISION
                                                COUNTY
                                                COURTS

Notes a. Courts of civil jurisdiction, having power to decide cases between private individuals, or in cases where an individual is suing the State or a local authority for some remedy such as damages.

b. The House of Lords, sitting as a court of law, with only judges (the 'Lords of Appeal in Ordinary' or 'Law Lords') present, but which is technically also part of the legislature.

Arrows indicate that there is a right of appeal from the lower to the higher court. A civil case will start before *either* the county court *or* the High Court according to the nature of the case and the amount of money involved.

(B) THE HIERARCHY OF CRIMINAL COURTS a

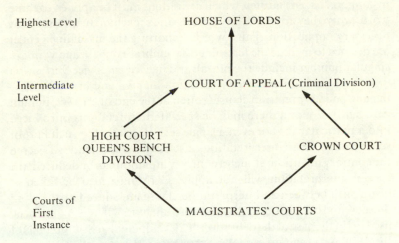

Highest Level   HOUSE OF LORDS

Intermediate Level   COURT OF APPEAL (Criminal Division)

HIGH COURT QUEEN'S BENCH DIVISION   CROWN COURT

Courts of First Instance   MAGISTRATES' COURTS

Note a. Some of these courts, it should be noted, appear also on the 'civil' diagram; as before *arrows* indicate a right of appeal. The right of appeal from the magistrates to the Queen's Bench Division is limited to points of law, 'by case stated'.

Courts of *criminal* jurisdiction can determine only cases alleging the commission of a *crime*, where the accused is charged with an offence against the State (murder, theft, or felling a tree contrary to a tree preservation order, etc.), for which he may be subject to a penalty (a fine or perhaps a sentence of imprisonment or Borstal training etc.). *All* crimes are tried at first instance before the magistrates; if a *prima facie* case is there made out against the accused, he will either be sent for trial before the local crown court (if the charge is a serious one), or the whole case will be heard and determined by the magistrates.

Now we must turn to consider the other form of law.

4. The Constituents of the Law: II Statute

When reading an Act of Parliament such as the Act of 1971 for the first time, one should start by glancing through the list of sections and Parts, so as to appreciate what topics are dealt with and in what order.

An English statute is a very precisely drafted piece of prose; each sentence is intended to be capable of having only one meaning, but it may not always be easy to ascertain what is that meaning. In this difficult task of statutory interpretation, there are a few guides, some provided by Parliament itself, and others have been worked out by the Courts.

Statutory Rules of Interpretation

The Interpretation Act 1978 gives definitions to some words or phrases in common use in statutes, which definitions must be applied to those words when they appear in any statute, unless excluded expressly or by necessary implication. Thus, words importing the masculine gender are deemed to include the feminine ('he' embraces 'she'), and words of singular number include the plural; and in each case, vice-versa.

Then the statute under consideration may — and usually will — include an interpretation clause[9] (often at the end of the Act, but not necessarily so), and there may be special interpretations introduced into a particular Part or even a single section relating to such Part or section only. These interpretations also are normally made subject to the contrary intention. If such a contrary intention can be deduced, the special interpretation will not apply. Care must also be taken to distinguish between an interpretation clause introduced by the word 'means', and one introduced by the word 'includes'. If 'means' has been used (as in the case of the definition of 'development' in section 22(1) of the 1971 Act), one must make a straight translation of the word so defined into the definition given. There is therefore no room for any ordinary meaning of the word 'development' in the 1971 Act; it can only mean what section 22(1) says it means (and this definition applies to every instance in the Act where 'development' appears).

On the other hand, if the interpretation of the word or phrase (such as 'engineering operations' in s.290 of the 1971 Act) is introduced by the word 'includes', this has the effect of expanding the ordinary meaning of the word so defined. Not only does the word bear the special meaning given to it by the interpretation clause, but it also retains any meaning that can reasonably be ascribed to it in ordinary everyday usage.

The reader must also ensure that the statutory provision in question is in legal operation. An Act of Parliament will normally acquire that status on the day when Royal Assent is given; and this date will appear in the Queen's Printer's copy of the Act immediately after the Preamble. But there may be a section — or sections — in the Act providing that the Act (or specified parts of the Act) shall not come into force until a day or days to be appointed by a Minister by subordinate legislation made under powers given in the Act.

This leads us to another feature of English legislation. The Act of Parliament itself is often an outline or skeleton, setting out only the principles of policy laid down by Parliament. The detail in such a case is left to be filled in by a Minister by regulations or orders made by him under authority given to him by the statute. In so far as he is using a power so given to him by Parliament he is making law, and his regulations[10] are just as much law as are the sections of the Act of Parliament itself. But he may not exceed those powers, and if he purports to make regulations that have not been so authorised, those regulations will to that extent be *ultra vires* (beyond the powers) and be void.[11]

Therefore the Town and Country Planning General Development Order 1977,[12] which provides for a number of classes of development in respect of which planning permission is to be deemed to have been granted, is part of the law, because it has been made by the Secretary of State for the Environment under powers given to him to do just that, under section 24(1), of the 1971 Act.

Circulars issued by the same Secretary of State, giving advice to local authorities on planning or other matters, are, however, not part of the law, as they have not been issued under any express power conferred on the Secretary of State in any Act of Parliament. They remain merely advice and are of no legal effect.

'Court' Rules of Interpretation

In addition, the courts have evolved a number of rules through the doctrine of precedent, which may be applied so as to assist in statute law interpretation, and which may be thought of as part of the common law.

In the first place, the *golden rule,* to be applied whenever possible, is that Parliament meant precisely what it said. Therefore (for example), to 'cut or lop' trees would not include a power to *top* them,[13] and a power given to a local authority to provide baths and wash-houses at the expense of the rates, did not include a power to provide a municipal laundry.[14] What Parliament has said to be law, is law, however unpleasant or unexpected may be the result. Therefore, when Parliament said in 1707 that the descendants of the Electress Sophia of Hanover (the mother of King George I) were to be British subjects, Prince Ernst Augustus of Hanover was entitled to claim British nationality in 1957, simply by proving that he was a descendant of Electress Sophia, although he had never been to Britain and had no real connections with this country.[15]

Nevertheless, words in a statute are to be understood in context, and given a meaning which agrees with the general purpose or 'intendment' of the Act in which they are to be found. Although section 29(1) of the 1971 Act allows a planning authority, when granting planning permission, to impose 'such conditions as it thinks fit', those conditions must relate to *planning* matters (and not, for example, purport to fix rents for caravans brought onto a site[16]) because the power to impose conditions is contained in a statute concerned exclusively with planning.

The courts also apply a few more technical rules of interpretation. In particular, there is the *ejusdem generis* rule. Where words of a general meaning are preceded by a group of words having a common meaning or significance which form a class of words, the general words are to be interpreted restrictively, in the same sense as the class of words that preceded them. Thus, in the expression, 'arms, ammunition, gunpowder or any other stores', the general words 'other stores' were construed restrictively as referring only to stores of a warlike kind.[17] When the Poole Corporation were given powers by statute to close streets in the town 'in all times of public procession, rejoicing or illuminations, and in any other case when the streets are thronged or liable to be obstructed', the words 'in any other case, etc.' were held not to be wide enough to cover the entire holiday season when the streets of Poole were crowded with tourists. Those words had to be construed restrictively in the light of the class of 'rejoicing', etc.[18] Nevertheless, the words 'building, mining, and engineering operations', which appears in the definition of 'development' in section 22(1) of the 1971 Act, do not amount to a class (because they are not sufficiently related to have a common significance) and therefore the general words 'or other operations', which follow them in the definition, are *not* to be construed restrictively, in the sense of operations *like* building, mining or engineering. 'Other operations' must therefore be construed generally, but in the sense of operations having a *planning* effect, as the phrase appears in a planning statute.[19]

The court will also, where appropriate, presume that Parliament intended its pronouncements to be understood in a certain way, unless Parliament has expressly provided to the contrary. Thus, it will be presumed that:

(a) Any discretionary power conferred on a government agency would not be exercised unreasonably. Therefore a condition in a planning permission requiring the developer to provide an estate road for the benefit of future potential developers in the neighbourhood was struck down as being unreasonable.[20] If the local authority had considered the provision of a new highway was necessary, then they should have acquired the necessary land from the developers and paid them compensation. They could not seek to achieve the same result in an unreasonable manner without paying compensation.

(b) Where the exercise of discretionary power by a governing agency affects an individual's employment, livelihood or property, the principles of natural justice must be observed. This means that the individual must be given the opportunity of a fair hearing before an unbiased judge. These principles were applied in a case where a market stallholder had his licence to trade taken away by the local authority as the result of an incident when the stallholder had urinated in public and, when reprimanded, had cheeked the market superintendent. The order cancelling his licence was quashed by the Court of Appeal, when it was established that the decision had been taken at a Committee meeting attended by the market superintendent; the stallholder had not been heard before an unbiased judge.[21]

This principle is most commonly raised in planning practice in connection with the conduct of an inquiry held into an appeal against a refusal of planning permission. Perhaps the inspector had refused the appellant permission to cross-examine a witness called by the planning authority,[22] or perhaps he had taken into account in formulating his report, some evidence that had not been placed before the parties at the inquiry.[23] The appellant in such a case must, as was said by one of the judges in a case before the House of Lords, 'have a fair crack of the whip'.[24]

(c) Other presumptions of less practical importance include the principle that no man is to be found guilty of a criminal offence until the case has been proved against him beyond all reasonable doubt. Therefore an individual charged with a statutory offence is entitled to strict proof of all the necessary ingredients of the particular offence. Thus, if a defendant is charged with failing to comply with the requirements of an enforcement notice, the prosecution must prove that the notice was duly authorised by the planning authority, that it was properly served, and that it complied with the requirements of the statute,[25] in addition to proving the essential facts as to the defendant's conduct, etc.

Other presumptions are that Parliament did not intend the words of the statute to lead to a ridiculous situation,[26] that it did not intend the statute to have retrospective effect, and that Parliament did not intend an effect that would be contrary to the terms of an international treaty to which the UK was a party.[27]

Further, when interpreting a statute, the court is not entitled to look at speeches made in the Houses of Parliament when the Bill that eventually became the statute, was under consideration. The court is not concerned with what the legislators *intended* to say, but only with what the legislator has said in the final form of the statute. This rule is contrary to the one generally accepted in continental courts, where the statute is construed according to its general purpose and the intention of the legislature, which may be deduced from the *travaux préparatoires,* such as the record of the Parliamentary proceedings.

English statutes are construed grammatically, each sentence, as a general rule, being considered in isolation, according to its ordinary meaning within the general context of the statute. There is also a firm rule that side notes and sub-headings are to be disregarded in interpreting the Act, as they are not part of the statute.

5. Subordinate Legislation

Because Parliament is invariably busy with the affairs of the nation, it cannot often afford to become preoccupied with detail. Moreover, circumstances change, unforeseen situations arise, and from time to time it may be desirable to carry out experiments in administration or government. For these and other reasons, Parliament is often content to confine itself to settling the general principles of legislation, leaving details to be determined by the appropriate government department (a Minister of the Crown) on its behalf. As we have seen Parliament may have entrusted the power of bringing an Act into operation to a Minister. Regulations may be required to specify the form of a notice that is to be used, the time within which an appeal is to be brought, the contents of a register, or the precise list of operations for which express planning permission is not to be required; all these matters are examples where Parliament in the 1971 Act has permitted the Secretary of State to make regulations filling in those details. Provided the Secretary of State keeps within the powers and duties so delegated to him by Parliament, the regulations he makes will be part of the law of the land in the same sense that the Act of Parliament is itself part of that law.

Regulations, orders, etc. so made under Parliamentary authority, must be read as if they formed part of the parent statute, and any definitions appearing in the statute (e.g. of 'development') will equally apply to those same expressions where they appear in the regulations, except insofar as they may be expressly excluded.[28] The courts cannot question the validity of subordinate legislation, any more than they can question the validity of a statute, except insofar as the subordinate legislation may exceed the powers conferred by the statute.

These remarks apply to all normal types of subordinate legislation made by Ministers of the Crown. However, local authorities and certain special bodies, such as British Rail and the National Trust, may be empowered by Parliament to make a special form of subordinate legislation, known as by-laws (or 'local', or 'town' laws). Such a power, to make by-laws for the good rule and government of their area, may be made by a local authority, under section 236 of the Local Government Act 1972. This form of subordinate legislation needs confirmation by a central government department before it acquires legal validity and it is also subject to questioning before the courts, not only on the ground (if this can be established) that it is *ultra vires,* but also if it can be shown to be *unreasonable* in operation.[29] Until recently, local authorities could make by-laws regulating the siting of buildings in new streets (Highways Act 1959, s.159), but this power has been withdrawn (Local Government, Land and Planning Act 1980), and by-laws will not often be met within the context of planning law.

Most forms (but *not* by-laws) of subordinate legislation are made by Ministers in the form of statutory instruments, in an annual series published by HM Stationery Office, and cited by year and number, and also by title[30] (e.g. the Town and Country Planning General Development Order 1977, SI 1977 No. 289).

6. The European Communities

Since the accession of the United Kingdom to the European Communities in 1972, the law of the EEC is part of English law, by virtue of the European Communities Act 1972. Legislative action of the various organs of the Communities may take any one of four forms, as follows:

(a) *Regulations* are binding in their 'entirety' on the Member States, and are 'directly applicable', and are therefore uniform throughout the Community. At present no regulations have been made that are of direct relevance to planning law, but this may, in a desire to seek harmonisation in the interests of the common market, not always be the case. If a regulation were made which was inconsistent with (for example) the GDO, the regulation would be held by the English courts to have varied the GDO to that extent. If there is any ambiguity about the meaning of a Community Regulation there must be a reference to the European Court at Luxembourg for them to decide under Article 177 of the Treaty.

(b) *Directives* are made by the European Commission, are addressed to the Governments of the Member States, and they require each Member State to introduce national legislation to give effect to the terms of the directive. They are not part of English law, but if the Government of this country failed to give effect to a Directive, it would be in breach of the Treaty and could be declared to be so by the European Court at Luxembourg. Recently a draft Directive (which was not approved by the British representative on the Council of Ministers, who must approve a Directive before it takes effect) proposed that each Member State should be required to provide for environmental impact analysis[31] to be undertaken before any major project for development was approved.

(c) *Decisions* of the court are binding in the laws of the Member States but are addressed only to the parties before the court.

(d) *Recommendations,* policy statements, etc., are of no legal effect, but they may have considerable influence on the future action to be taken in the Member States. The *European Community Policy and Action Programme on the Environment for 1977-1981,* published by the Community in December 1976[32] is a case in point. Among the principles there recommended to the Member States was the following: 'The best protection of the environment consists in preventing at source the creation of pollution or nuisance, rather than subsequently trying to counter their effects.'[33] This surely should be the principal objective of our planning control legislation and administration.

7. Conclusion

English law thus consists principally of statute law, although the statutes are applied in practical situations in accordance with rules spelt out in the statute where relevant, and also in accordance with principles worked out by the courts. In so far as there is no statute dealing with a particular situation coming before a court, the judge will have to solve the problem by applying principle of the common law as worked out by the doctrine of precedent. Subordinate legislation and the law of the EEC is merely an extension of statute law, but it is an extension kept strictly in check by the courts (either in the UK or in

Luxembourg) so as to ensure that the extension does not exceed the bounds set by the enabling statute and the Treaty of Rome. Generally in planning law, we are concerned only with statutes and regulations made thereunder, but the rules for interpreting statutes may often be of the very first importance — and the evolution of those rules has also depended on the doctrine of precedent. Once a court has applied *the terms* of a statute to a particular factual situation, precedent may demand that this ruling is followed in future cases. Statute law thus cannot be considered in isolation without also considering the basic principles of the common law such as the rules of natural justice.

Notes

1. *Bendles Motors Ltd* v. *Bristol Corporation* [1963] 1 All ER 578.
2. In his Hamlyn lectures for 1975, 'The Land and the Development'.
3. *Coleshill Investment Co.* v. *Minister of Housing and Local Government* [1969] 2 All ER 525.
4. As to the *ejusdem generis* principle, see page 26.
5. *Donoghue* v. *Stephenson* [1932] AC 562 (a decision of the House of Lords).
6. (1935) 51 TLR 551.
7. *Hedley Byrne* v. *Heller and Partners* [1964] AC 465; another decision of the House of Lords.
8. House of Lords direction of 1966, reported at [1966] 3 All ER 77.
9. See, for example, 1971 Act, s.290, read with s.22(1).
10. Regulations, orders, directions, approvals, etc.; these words are used indiscriminately in statutes conferring power to make subordinate legislation.
11. This will be so if the substance of the regulation is not within the terms of the enabling statute, and the regulations will also be void if some procedure required to be followed by the statute when the regulations are made, has not been complied with.
12. SI 1977 No. 289, as amended.
13. Under the Public Health Act 1925.
14. *Att.-Gen.* v. *Fulham Corporation* [1921] 1 Ch. 440.
15. *Att.-Gen.* v. *Prince Ernst Augustus of Hanover* [1957] 1 All ER 49.
16. *Mixnam's Properties Ltd* v. *Chertsey UDC* [1964] 2 All ER 627.
17. *Att.-Gen.* v. *Brown* [1920] 1 KB 773.
18. *Brownsea Haven Properties* v. *Poole Corpn* [1958] Ch. 574.
19. *Coleshill Investment Co.* v. *Minister of Housing and Local Government* [1969] 2 All ER 525.
20. *Hall & Co Ltd* v. *Shoreham by Sea UDC* [1964] 1 All ER 1.
21. *R* v. *Barnsley Corpn, ex parte Hook*, [1976] 3 All ER 452.
22. *Bushell* v. *Secretary of State for the Environment* [1980] 2 All ER 608.
23. *Fairmount Investments Ltd* v. *Secretary of State for the Environment* [1976] 2 All ER 865.
24. *Ibid., per* Lord Russell.
25. See pp. 181.
26. Subject to any contrary intention appearing. Parliament is supreme and therefore it can, if it really says so, do stupid or unexpected things (as in the *Prince Ernst Augustus case, Note 15 supra*).
27. This is of course particularly important if some aspect of the law of the EEC is

involved. Although a statute passed subsequent to the UK's accession to the Communities may over-rule European law, in the absence of such an express provision, European law must be applied by the English courts.

28. But a definition contained in subordinate legislation may not *widen* the meaning of a word beyond the meaning given to the same word in the parent statute.

29. See, for example, the argument in *Kruse* v. *Johnson* [1898] 2 QB 91. It is also essential that any procedural rule for the making of by-laws laid down in the parent statute, has been observed.

30. Statutory Instruments Act 1946.

31. Chapter 10, p.122.

32. Bull. EC Supp. 6/76; *Official Journal* 1977 C 139.

33. See article at [1980] JPL 638.

3 Private Law Controls Over Land Use

1. Introduction

The common law, without the supplement of statute, knew nothing of land use control in the modern sense. This did not mean that the English landowner could do exactly as he wished with his own land without regard to the rights of others. On the other hand the landowner could use his physical and economic position to control in some measure the manner in which those who derived their estates or interests in a particular parcel of land from him. These common or private law restrictions and controls in many instances still exist today and so they must be explained in some detail. First, however, it should be understood that while the ownership of all land in England has since 1066 in theory belonged to the Crown, individuals have always been able (originally by grants from the Crown) to own *estates* in the land. An estate is an abstract concept protected by the law which allows the holder to exercise the normal rights of ownership[1] over the land for a specified (or indefinite) period of time. Since the reform of the land law in 1925,[2] legal estates have been of two kinds only; the fee simple absolute[3] (or freehold), and the leasehold.

The fee simple absolute is the largest estate known to English law, as it is capable of existing for as long as there are members of the family of the holder of the estate, or of anyone to whom he may have transferred it. A leasehold estate, on the other hand, will last only for a precise, stated, period of time such as 999 years, 21 years, or possibly only for a week. A leasehold estate may be granted to a 'tenant' by an owner of the fee simple (the 'landlord') in the same land, and so there may be more than one legal estate existing in the same land at any one time. This may be shown as follows:

BLACKACRE
The owner of the fee simple (A) grants to
(B) a lease for 99 years, who grants to
(C) a sub-lease for 21 years, who grants to

(D) a weekly tenancy (who will be entitled to
occupy the land).

A, B, C and D all may have legal estates in Blackacre, and each person
in the hierarchy will normally pay a rent to the landlord above. So D
may pay £15 a week to C, C may pay £250 a year to B, and B may pay a
ground rent of £10 a year to A. As we shall see, each landlord will be
entitled to impose and enforce conditions against his tenant as to the
use to be made of the property. In the example given, A, B and C, will in
effect only enjoy their respective rents; D alone will be entitled to
occupy the land itself (while his weekly tenancy lasts), but all four will
have estates in the land. This method of breaking up ownership has its
own consequences in land use control, as will appear.

2. Nuisance

First, however, we must say something about the law of nuisance, as
this may be of relevance to every type of estate owner. Every landowner
may, subject to statute law to be discussed later,[4] do what he likes with
his own property, provided he does not interfere with the enjoyment by
his neighbour of those same rights over his land.[5] So, a landowner may
not allow smoke from his bonfire to escape onto his neighbour's
garden so as to cause the neighbour substantial inconvenience, nor
may he play his guitar all night so loudly that his neighbour cannot
sleep, nor cause his downspout to eject rainwater onto his neighbour's
lawn, nor operate a pile-driver to such effect that it shakes his
neighbour's house; in all these, and many other situations, the offender
will be guilty of the civil wrong (or *tort)* of nuisance, and the neighbour
can sue him in court for an order (an *injunction)* requiring him to stop
the nuisance, and possibly recover money damages as well.

Action of this kind can in serious cases operate to effect some
measure of land use control. A factory starting up in a residential area
may become the subject of nuisance proceedings; so may, for example,
the operation of a petrol depot.[6] In the United States proceedings in
nuisance have even been taken against the use of premises as a funeral
home in a high-class residential district[7] in St Louis, Missouri,
although nuisance has never been applied in this kind of context in
England.

If the nuisance in question is, or becomes, so serious as to affect the
ordinary convenience or enjoyment of life of a substantial number of

members of the public, then there may be a *public* nuisance. This arose, for example, when noise, fumes and vibrations from a neighbouring quarry made living conditions in a small group of houses in a country district virtually unbearable.[8]

In such a case, proceedings to require an abatement of the nuisance may be commenced by an individual (as for a private nuisance), but the Attorney-General. as protector of Her Majesty's subjects, may be asked to institute the proceedings, and obtain an injunction from the court.

3. Leaseholds

By the device of granting a long lease of land (for, say, 999 or 99 years), to a prospective developer, the owner of the freehold is able to retain very considerable control over the use made of that land by his tenant. In any lease the landlord normally inserts convenants which must be obeyed by the tenant (or any subsequent tenant who may acquire the benefit of the lease), under penalty of losing his leasehold interest in the land. These covenants will stipulate for a rent to be paid, which would often be quite small in the case of a long building lease. If the property let is an existing building, the covenants may provide (for example) that the building is to be used as a single private dwelling house only, and not be split into flats. If the lease is of undeveloped land and is granted to a builder for development, the covenants will often stipulate the kinds of buildings to be erected. They may specify a particular layout and require that the designs of the building shall conform to the wishes of the landlord or his architect. Many residential estates in England were laid out in this way by large country landowners in the eighteenth and nineteenth centuries; the Russell estate in Bloomsbsury (London), the Royal Crescent in Bath, and parts of such towns as Leamington Spa, Weston-super-Mare, and the Calthorpe estate in Edgbaston, Birmingham, are examples of leasehold development. By the economic power given by ownership of the fee simple, the landlord is able to dictate a local land use law that must be observed by his tenants, under penalty of forfeiting their interests for non-compliance.

In more recent years the leasehold device has been adopted by legislation. The new town development corporations in particular have been empowered to grant long leases for development purposes of land purchased by them, and covenants as to land use are imposed in these leases.[9] The device was also used in the abortive Community

Land Act 1975, and has now been continued by the 1980 Act and can be used by local authorities and the Land Authority for Wales.[10]

4. Easements

Ownership of an estate in land may be thought of as bundle of sticks; an unlimited number of rights to enjoy the land (including the right to grant a lease, in which event the tenant will have the present right to physical enjoyment). Nevertheless, an owner can, if he wishes, grant away to another person one (or more) of those 'sticks' or rights from his total bundle. He can, for example, permit his neighbour to walk across his garden so as to have access to the local village; or he can allow a neighbour to run a drain or a water pipe through his land.

Such arrangements depend primarily on a *contract*[11] (legally enforceable agreement) between the landowner and his neighbour, but these rights may be given, or acquire, a more lasting effect than one merely between the original parties. If the right (easement) over the garden (A) is given for the benefit of the owner of the adjoining land (B), as the owner of (B), then that right if granted by deed, will survive the original parties to the agreement. It will be enforceable by any subsequent owner of (B) against any subsequent owner of (A). The existence of such a right of way, water, drainage, etc. may have important land use consequences. For example, it may make the development of (B) simpler, because of the right of way to the village or because of the right of drainage, but also it may mean that (A) cannot be developed as its owner might have wished, owing to the existence of the easement. It may be difficult to contemplate building a house on (A) if this means that the owner of (B) will have a right to walk through the front door and out by the drawing room french windows!

A special kind of easement[12] is known as the right to light. This is a right to the effect that the light to a certain window in a particular building shall not be obstructed by an adjoining building subsequently to be erected on a neighbour's land. This right, like all easements can either be created expressly by deed, or it will come into effect by uninterrupted use over a period of at least 20 years.[13] When such a right exists, it may have the effect of prohibiting virtually any building on the land adjoining the window in respect of which the right to light is enjoyed. This may of course have a quite drastic control over land use.

Easements can be abolished only by agreement (or by statute) which will usually mean that the dominant owner — the owner of the land for the benefit of which the easement attaches — can hold the servient owner to ransom. If the servient owner of the land subject to the easement wants to develop his land in a manner that will conflict with the easement, he will probably have to pay the dominant owner a substantial sum of money for his agreement.

Public rights of way are not easements at all, although they may be confused with private rights of way, which are a very common type of easement. Public rights of way are really highways and are subject to their own rules; they are considered in Chapter 19.

5. Restrictive Covenants

When V sells off a piece of his garden to P, so that P can build a new house in the garden, V may well wish to impose covenants on P, restricting him in the use that he may make of the piece of the garden that he is buying. Perhaps V wants to prevent P from building a public house or some business premises on the land, or he may wish to ensure that no building will be erected unless the plans have first been approved by V's surveyor, and this will operate much in the same way as a landlord may impose covenants on his tenant in a lease (see above). Originally these covenants, being a part of the contract of sale and purchase of the land between V and P, were regarded by the law as being enforceable only by V and only against P, as these were the parties to that contract. Restrictions of this kind could not be created as easements, as an easement confers a positive power to exercise a single right of ownership over another's land (to walk across it, cause water to flow through it, etc.). A restrictive covenant is negative in concept; it prevents the landowner affected by it from using his land in a specified manner, and it does not confer any positive rights on the person entitled to the benefit of the covenant.

The famous case of *Tulk* v. *Moxhay*[14] was decided by the court of Chancery in 1848, and this concerned the garden in the centre of Leicester Square in London. When V sold the garden to P he had imposed a covenant, prohibiting any building on the garden. It was held that it would be unfair to allow a purchaser (X) from P, who had purchased the garden knowing of the existence of the covenant, and who probably had paid less for the land because of the covenant, to snap his fingers at the covenant. So, although X was not a party to the contract between V and P, he was compelled by the courts in an action brought by V, to observe the terms of the covenant. Today this principle is well established, and even a subsequent purchaser from V of the land for the benefit of which the covenant was imposed (in *Tulk* v. *Moxhay,* the land surrounding the garden in Leicester Square) could enforce (by means of a court order, if necessary) the covenant against P, and any subsequent purchaser (X) of the garden from P, or even against any person buying from X who is aware of the covenant. And as these covenants now[15] are registrable in a central public registry, it is a simple matter to ensure that everyone is made aware of the covenants, because it is common form before purchasing land for a purchaser to search the register. But for these principles to operate, the covenants in question must be *restrictive* of the user of the land affected.

The rules about restrictive covenants are much too complicated to be explained in any more detail here, but it must be obvious that they offer a most effective means in the hands of a vendor of ensuring some measure of control over the use to be made of land. Like easements, they can be abolished by agreement, but they can also be modified or abolished by proceedings before a specialised administrative court, known as the Land Tribunal.[16] When the Tribunal is satisfied that the covenant in question has become obsolete or is no longer of any value, the Tribunal can order its abolition or modification.

The concept of the restrictive covenant has been adopted in modern planning legislation. When a planning authority disposes of land that it has purchased to ensure that some desirable development will be carried out, the authority may as a term of the sale, impose restrictive covenants providing that the land shall not be used otherwise than in a specified manner. Those covenants will then be enforceable against not only the purchaser, but also any subsequent owner of the land. Similarly clauses in an agreement under section 52 of the 1971 Act (see Chapter 12, page 140) will be enforceable against all subsequent owners of the land as if they were restrictive covenants.

6. Building Schemes

During the Edwardian period of rapid expansion in house building, the courts extended the theory of the enforceability of restrictive covenants. In *Elliston* v. *Reacher* in 1908,[17] it was held that if it could be shown that a developer had made a building scheme covering a number of plots on an estate, and had imposed the same restrictive covenants on all the purchasers of the plot, then the court would allow each purchaser (and each subsequent purchaser from an original purchaser) to enforce the covenants against each other purchaser or sub-purchaser. By this means an estate developer is able to establish a kind of local land use control for all the plots (and eventual houses) on the estate. So anyone seeking to buy a house on that estate can be assured that all his neighbours on the estate will be obliged to observe the same covenants that are binding on him.

Such a scheme may be used to enhance the value of the houses on an estate subject to the building scheme. Each prospective resident will know that, for example, none of the houses on the estate will be used for commercial purposes, that none of them will be of such poor quality that they can be built for less than (say) £20,000, that no-one on the estate will be able to hang out washing on the line in a garden on Sundays, etc.

Originally the rules laid down in *Elliston* v. *Reacher* for the establishment of a building scheme that would be recognised by the courts, were very detailed and strict. More recently the courts have been able to accept a scheme in any case where it can be shown that it was the intention of the developer to establish a scheme and to impose substantially the same restrictive covenants on all the plots.[18] Building schemes today are very popular. Some survive from the periods of before the First World War and others from the years between the wars; yet others are of more recent origin, dating from the 1950s or 1960s or even more recent times.

It must be emphasised, however, that the recognition of a building scheme by the courts for the purpose of the mutual enforcement of covenants as between the several owners of property subject to the scheme, applies only to those covenants that are restrictive of the user of the land. This is because the whole principle depends on the doctrine of *Tulk* v. *Moxhay*. Only those covenants that are restrictive will be allowed by the courts to be enforced beyond the strict confines of the contract made between the original parties to the covenant. The court will, however, look at the substance of the covenant, and not be bound too narrowly by the actual words used. Thus, a covenant providing that, for example, 'a single private dwelling house only may be erected' on any plot in question, is none the less restrictive in substance although it may appear positive in its wording. A covenant 'to erect and maintain fencing' is, however, positive in nature and will be enforceable only between the original parties, unless it is contained in a lease, when it will be enforceable by the landlord against his tenant and the tenant's successors in title.

7. The Relationship Between Private and Public Law Controls

The two forms of control over land use, under private law and public law respectively, exist quite independently of one another. Indeed, the several different private law controls explained above also operate separately.

Thus, if a particular form of development causes a common law or a public nuisance, or if it infringes property rights such as an easement or a covenant in a lease, or if it amounts to a breach of a restrictive covenant, whether or not contained in a building scheme, it will be no defence for an offender to plead that he has obtained planning permission for that development. He must meet the requirements of the person entitled to enforce the covenant or easement or who may take proceedings against him in nuisance, and the fact that he has obtained a valid planning permission will be quite irrelevant. Similarly, the fact that the developer may have obtained a dispensation from the restrictions imposed under a building scheme or from a particular restrictive covenant, either by agreement or by obtaining an order from the Lands Tribunal, will in no sense permit him to dispense with the need to obtain planning permission for the projected development. Nor will such a dispensation be of any use as an argument to persuade the planning authority to give him planning permission.

The several forms of control thus operate quite independently of one another. The only exceptions from this are the following:

(a) If a house owner wishes to be relieved from a covenant in a lease or from a restrictive covenant between freeholders, to the effect (only) that his house may not be converted into two or more separate dwellings (flats or maisonettes), he can apply to the local county court for an order modifying or abolishing the covenant. On such an application he will have to prove that he has already obtained planning permission authorising such a conversion.[19]

(b) On some applications to the Lands Tribunal for the modification or abolition of a restrictive covenant (whether or not contained in a building scheme), it may be necessary to establish that the proposed development (which infringes the covenant as it stands) is in accordance with the established planning policy of the local authority.[20]

Apart from these two instances, however, there is no link between the private law controls and the statutory public law controls of the Town and Country Planning Acts.

The private law controls have been developed by the courts primarily for the purpose of protecting the interests of private landowners; the Russells of Bloomsbury, or the big developers of our own day desirous of making their estates seem as attractive as possible so as to obtain maximum profits. In the days of the Welfare State, and the ever increasing pressures on our exiguous land stock, needs for roads, airports, housing, schools and leisure activities, make themselves obvious. It also becomes essential to preserve our heritage of countryside and coast, and to save some land for agriculture and forestry. In these conditions some more elaborate and more effective machinery was clearly needed to control these competing claims, than can be provided by the private interest oriented land use controls of the common law. Building schemes may be of considerable value in maintaining the quality of building and the value of property in the open market, and we have seen that leasehold covenants of the past have often been successful in these respects. But these controls were not imposed in the public interest, and they always depend on private initiative for their implementation.

The preservation of our physical and social environment is also an essential objective, and controls over future land use, exercised imaginatively, are a much more powerful weapon than attempting to cure the ills caused by pollution from industrial or domestic sewage and chimneys.

Parliament therefore has had to intervene, and the remainder of this book will be concerned with the resulting highly complicated statutory controls, which can be traced back at least to 1909.[21] Nevertheless the legislature has adapted the private law processes of land use control for use in the public sector. The Town and Country Planning Act 1944, aiming at rapid reconstruction after the war, empowered local authorities to arrange for the development of extensive areas of war-damaged land by private enterprise through the medium of long leases, and these powers, no longer restricted to war damage, are still used today, especially in the context of town centre redevelopment. When housing authorities sell off council houses, they can impose restrictive covenants under the Housing Acts on the future use of those houses.

We must now discuss the nature and powers of the statutory agencies, at both central and local levels, established to administer these public controls over land use. This will be the subject matter of the next chapter.

Notes

1. This means in practice the right to enjoy the land in the widest sense, except only in so far as may be prohibited by law, and also the right to alienate or dispose of the land, by sale, exchange, lease mortgage, or by a devise on death, etc.

2. The Birkenhead legislation, especially the Law of Property Act 1925.

3. 'Fee' means that at common law the estate passed on the death of the owner to his heirs; 'simple' means it could pass to *any* of his heirs, both lineal and collateral, and 'absolute' means it was not subject to any condition or limitation.

4. In particular, under the Town and Country Planning Acts.

5. Liberty must not be allowed to become licence; as the Romans said 'sic utere tuo ut alienum non laedas' (use your own so as not to harm others).

6. *Halsey* v. *Esso Petroleum Ltd* [1961] 2 All ER 145.

7. *Street* v. *Marshall,* 291 S.W. 494 (1927), extracted in Milner's casebook *Community Planning,* (University of Toronto Press, 1963) p. 9. A recent American textbook says that 'Nuisance theory and case law is the common law backbone of modern environmental and energy law' in William H. Rodgers, *Environmental Law,* p. 100.

8. *Att.-Gen.* v. *P.Y.A. Quarries Ltd* [1957] 1 All ER 894.

9. As to the new towns, see p.67.

10. As to the Land Authority for Wales, see Chapter 4, p.57.

11. As a general principle of English law, a contract is enforceable only as between the two (or more) original parties to that agreement: this is what is meant by the expression 'privity of contract'.

12. There are many kinds of easement in addition to those mentioned; a right to park vehicles on a defined piece of land, a right to wander at will in a town garden, and a right to place a board on the defendant's land advertising the plaintiff's nearby public house, all have been found by the courts capable of existing as easements, as well as the more usual ones of the right of way, water, drainage, and support. 'The list of easements is not closed.'

13. In practice, the right to light most commonly comes into existence by such long use. Other easements can be created in the same way, but more commonly a right of way or drainage, etc. will be created by deed as a consequence of the sale of part of a property.

14. (1848) 2 Phill. 774.

15. Law of Property Act 1925; Land Charges Act 1925 (now replaced by the Land Charges Act 1972).

16. Law of Property Act 1925, s.84, as amended by the Law of Property Act 1969. The Lands Tribunal Act 1949 established the Lands Tribunal.

17. [1908] 2 Ch. 374.

18. See, for example, *re Dolphin's Conveyance* [1970] 2 All ER 664.

19. Housing Act 1957, section 184.

20. Law of Property Act 1925, s.84, as amended by the Law of Property Act 1969.

21. Housing and Town Planning, etc. Act 1909; see Chapter 5, p.61.

4 Local Government and the Planners

1. Local Authorities

A local authority may be described as being a separate *person* in law (i.e. it may sue and be sued in the courts in its own name, and it may own property), separate from the members of its governing body (the 'council'), which exercises those governmental functions that have been entrusted to it by Parliament. It will exercise those functions over a precisely delimited geographical area, and the members of its council will be elected, on a universal adult suffrage, from the residents in that area. A local authority also draws a substantial part of its operating income from those same residents, by means of an annual 'rate', levied on landed property in that area. These are the essential special features of an English (or Welsh) local authority, which distinguish such an authority from other government agencies, such as gas or electricity boards or a local employment exchange.

Local authorities are of two principal kinds, with a third tier in country areas. Principal councils, as they are called in the major local government constitutional statute, the Local Government Act 1972, are the county councils and the district councils. Every part of England and Wales outside the Greater London area, is within the area of a district and also of a county. Some functions are entrusted by Parliament to the counties, others to the districts. Counties and districts may therefore be thought of as being in partnership in the business of local government. Counties, although obviously much larger than any district and therefore having more considerable resources, are in no sense in a superior legal position to the districts, and they cannot give orders to the districts or supervise them in any way.

There are six special or 'metropolitan' areas,[1] where the districts enjoy somewhat wider functions than districts do outside the metropolitan areas. In rural areas a third kind of authority, having but few functions, will be found. These are the parishes, known in Wales as communities. Then in Greater London, there is one 'county council', the Greater London Council (GLC), 32 London Boroughs, and also the Common Council of the City of London. This complicated organisation may be shown diagrammatically as follows:

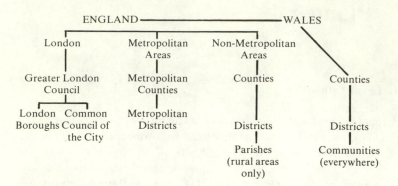

It must be emphasised that this diagram in no sense portrays a hierarchy of authorities. The districts are not subservient to the counties, nor are the parishes subservient to their districts; each local authority derives its powers direct from Parliament. Each local authority can exercise those powers within the law and (subject also to the supervisory powers of the central government, to be mentioned below) can be kept within those powers only by the courts, whose principal duty it is to see that the law is obeyed.

Each local authority on this diagram has some planning functions. The counties (and the GLC) are responsible, in consultation with their district councils, for the preparation of the structure plans, while the district councils, again in consultation, are responsible for the preparation of the local plans (which, together with the structure plan, make up the 'development plan' for the area — usually the area of the county council).[2] All applications for planning permission must be sent to the district council, who will be responsible for determining the application in most cases, but exceptionally they will have to refer the application to the county council. The subsidiary controls (over buildings, advertisements, etc.) and enforcement action are the responsibility of the districts although before the coming into operation of the 1980 Act the county councils had concurrent powers. The parishes and communities have a right, if they decide to exercise it, to be consulted by the district council on any application for planning permission that may affect their parish or community. London Boroughs and the City Council are in virtually the same position for these purposes, as are the district councils. Housing and public health functions are the concern of district councils, but highway functions are assigned to county councils.

2. Councils and Their Procedures

Each local authority[3] has a governing body consisting of a council with a number of councillors,[4] each elected by the local residents for periods of four years. The council will elect a chairman from among its members and will meet periodically, usually once a month. All decisions on planning (or other matters) must in law be taken by the council, at a meeting, by a majority vote of those present and voting. Council meetings must be open to the press and public, although the press and public may be excluded while some specific matter is under consideration if the council pass a resolution to exclude them in the public interest.

Nevertheless, English local government business is in practice conducted by the 'committee system'. This means that by convention, no item of business will come before the council for a decision until it has been considered by a committee of selected members of the council. Committees will be appointed by the council members annually to consider particular functions of the council. Thus a district council may appoint a housing committee, a finance committee and a leisure services committee, while both counties and districts will probably appoint a planning committee. Committees may in turn appoint sub-committees; perhaps a district planning committee will appoint a 'plans sub-committee', which would be required to consider applications for planning permission. When a committee or sub-committee has been appointed, all matters within its terms of reference will be considered first by them, and they will either make a recommendation to the committee or council as to what action should be taken, or they will have been empowered to decide the matter themselves on behalf of the council.

A committee (or a sub-committee) will be able to conclude a matter on the council's behalf, without referring it to the full council for a decision, only where the power to make that decision has been expressly *delegated* to the committee (or sub-committee) by the council. This is because the power to decide any matter has been conferred by Parliament on the local authority, but Parliament also has authorised that power to be delegated by the authority to a committee or sub-committee of members of the council. Where the council has so delegated its functions within a specified area (for example, decisions on applications for planning permission), the committee or sub-committee concerned can make the decision on behalf of the council. Even if the council as a body disagrees with the decision, it cannot reverse the decision, although thé council could withdraw the delegated power from the committee for future cases. Where there is no such delegation,[5] the committee will be confined to making a recommendation on which the council will make the decision.

The result of this committee system is that no matter is considered by the council until it has first come before a committee, who will either make a recommendation as to the action that they suggest the council should take, or the committee will report to the council on the action they will already have taken in the council's name under delegated powers. The principal advantage of this procedure is that any matter, such as an application for planning permission, can be fully discussed in the informal atmosphere of a committee room, with the council's technical and legal advisers present. Strict rules of debate will not normally apply as they do at a council meeting, and political party considerations are not so likely to govern the decision as they are when a matter is discussed in the glare of a full council meeting. However committees are now open to the public and the press.

The power to delegate a function also extends in favour of one or more officers of the council. Therefore many planning committees, with the authority of their councils, have authorised their planning officers to make planning decisions of specified kinds (usually limited to comparatively trivial matters, such as the erection of a garage in front of the building line, or perhaps development on land not exceeding an acre in extent).

3. The Elected Members

The decision-making power is given by Parliament to the local planning authority, and this can be exercised definitively by a committee or an officer only in so far as it has been expressly delegated as above mentioned. However, even if the power to make decisions on most planning applications has been so delegated to an officer, this does not mean that the councillors, members of the planning committee, are denuded of all powers. They will still have considerable influence over decisions because:

(a) they can always revoke or modify the terms of the delegation, although they cannot reverse a decision actually taken under the delegated power;[6]

(b) they select and appoint the officers, and allocate staff and resources within the limits of their (the council's) budget;

(c) they can dictate general lines of policy to be observed in planning decisions;

(d) they should receive reports on all decisions taken under delegated powers.

4. Controls Over the Activities of Local Authorities

In law, local authorities in England and Wales are independent legal bodies entrusted by Parliament to make decisions (right or wrong) without recourse to any other administrative body. They are of course subject to political control through the democratic process of elections, their meetings are open to the public,[7] and many documents are required to be made available to public inspection.[8] Apart from these controls by the public, discussed below,[9] there are a number of controls imposed by law.

The Courts

As we have said, the principal task of the courts is to ensure, in the widest sense, that the law is obeyed. In the field of local government and land use planning, this means that the courts will ensure that local authorities — and the central government — do not exceed the powers conferred on them by Parliament. Individual citizens may invoke the aid of the courts to prevent a government agency or local authority from interfering with their property or personal liberty without the authority of statute; the principles that the courts will follow in interpreting such statutory powers have been discussed;[10] here we will concentrate on the procedures whereby the courts may be asked to intervene. Although we return to this topic in more detail, with particular reference to planning matters, the principal remedies available to a member of the public may be summarised as follows:

(a) Applications for Judicial Review. Under Order 53 of the Rules of the Supreme Court an application may be made for judicial review of a decision of a government authority, central or local. On such an application the applicant may ask for an order of *certiorari* to quash

the decision of the authority on the ground that it was *ultra vires*[11] or was arrived at in a manner that was contrary to law. The applicant may alternatively, ask for an order of *prohibition* which, if granted, would have the effect of preventing the agency from acting in an illegal manner. An order of *mandamus* will be issued if the court finds that the agency is not carrying out its statutory duties; for example, if a local authority has failed to consider an application for planning permission that is legally in order, *mandamus* will be granted, requiring the authority to hear and determine the application according to law. Yet other remedies that may be obtained on an application for judicial review are a *declaration,* which is a judgment of the court stating what the law is when a dispute has arisen,[12] and an *injunction,* ordering the defendant agency to stop some unlawful action which is causing harm to the applicant.

(b) Contracts, etc. If the government agency is guilty of a breach of contract or a tort,[13] the agency may be sued in the ordinary courts in the same manner as an ordinary citizen.[14]

(c) Statutory Appeals. In some cases a statute may give a special right of appeal to the courts against some order made by a government agency on the grounds specified in the statute. Thus, there is a right of appeal on a point of law against a decision of the Secretary of State on an appeal to him from a refusal by the local planning authority to grant planning permission, under section 246 of the Act of 1971. Similarly, there are rights to ask the court to quash a development plan, a variety of orders (including a decision on an appeal against an enforcement notice) made by the Secretary of State under the 1971 Act,[15] or to quash a compulsory purchase order made under the Acquisition of Land (Authorisation Procedure) Act 1946. Appeals and applications of this kind are extremely common in planning practice, and many of the cases to be discussed later had reached the courts by this route.

(d) Which Court?[16] Applications for judicial review and appeals under the 1971 Act, and against compulsory purchase orders, will be brought before the High Court, usually in the Queen's Bench Division but sometimes in the Chancery Division. Actions in contract or tort will be brought in the local county court, unless the amount of the claim involved exceeds a specified amount,[17] in which event proceedings will have to be commenced in the High Court (Queen's Bench Division).

(e) Criminal Proceedings. Some planning cases will be criminal in nature, in that the defendant is being charged with some offence; for example, failing to comply with the terms of an enforcement notice, displaying an advertisement without consent, or felling a tree which was the subject of a tree preservation order. In such cases, proceedings will commence in the local magistrates court. Generally, the case will be determined finally by the magistrates, but in some instances the accused may have a right to be tried before a jury. If he decides to exercise that right, he will be tried before the local crown court. In either event there will be the usual rights of appeal available in criminal proceedings (see Chapter 2, p.23).

It will always be possible for the defendant to argue by way of defence that the notice or order, etc., in question was not authorised by law, or that it had not been properly served on him, or that there was some other procedural defect of substance as a consequence of which he has been prejudiced.

(f) Other Proceedings. In some cases, if a citizen fails to comply with, for example, an enforcement notice served on him, the local authority may have power to take default action, i.e. to enter on his property and carry out the work (e.g. demolish a building constructed without planning permission having first been obtained) required by the notice. In such a case they may then recover the expenses they have incurred, if necessary by action in the courts. If such a defendant is certain that the notice was for some reason bad in law, he would be entitled to resist the illegal entry on his property, and either sue the local authority for damages for the trespass on his land, or wait to be prosecuted by them for obstructing their officers or servants in the execution of their duty, and plead the illegality of the entire proceedings in defence. Such 'self help' is rare in practice, partly because it is a dangerous course unless the individual is quite sure of his legal rights, and also, of course, because local authorities rarely act in practice in an *ultra vires* manner.[18]

The Secretary of State

In addition to the controls exercised by the courts, local authorities are in many circumstances subject to control by a Minister of the central government,[19] usually the Secretary of State for the Environment. Local authorities are, as we have said, independent bodies in their own right, being entrusted with functions, often of a discretionary nature,[20] by Parliament but this does not mean that they can always do as they wish, even if they scrupulously keep within the law. The Secretary of State can exercise a number of controls over their functions, as referred to in Chapter 1. In the planning context, the most important of these controls are his powers to hear and determine appeals against refusals or conditional approvals of planning permission, and against enforcement notices, and also his power to approve (with or without modifications) a structure plan submitted to him. Compulsory purchase and many other orders such as those diverting or stopping-up rights of way under the Highways Act 1980, may also be subject to his confirmation.

Under s.276 of the 1971 Act the Secretary of State has wide default powers. Whenever he considers it expedient, after consultation with the planning authority, he may require them to submit an order to him for confirmation, or may himself make an order under any of the provisions of Part III (as to ordinary planning control) or Part IV (as to special controls) of the 1971 Act. For example, some years ago the local authority had granted planning permission for the erection of a large hotel overlooking the Clifton Gorge at Bristol. The Secretary of State ordered this permission to be revoked by an order under section 45. This order took effect as if it had been made by the local authority, and consequently they were liable to pay compensation as provided for in the Act (see Chapter 15, p. 164).

The Public

Control by the public over the activities of a local authority is of a kind different from that of others. This control is exercisable only in a general way, either by the pressure of public opinion, or ultimately through the ballot box, which, crude means of control as it is, is exercisable in respect of most authorities[21] only once every four years.

But in order that this control can be exercised at all, the public must be adequately informed about the actual and proposed decisions of the local authority. This the law ensures in some measure by the following devices:

(1) meetings of councils and of their committees (but not sub-committees) must be open to the press and the public, except in cases where in the public interest the council (or committee) pass a special resolution to exclude the press and public while a particular matter is being discussed;[22]
(2) a number of documents must be made available at the Council's offices for inspection by members of the public. This applies to the

development plan,[23] compulsory purchase orders and similar documents, the annual statement of a Council's accounts, and the minutes of a Council.[24] Members of the public are allowed to take copies of or extracts from the minutes, on payment of a reasonable fee;[25]

(3) registers must be maintained by the district planning authority of all applications for planning permission[26] and of applications for consent to the display of advertisements;[27] these registers must show how each application has been dealt with. The registers must be open to public inspection at the authority's offices at all reasonable hours;

(4) inquiries convened on behalf of the Secretary of State into appeals against planning permission, etc., are customarily advertised in the locality[28] and interested members of the public are allowed to attend the inquiry and to take part in the proceedings;

(5) some types of application for planning permission[29] must be advertised in the locality and an opportunity for observations to be submitted by members of the public within 21 days, before the application is considered by the planning authority;

(6) elaborate provisions are laid down in Part I of the 1971 Act for the participation of members of the public in the preparation of a structure plan and of a local plan.[30]

These various forms of public participation were in part the result of a report published in 1969.[31] Since then the enthusiasm for public involvement has waned somewhat, with the realisation that only a well-informed public can usefully contribute to the planning process, and that any amount of publicity and education (in the form of handouts, public meetings and 'forums') can do little if the public is not willing to be educated or informed. Pressure groups and amenity societies often play a very useful role, but individuals who concern themselves in planning matters tend to be those who have a personal interest as landowners or local residents, and they can rarely be provoked — or inspired — into doing more than *oppose* a particular planning project of either a developer or a public authority.[32]

5. Local Authority Finance

This book is only incidentally concerned with local government administration, but the activities of a planning authority must be very considerably affected by the extent of its financial resources; if only in the number of staff it can afford to employ in the planning office. The subject matter of finance will be considered for present purposes under two headings, the sources of local authority income, and the controls over expenditure:

(1) Income

This comes from two principal sources; the general rate, and contributions and grants from the Central Exchequer. Rates are levied by each district and London borough (and the City) council on the rateable occupiers of all buildings within the authority's area, expressed as a fixed number of pence in the pound, on the rateable value of each 'hereditament' or building.[33] The rateable value is fixed by the local valuation officer (subject to a right of appeal to a special administrative tribunal, known as the local valuation court), an officer of the Board of Inland Revenue. If, for example, a dwelling house is given a rateable value of £300, and a rate is 'struck' by the local authority for the particular year, at 90 pence in the pound, the occupier of that dwelling will be liable to pay $300 \times \dfrac{90}{100} = £270$ in rates for the year.

The amount of the rate for the year will be computed by the district or London borough council according to the following formula:

Total requirements of the local authority needed to meet the expenditure decided upon by the Council for the forthcoming year:	£X
LESS amount of central government grants and subsidies payable:	£Y
LESS other income of the council (product of entertainments, council house rents, etc.)	£Z
Net requirement of the council:	X — (Y + Z)
Total of the rateable value of all the hereditaments in the district of London Borough	£a
Therefore the rate to be struck for the Council's requirements:	$\dfrac{X - (Y + Z)}{a}$

and the answer to this sum will probably be *less* than £1. Then to this must be added the rate in the £ required by 'precepting' authorities to meet *their* requirements for the financial year in question. These will be the county council (a large sum — sometimes larger than the district's rate — to pay for the education, police, fire and other county services). In addition, in rural areas, there may be a small rate to pay for the requirement of a parish or community council.

The total rate payable by an occupier of a hereditament,[34] will therefore be:

$$\frac{X - (Y + Z)}{a} + c\,(\text{county}) + c\,(\text{parish})\,pence$$

The district council's share of the general rate, computed in this way, is the only part of a local authority's income over which they have complete control,[35] and in modern practice it amounts to barely 40 per cent of their total income, omitting council house rents, which in any event have to be kept in a special account which can be used only for housing purposes. The other 60 per cent of necessary income comes from the central exchequer in one form or another.

By far the largest of the contributions from the central government is the general exchequer contribution. Each year the Secretary of State in consultation with the Treasury, decides on the total amount of government money that is to be paid to local authorities. This is then broken down into specific amounts for each district and London borough, by an elaborate statutory formula which takes into account any special needs in the authority's area and the discount from rates required to be made in favour of all domestic ratepayers. Then in addition some local authority services (in particular education) attract percentage grants towards the cost of approved expenditure. Similar percentage grants are payable in a few special cases for particular projects, such as the reclamation of derelict land,[36] and expenditure in connection with the needs of immigrants in an authority's area.[37]

This considerable dependence of local authorities on central government financing tends to place them further under central government control. The Secretary of State could withhold the whole, or part, of the general exchequer contribution from a particular authority if he considers they are not performing their functions efficiently.[37] This would be, however, a very serious step for any Minister to take, and it has not been used in modern times; but the threat of its use is real. Specific grants for particular projects bring detailed Ministerial control as to how the project in question is to be carried out; so does the requirement that Ministerial sanction is required to the raising of a loan for capital expenditure.[38]

(2) Controls over Expenditure

These are of two kinds, those exercised by an authority themselves, and those exercised by the auditor.

Every local authority will in practice, although they are not required by law to do so, operate some system of internal audit, and by means of standing orders, ensure that strict procedures are followed to regulate the payment of accounts.

In addition all the accounts of a local authority have to be subjected to an annual external audit; this may (at the choice of the authority) be carried out by a professionally qualified accountant in private practice, or by the 'district auditor', who is an officer of the Department of the Environment.[39] Any ratepayer in the authority's district has certain rights to appear before the auditor and make objections to items appearing in the accounts. A district auditor either in response to such an objection or on his own initiative, may ask the High Court for a declaration to the effect that a payment by the local authority was 'contrary to law' (*ultra vires* the authority). In some cases a councillor (or an official) who had voted for or advised such an *ultra vires* course of action, may be required to repay out of his own pocket the loss sustained on the public accounts in consequence. This will not often arise in a planning context in practice, but the existence of the auditor (and the district auditor in particular) does operate to dissuade the members of an authority from undertaking novel courses of action that involve expenditure, in case such action should subsequently prove to have been *ultra vires*.

If expenditure of a capital nature is involved, a local authority will be subject to further central control. Under the Local Government Act 1972, separate loan sanction had to be obtained from the Secretary of State in any case where the authority finds it necessary to raise a loan (even if they propose to borrow from funds under their own control). Under the Local Government Planning and Land Act 1980, the Secretary of State will prescribe for each local authority in any one year the total expenditure that may be incurred by them on projects of a capital nature. Within this global sum so prescribed the Secretary of State may also give directions as to how much is to be expended on projects of national or regional importance by the authority concerned.

(3) Grants

The Secretary of State may make grants towards specific items of expenditure of local authorities. Section 250 of the 1971 Act provides for regulations for the making of grants from the central exchequer towards the cost of specified local authority development, but these regulations have not yet been made. However, grants are available under the following provisions:

(i) for expenses incurred under the Town Development Act, 1952;

(ii) towards the cost of re-claiming derelict land (Local Government Act 1966, s.9, as amended by the 1980 Act, s.117);

(iii) for research and education with respect to the planning and design of the physical environment (1971 Act, s.253);

(iv) towards schemes that preserve or enhance an 'outstanding' conservation area (Town and Country Planning (Amendment) Act 1972).

Some 500 areas had been the subject of these grants by 1980, but it is understood that the word 'outstanding' has led to some controversy in this context, and the DoE is intending to propose alterations to the scheme.

6. Supervisory Agencies

In addition to the specific controls over functions of local authorities exercisable by the courts, the central government, the financial controls and the less specific control of public opinion, two specialised agencies have been established in recent years. These also supervise local authorities in the exercise of their functions especially in the land use area, without actually being able to inhibit or reverse any decision.

The first (though not chronologically) are the two *Commissions for Local Administration.* These bodies consist of a Commission and three full-time Commissioners, in England, and a separate Commission (having a single Commissioner) in Wales. Any member of the public who considers he has sustained injustice as the consequence of some act of maladministration on the part of a local authority, may complain to a Commissioner ('Ombudsman'). He has to route his complaint through a member of the local authority, who may send on the complaint to a Commissioner, but if the member refuses or fails to do this, the complainant concerned may send his complaint (in writing) direct to a Commissioner. On receiving a complaint, the Commissioner will investigate it and make enquiries of the local authority and other persons concerned. If he is satisfied that the complaint was well-founded,[40] he will report accordingly to the local authority, and perhaps recommend some action that he considers the authority should take by way of redressing the injustice. On receipt of any such report, the authority must consider it and inform the Commissioner as to what action (if any) they have taken, or propose to take, on the matter (perhaps to make an *ex gratia* money payment to the complainant). The report must also be made available to the public, but the local authority are not legally obliged to take any action on the report, whether or not recommended by the Commissioner. The sanction (such as it is) for such a case thus depends on the goodwill of the authority, and possibly on any pressure exerted by an opposition group on the Council, or by public opinion in the locality. A considerable proportion of the complaints made in recent years has concerned land use planning matters. One of the commonest set of circumstances has concerned cases where the planning authority had granted planning permission without adequately considering the effect that the proposed development would have on a neighbouring landowner.[41]

At national level there is a similar institution known as the *Parliamentary Commission for Administration (PCA).* It considers complaints, received through Members of Parliament, alleging acts of maladministration that have caused injustice, caused by an agency of the central government. An example of such a complaint might involve some faulty procedure followed by the Secretary of State for the Environment when confirming a development plan or considering a planning appeal. On receipt of such a complaint the PCA will investigate and if he finds the complaint well founded, he will report to the Member of Parliament who sent the complaint to him, and he will also send a copy of his report to the government department concerned. Once more there is no effective sanction; but the MP may stimulate the House of Commons to take appropriate action.[42]

There is also the *Council on Tribunals.*[43] This is a body of part-time experts, with a small paid secretariat, which has the duty to supervise the conduct and procedure of administrative tribunals and enquiries. Rules of procedure, for example, for planning enquiries,[44] must be submitted to the Council for their observations, before they are made by the appropriate Minister. The council may also receive and investigate complaints about the procedure followed at a particular tribunal or enquiry. Like the Commissioners, however, they are in no sense a court of appeal from the tribunal or enquiry, and as a consequence of an investigation, all they can do (if they see fit) is to report on the complaint to the Lord Chancellor and their report is then made public. This occurred in the 'Chalkpit' enquiry in 1961, which concerned a complaint to the effect that the Minister had decided an appeal to him against a refusal of planning permission on the basis of evidence that had not been placed before the local enquiry. The Council on Tribunals found the complaint justified and reported accordingly to the Lord Chancellor. The decision in the actual case was not affected, but a short time later the rules of procedure regulating the conduct of planning enquiries were amended so as to prevent such an occurrence in future.[45]

7. The Land Authority for Wales

This is a special body, having separate legal personality, like a local authority, but standing mid-way between central and local government. The Land Authority is unique to Wales as there is no corresponding body in England. It was first constituted by the Community Land Act 1975, but when that Act was repealed in 1980, the Authority was kept alive and given revised functions by the Local Government, Land and Planning Act 1980. The principal function of the Authority is to acquire land in Wales which in the opinion of the Authority needs to be made available for development, and then to dispose of it to other persons for development at an appropriate time.[46] Acquisitions by the Authority may be by agreement, or the Authority may be authorised to acquire land compulsorily, very much as if it was a local authority. The Authority is not a planning authority, but it must consider whether planning permission would probably be granted before deciding to acquire particular land for development; they will therefore be obliged to work in close co-operation with the local authorities.

The Authority consists of 6 to 9 members (including a chairman) all of whom are nominated by the Secretary of State, and four of these members must appear to the Secretary of State to be representative of Welsh local authorities.[47] The Authority has a constitution very similar to that of a local authority; it derives its funds, principally of a capital nature, partly from receipts from the sale of land, and partly from loans guaranteed by the Treasury.

8. Conclusion

Under the system in force in this country, the planners are, in the eyes of Parliament and the nation, the local authority. As to which local authority is meant, the answer, especially since the passing of the 1980 Act, is generally the district or London Borough Council. But because of the wide powers of delegation, the actual planners taking decisions are most commonly the planning committees and, in many cases, the planning officers. The Secretary of State (acting through his civil servants) can also make out a good claim to be included among the 'planners'. Not only because of his power to confirm and modify structure plans, and his default powers, but also because of his power to determine appeals, he can have a very considerable influence on planning policies in any area. His decisions, moreover, have the effect in law as if they were decisions of the local authority.

Notes

1. These are, Tyne and Wear, West Yorkshire, South Yorkshire, Merseyside, Greater Manchester, and West Midlands.
2. See Chapter 7, p.83.
3. Some parishes are too small to have separate councils; their affairs are then conducted at an annual parish meeting, presided over by an elected chairman. In Wales, every community has an elected council, and these will be found in urban as well as rural areas.
4. The precise number of councillors varies from one local authority to another, according to the population of the area.
5. Authorised by section 101 of the Local Government Act 1972. Perhaps the power to decide development applications has been limited by the council to cases where the area of land concerned does not exceed a specified amount, such as five hectares.
6. 1971 Act, section 45.
7. Public Bodies (Admission to Meetings) Act 1960.
8. E.g. 1971 Act, section 5 (development plans).
9. See, p.50.
10. Chapter 3, p.25.
11. See, e.g. *R* v. *Hillingdon LB ex parte Royco Homes Ltd* [1974] 2 All ER 643, discussed on p.129.
12. This remedy is unlike the others in that there is no machinery whereby the defendant can be compelled to act on or accept the court ruling, but in practice this does not cause any difficulty because public bodies invariably feel themselves obliged to observe the law as declared by the courts. Failure to comply with an order of *certiorari, prohibition* or *mandamus,* on the other hand would cause a recalcitrant defendant to be guilty of contempt of court and liable to severe penalties.
13. For example, if a local authority takes a person's land under the terms of a compulsory purchase order which is subsequently proved to have been *ultra vires* (either because there was some serious error of law or procedure), the local authority will be liable for the tort of trespass.
14. If the defendant is the Crown, certain special procedures may have to be observed under the Crown Proceedings Act 1947.
15. See 1971 Act, sections 242-246.
16. For a diagram showing the hierarchy of courts, see Chapter 2, p.22.
17. At present fixed normally at £2,000.
18. Self help was successful in the case of *Stroud* v. *Bradbury* [1952] 2 All ER 76, where a householder, exercising 'the rights of a freeborn Englishman', repelled unlawful entry by a sanitary inspector, armed with a 'clothes prop and a spade'.
19. Chapter 1, p.12.
20. E.g. to grant or refuse planning permission.

21. General elections are held only once every 4 years, but there may be intermediate by-elections.

22. Public Bodies Admission to Meetings Act 1960, as amended by section 100 of the Local Government Act 1972.

23. As to the procedure governing the making of development plans, see Chapter 7, p.85.

24. But *not* the minutes of a council's committee, even if the committee is acting under delegated powers: *Wilson* v. *Evans* [1962] 1 All ER 247.

25. Local Government Act 1972, section 228.

26. Town and Country Planning General Development Order 1977, article 21 and 1971 Act, section 34.

27. Town and Country Planing (Control of Advertisements) Regulations 1969, Reg. 31.

28. This is not provided for in legislation, but the Secretary of State commonly directs the local authority to make arrangements to this effect.

29. These are cases where some person other than the owner of the land affected is submitting the application (1971 Act, section 27), where the application is for a prescribed 'noxious' use (including the erection of a building more than 20 metres in height; 1971 Act, section 26; General Development Order 1977, article 8), where the development may affect the character of a conservation area or the setting of a listed building (1971 Act, section 28), or is not in accordance with the provisions of the development plan (Town and Country Planning Development Plans Direction 1975, made under the 1971 Act); see Chapter 9.

30. See Chapter 7, p.85.

31. The 'Skeffington' Report, *People and Planning*.

32. More on this theme will be found in the contributions of the author and others to the symposium appearing in the *Town Planning Review* for October 1979, p.412.

33. Rating law, contained in the General Rate Act 1967, as subsequently amended, is extremely complex, and consequently only the barest outline is given here.

34. A domestic ratepayer is entitled to a discount from this total rate assessed on him, which is reimbursed to the district council in part of the exchequer contribution (see below).

35. An authority can of course vary the prices it charges for various services, such as entertainments, the collection of commercial waste, deck chairs in the parks and the use of public conveniences, but the income from these sources rarely pays for the services provided and is in any case a minute proportion of the total income.

36. Local Government Act 1966, section 9 (as amended by the Act of 1980).

37. Local Government Act 1966, section II.

38. Local Government Act 1972.

39. For the law on local authority audit, see Local Government Act 1972, ss. 156-167. Most local authorities prefer their accounts to be audited by the district auditor.

40. I.e. related to an act of maladministration that had caused injustice to the complainant.

41. The law regulating the Local Government Commission will be found in Part IV of the Local Government Act 1974, as amended in 1978 by the Act of the same name.

42. The law regulating the PCA is contained in the Parliamentary Commissioner Act 1967.

43. Established by the Tribunals and Enquiries Act 1958; see now the Act of the same name of 1971.

44. See Chapter 13, p.144.

45. As to the rules of procedure, see Chapter 13, p.144.

46. 1980 Act, section 79.

47. Ibid., Schedule 14.

5 Planning Legislation

1. Introduction

There are of course vestigial examples of land use control legislation in very early times; Edward I, for example, provided that a space of 200 feet should be left free of bushes and woodlands on either side of main roads between market towns,[1] and Queen Elizabeth I passed an ordinance prohibiting the use of 'sea coal' near her palace of Westminster;[2] William Shakespeare's father was fined by the town council of Stratford-on-Avon for allowing a dung heap to remain outside his house in Henley Street.[3]

The Victorian age saw the first comprehensive statutes on sanitation; prompted by the cholera epidemics of the middle of the century, the Public Health Acts of 1848 and 1875 gave considerable powers to the newly created boards of health — sanitary authorities as they became in 1875. The Housing of the Working Classes Act 1890 heralded a first step in positive planning by municipal enterprise. However, we had to wait until 1909 for the first 'planning' statute. The Housing and Town Planning, etc., Act of that year empowered borough, urban and rural districts to make town plans for urban areas, subject to the approval of the Local Government Board (the central government department of the day).[4] Such a scheme was, however, restricted to the items (streets, open spaces, lighting, etc.) listed in the Fourth Schedule. Further statutes were passed in 1919 and 1925, but no important step forward was taken until 1932. The Town and Country Planning Act 1932 was the true midwife of planning law in a modern sense, although, as we shall see, that law did not come of age until another war and a further 16 years had passed.[5] The Act of 1932 had the following important features:

(a) Land use planning was now no longer confined to urban areas; as the title of the Act suggests, planning was to extend into the countryside.

(b) Accordingly, every borough, urban district and rural district (of which there were in 1932 some 1600[6] throughout England and Wales) was required to pass a resolution (which needed the approval of the

Ministry of Health) to prepare a planning scheme for their area.

(c) In areas where such a resolution had been approved, developers could apply to the local authority for 'interim development consent', to the carrying out of 'development'.[7] If such consent was refused (or not applied for) and the development in question proved eventually to have been in contravention of the terms of the eventual operative planning scheme, the developer might be compelled to cease or demolish his development, without any compensation. If on the other hand consent was obtained and the resulting development proved eventually to contravene the operative scheme, the developer would be entitled to compensation if he were then required to comply. There was, therefore, a considerable incentive to apply for consent, and this became common form.

(d) The resolution to prepare a scheme was intended to be followed by the actual preparation of the scheme, which would be adopted by the local authority and submitted to the Ministry for approval. This was, however, a slow process, especially as interim development control had to be administered concurrently. Planning in the 1930s was an infant discipline and there were very few local government officers with adequate skill or training. Consequently, by the time war broke out in 1939 very few schemes had become operative; after 1939 local authorities had too many other things to do with a staff creamed off for military service.

Nevertheless, Parliament did not ignore the subject, and prompted by the Barlow and Uthwatt Reports,[8] passed the Ministry of Town and Country Planning (Interim Development) Act 1943. This statute extended interim development control to the whole country, whether or not a resolution to prepare a scheme had been passed, and also provided for enforcement action. A local authority could thenceforth take action against a developer who undertook development without first obtaining interim development consent.

This was followed by the Town and Country Planning Act 1944, which gave extensive powers to local authorities to acquire land which had been 'blitzed' or 'blighted' by or as a consequence of enemy action during the war. The stage was now set for the passing of the seminal Act of 1947. This was foreshadowed by a White Paper[9] published by the Coalition Government of 1944, while the war was still being waged, which outlined the legislation that would be necessary for post-war reconstruction.

2. The Town and Country Planning Act 1947

This statute, passed by the first post-war Socialist Government, was therefore very largely not a party-political measure, except in relation to the financial provisions.[10] The main features of this Act, which are the basis of the modern legislation of 1971, may be summarised as follows:

(1) A reduction in the number of local planning authorities from the 1500 or so of the 1930s to the 150 or so counties and county boroughs. On local government reorganisation in 1974[11] this picture changed again, so that today there are some 440 district (metropolitan and non-metropolitan) planning authorities, 32 London boroughs and 52 county authorities, throughout England and Wales, *plus* the Greater London Council and the Council of the Isles of Scilly.

(2) Planning authorities were given (and still possess) very wide powers of compulsory acquisition of land for planning purposes.[12]

(3) Planning authorities were required to prepare a development plan, to show the optimum use that should be made of land in their area over a period of 20 years, which would be much less rigid than the interim and operative development schemes of the 1932 Act. This was subsequently changed considerably by the 1968 Act, as will be explained later (see Chapter 7).

(4) The Act followed the precedent of the earlier Acts by defining 'development' widely and requiring permission to be obtained, subject to minor exceptions on detail, before development was carried out.

(5) This amounted to 'nationalisation' of the right to develop — the landowner had to apply to a State agency for permission to exercise what would normally be regarded as one of the incidents of his ownership of the land: the right to develop. Therefore the Act provided for compensation to be paid to those landowners whose land was 'ripe' for development on the 7 January 1947[13] while the developer would also be required to pay the State if he was successful in obtaining permission to develop. These financial provisions were subsequently drastically altered, and the whole topic might be described as a game of Parliamentary 'ping-pong' between the two main opposing political parties.[14]

The purposes or objects of the 1947 Act have been judicially described as follows:

[the legislation] is for the orderly development of the countryside, to prevent unsightly development, to prevent the development of too crowded areas, to prevent the development taking place of industrial buildings and plant in what should be a residential district, and for the mapping out of residential districts and industrial districts, and so forth.[15]

Until the end of this passage, the emphasis here is on *restriction,* understandably enough, as it is the restrictive control exercised by the planning authority that has had the most significant impact on the landowner, and this is therefore the aspect of planning legislation that is most likely to be the subject of litigation. The *positive* side of the planning process, the 'mapping out' is, however, also of great practical importance, and will be discussed in the next Chapter.

3. Subsequent Planning Legislation

Not many years have passed since 1947 that have not seen some tinkering by Parliament with the 1947 Act, but, as we have said, the main structure of that Act (described at the time as a revolution in our land law) remains, swollen and staggering under the weight of many complicating provisions, but still substantially the same. The amending Acts can be listed as follows:

1953, 1954 Town and Country Planning Acts of these years, amended the financial provisions (see Chapter 18).
1953 Agricultural Land (Removal of Topsoil) Act, expanding the definition of development.
1959 Town and Country Planning Act, mainly concerned with cases of compulsory acquisition and compensation, now replaced by the Local Government Act 1972 and the Act of 1971.
1960 Caravan Sites and Control of Development Act; only the provisions on caravan sites remain important.
1962 Town and Country Planning Act, replacing the Act of 1947 and consolidating, with certain minor amendments; repealed in 1971.
1963 Town and Country Planning Act, now repealed.
1965 Control of Office and Industrial Development (also repealed).

1968 Town and Country Planning Act, introducing the new style development plans, but mostly repealed.

1971 Town and Country Planning Act, replacing the 1962 and most of the 1968 Acts; the operative (consolidation) statute at the present time.

1972 Town and Country Planning (Amendment) Act, amending the procedure for the preparation of development plans and in particular introducing the device of the 'examination in public'.

1974 Town and Country Amenities Act, dealing with conservation areas, trees, and historic, etc., buildings.

1977 Town and Country Planning (Amendment) Act, dealing with stop notices (part of enforcement procedure).

1980 Local Government, Land and Planning Act — a massive statute dealing with many topics, only some of which are relevant here.

In addition, there were the New Towns Acts of 1946 and 1965, and the 'financial' statutes, the Land Commission Act of 1967 and its dissolution in 1970, then the Community Land Act 1975, almost completely repealed by the Act of 1980. Minor matters are dealt with in the Countryside Act 1968 and the Petroleum and Submarine Pipe-lines Act 1975, and the Local Government Acts of 1972 and 1974.

Compensation for compulsory acquisition and in respect of certain planning restrictions, was dealt with in the Acts of 1947, 1953, 1954 and 1959, and by the Land Compensation Acts of 1961 and 1973, as amended by the Act of 1980. The procedure for compulsory acquisition itself is governed by the Authorisation of Land (Acquisition Procedure) Act 1946, and the procedure for claiming compensation by the Compulsory Purchase Act 1965 and the Lands Tribunal Act 1949.

This mass of what is often disjointed legislation is considered in the Chapters that follow, but we must not overlook the many pieces of subordinate legislation made under the authority of the Planning Acts, such as the General Development Order (now of 1977), the Use Classes Order, and the several Inquiries Procedure Regulations, to name but a few.

Notes

1. Statute of Winchester (1285); 200 feet was an estimate of the distance of a bow shot. See The Webbs, *English Local Government,* vol. 5, p. 7.

2. This had been preceded by an Ordinance, much to the same effect, of 1307.

3. *Shakespeare* by Ivor Brown, p. 41.

4. The Board was replaced by the Ministry of Health in 1919; this was followed by the Ministry of Town and Country Planning in 1943, itself superseded first by the Ministry of Local Government and Planning, and then by the Ministry of Housing and Local Government in 1950. This latter Department was to remain responsible for the supervision of local government generally and their land use control functions in particular until 1970, when it was superseded by the Department of the Environment, headed by a Secretary of State.

5. Until 1 July 1948, when the Town and Country Planning Act 1947 came into force (see below).

6. This number had shrunk by some 50 or so amalgamations of small authorities effected during the period 1925-35 or so.

7. 'Development' was widely defined in the 1932 Act in terms very similar to those subsequently to appear in the 1947 Act (see Chapter 8, p.96).

8. Scott Report, *Land Utilisation in Rural Areas,* 1942, Cmd. 6378; Uthwatt, *Compensation and Betterment,* 1942, Cmd. 6386.

9. *The Control of Land Use,* Cmd. 6537.

10. The history of the financial aspects of town and country planning controls is traced in Chapter 18, p.203.

11. By the Local Government Act 1972, which came into force on 1 April 1974.

12. See Chapter 20, p.219.

13. The date when the Bill which eventually became the 1947 Act, was introduced in the House of Commons.

14. See Chapter 18, p.201.

15. *Per* Lord Goddard, CJ, in *Attorney-General v. Smith* [1958] 2 All ER 557, p. 562.

6   Positive Planning

1. Introduction

Generally land use planning law is thought of in restrictive terms, as it is concerned primarily with the control of development and the imposition of restrictions on what an owner may do with his land. These are imposed to ensure that an owner will not offend against the basic principles of good planning as laid down in the development plan for the area. It is, moreover, this restrictive aspect of planning law that has the greatest impact on members of the public as landowners, and so it is restrictive planning that is the subject matter of litigation and so of the many detailed rules of statute and case law.

However, the law does also provide machinery whereby the planning authorities can ensure that desirable planning projects can be carried out. This is the positive aspect of planning law, and it consists mainly of a series of powers given to public authorities by various statutes, enabling them to acquire land, by agreement or compulsorily, and to develop the land so acquired.[1] Some of these powers are contained in Acts of Parliament conferring major functions on authorities, such as the Public Health Acts, empowering them to acquire land for sewage farms, refuse disposal sites, burial grounds and crematoria, etc. The Housing Acts, commencing with the Housing of the Working Classes Act 1890, have for years enabled district councils to purchase land for the construction of houses and the clearance of slums. These are but two examples: there are many other statutes authorising the acquisition of land for particular purposes. In this chapter, however, we shall confine ourselves to a consideration of those statutes that are more closely concerned with land acquisition and subsequent disposal or development in order to secure the optimum land use. The powers here to be considered are therefore those given primarily so as to ensure positive planning.

2. New Towns

One of the most important pieces of post-war legislation of this kind, and certainly one of the most successful in practice, has been the New

Towns Acts of 1946 and 1965 (subsequently amended in matters of detail). Under these Acts, the Secretary of State is empowered to designate areas of land (normally undeveloped but not necessarily totally so) as sites for 'new towns'. When a designation order has been made he then, also by order, constitutes a public corporation, known as the '[according to the name of the town] development corporation'. This corporation will have a governing body consisting of a chairman, deputy chairman and not more than seven other members, all appointed by the Secretary of State. It will be their duty to plan[2] and to arrange for the construction of the new town, with all necessary facilities, within the designated area. They will be put in funds by the Treasury and will contract with firms (and possibly a local authority) for the construction of the roads, sewers, houses, shops, commercial and industrial premises, and they will let tenancies (sometimes on long leases [3]) or sell[4] plots or buildings to developers and potential residents.

Until the new town has been developed, the development corporation will act as a kind of estate manager and developer. They will have no governmental functions except as landowner and planner, but they are not the planning authority for their area, although they may become such if they are invited to make a scheme for an enterprise zone (see below). Eventually the houses constructed by or for the corporation will be handed over to the local authority as the normal housing authority while the other assets of the corporation (factories, shops, etc.) will be transferred to a separate corporation organised on a national basis, the New Town Commission.[5]

The new towns movement in Britain, considerably influenced by the writings of Ebenezer Howard[6] and the pre-war private enterprise experiments[7] at Welwyn Garden City and Letchworth, has established over 25 new towns throughout the United Kingdom since the Second World War, some of which are now (1980) fully developed. These towns were originally conceived to meet the needs of 'overspill' from the conurbations in London, the Midlands and elsewhere, 'blitzed' or 'blighted' as a consequence of the war. It was possible to plan and build them quickly, because of this special administrative and financial machinery provided by the New Towns Acts. The corporations, as they have had but a single urgent task to perform, have achieved their objectives with drive and enthusiasm.

A different type of machinery was invented by the Town Development Act 1952. Rather than start with a new town in open fields, the sensible concept of developing an existing town and using existing resources was attempted. A small market town, already supplied with most of the necessary infrastructure such as shops, sewage farm, railway communications, etc., was chosen for development. An 'exporting local authority', such as London or Birmingham, would then enter into an agreement under the Act of 1952 with the 'importing local authority', under which the exporting authority would bear a substantial proportion of the cost of constructing roads, sewers, houses, commercial premises, etc. in the importing authority's area. The importing authority would be responsible for supervising the construction and managing the estates when completed, but the exporting authority would have the right to nominate prospective tenants for the houses and to assist in finding industry and commercial businesses prepared to move to the developing towns and so provide employment. Additional subsidies towards this expenditure are payable by the importing authority's county council, and by the Secretary of State for the Environment.

This system has proved much less successful than the device of the new towns. The administrative machinery under the 1952 Act has to be very complicated, requiring the agreement of many committees of both exporting and importing authorities, and of the county council; then the whole scheme needs the approval of the Secretary of State. All this consumes much time and mountains of paper. Nevertheless, four small towns[8] have been developed by this means over a period of some 20 years, and these have provided some relief to overcrowded areas in London and Birmingham.

New and developed towns cannot consist only of housing; commercial firms and industries must be encouraged to establish themselves in these areas so as to provide employment. The development corporations from the beginning were most active in attracting employment; their efforts were assisted by the Location of Offices Bureau. This was a special public corporation established by Ministerial order,[9] originally with the task of persuading firms to move their offices out of London, but in view of more recently changing conditions, it was abolished in 1979. Using the device of the industrial development certificate, the Department of Trade and Industry has been able to direct industrial development into these new and developing centres.

3. Urban Development

Under the Local Government, Land and Planning Act 1980, a new type of public corporation, modelled on the successful new town development corporations, may be established by order of the Secretary of State. Under Part XVI of the Act, the Secretary of State may create such a corporation when he considers it 'expedient in the national interest' (s.134) for the purpose of regenerating an area within a metropolitan district or in London. It is presently intended to establish six or so such corporations for the inner areas of the larger cities in the country. Each corporation will consist of a chairman, deputy chairman and 5-11 other members, all appointed by the Secretary of State; in selecting members he must have regard to the desirability of securing the services of persons having special knowledge of the locality.

A corporation would receive grants from the Treasury and be able to raise loans. They would operate independently of the local authority for the areas and would take over from that authority a number of functions. Thus:

(a) they would have power to make proposals for development of land within the urban development area. The Secretary of State may, after consultation with the local authority, approve those proposals and then he may make a development order under section 24 of the 1971 Act, giving planning permission for any development of land in accordance with such approved proposals (s.148);

(b) they will become the planning authority for their area, if the Secretary of State so provides by order (s.149);

(c) a similar order may make the corporation responsible for building regulation control in their area (s.151);

(d) similarly, they may be made the housing authority, and in that event they will be required to allow rent rebates (s.153);

(e) they will have certain highway powers in relation to new streets (s.157);

(f) they will also have the powers and duties in relation to the provision of public sewers normally vested in a water authority under the Water Act 1973 (s.158);

(g) The Secretary of State may make an order vesting land belonging to a local authority in a corporation (s.141), and all corporations will have wide powers of acquiring and disposing of land so acquired (s.136).

The urban corporations have obvious affinities with the new town corporations, but as they will operate in developed areas having established local authorities with long traditions of housing and planning functions, their tasks will be carried out under very different conditions. Liaison between the nominated corporation and the elected local authority will be essential.

Quite apart from urban development as above described, a district council, London Borough, new town development corporation or urban development corporation may be 'invited' by the Secretary of State to prepare a scheme relating to the development of some part of their area. If the invitation is accepted by the authority concerned, they will be expected to prepare a scheme, which must be duly advertised in the locality. The authority may adopt their scheme, and after further advertisement, time for objections, and determination of those objections by the High Court (there is no provision for a local inquiry), the scheme will come into operation. The Secretary of State may then make an 'enterprise zone' order for the area covered by the scheme, specifying the commencement date and the period for which the area is to remain such a zone.

The significance of an enterprise zone order, from a land use point of view, is that the order will have the effect of granting planning permission for development specified in the scheme or for development of a class so specified (Sched. 32, para. 17) but any such permission may be made subject to specified conditions or limitations. The Act also provides that the enterprise zone authority (the body originally invited to prepare the scheme) will be the planning authority for their area (ibid.).

The authority for an enterprise zone will apparently be expected to undertake and encourage development in the zone, but they will not have as extensive powers, nor will they be funded to the same extent by the central exchequer, as will the urban development corporations.

4. National Parks and the Countryside

The 'national park' concept is of North American origin; the great national parks of the United States, such as Yosemite, the Everglades in Florida and Platt in Oklahoma, have been established for many years, and are managed as reserves by a national (Federal) parks service. In the United States, all the land in a national park is owned by the Federal Government,[10] and no substantial development is there permitted; indeed, members of the public are on occasion totally prohibited from access.

(a) National Parks

In Britain, the national park is basically different, in that the land in the park is not acquired by any State agency. Under the National Parks and Access to the Countryside Act 1949 (since expanded by the Countryside Act 1968), a public corporation, the Countryside Commission,[11] can recommend to the Secretary of State that he should designate an area of the country which is of particular beauty, as a 'National Park'. Such areas as the Lake District, the Peak District, the Norfolk Broads, Exmoor and Dartmoor, have been so designated.[12] The effect of a designation order is in law comparatively slight. Land ownership is left in private hands, but a special organisation is established for planning administration. This will be *either* of a joint planning committee consisting of representatives from the several planning authorities within whose area some part of the park area is situate, *or* (in two cases only[13]) a joint planning board. The board is a corporation with legal existence separate from the constituent local authorities, and it is entitled to issue a rate precept on them for its finance. All the members are appointed by the Secretary of State.

A national park planning authority (of either kind) will exercise all the normal powers of a planning authority within the park area, but it will (presumably) not willingly grant planning permission for any development that may adversely affect the environment of the national park. In law, however, the provisions of the 1971 Act are applied in exactly the same manner in a national park as they are elsewhere in the country.

A national park planning authority will have a few special powers — to provide a warden service for the park and to construct car parks, public conveniences, refreshment facilities, etc., at appropriate places.

The Secretary of State may also declare an area, normally much smaller than a National Park,[14] to be an 'area of outstanding natural beauty'.[15] This also has even less legal effect, as there is no special planning authority for such an area, but designation operates as a warning to local authorities to be chary in granting planning permission for development that may adversely affect the physical environment of the area.

(b) Access to the Countryside

A planning authority may arrange for public access to be assured to 'open country' in their area. This expression is defined in section 59 of the Act of 1949 (as subsequently amended[16]), and access may be obtained by an agreement with the landowner(s), or by the authority making a compulsory 'access order'. Such an order will be subject to objections made to the Secretary of State. There will then be a public inquiry, if the order is objected to and the objections are not withdrawn;[17] it will then be a matter for the Secretary of State to confirm, quash or modify the access order.

(c) Special Areas

Smaller areas that are the habitat for some rare fauna or flora can be designated by the Nature Conservancy Council as areas of 'special scientific interest'; members of the public will then be excluded from such areas, unless they obtain a special licence from the Council.[18]

(d) Country Parks

Under the Countryside Act 1968, ss.6-8, a county or district council may establish, on land owned (or acquired for the purpose) by them, a *country park*, of perhaps a few acres in extent, and this may include land covered with water. At such a park, the authority may provide refreshment facilities, car parks and conveniences, and facilities for a wide variety of outdoor pursuits, such as camping and caravanning, boating and yachting, swimming, fishing, and the playing of games and sports. Charges may be made for the use of the facilities provided, but the public must be allowed access free of charge. The country park concept, like the sports forum, has become very popular in recent years.

(e) Conservation Areas

These may be designated under section 277 of the 1971 Act (as amended); it then becomes the duty of the planning authority to formulate proposals for their protection and improvement (s.277A).

(f) Rights of Way

Under the 1949 Act, county councils were required to carry out a detailed survey of public rights of way (footpaths, bridleways, and carriageways) in their area; these have for the most part been completed and in many instances the rights of way have been recorded on the county council's 'definitive maps'. Many of these are now indicated on the Ordnance Survey maps in general public use. The county council has a duty to protect public rights of way, and they can establish a new right of way where required in the public interest,[19] either by agreement with the landowner's concerned, or by a compulsory public path order.[20] Long-distnce routes may be established by this means, such as the Pennine Way and the coastguard path in Cornwall.

(g) Wildlife and Countryside Act 1981

Under the Wildlife and Countryside Act 1981, new powers were given to the Secretary of State and in some cases to local authorities, to protect certain features in the countryside. Thus:

(i) The Secretary of State may designate an area as being of special scientific interest by reason of its flora, fauna, or geological or physiographical features; in such a case the owner or occupier of the land may not carry out any 'operations' (a word that is not defined) that are likely to destroy or damage those features, without the prior written permission of the Nature Conservancy Council, unless planning permission has been granted or there is a case of 'emergency'. Compensation may be payable if permission for particular operations is refused.

(ii) On the prompting of the Nature Conservancy Council, the Secretary of State or the local planning authority may by order designate an area of land in the countryside consisting substantially of exposed limestone or of limestone lying near the surface ('limestone pavement'); such an order would prohibit the removal or disturbance of limestone on or in the area so designated, unless the removal or disturbance had been authorised under a planning permission granted under the 1971 Act.

(iii) The district planning authority (or, in a National Park, the county) may make a management agreement with the owner or occupier of any land in the countryside in their area for the purpose of conserving or enhancing the natural beauty of the land or for promoting its enjoyment by the public (these two purposes may in practice be inconsistent).

(iv) Where the Secretary of State has made an order in respect of specified land in a National Park, the owner or occupier of any part of that land that is moor or heath and that has not been in agricultural use for at least 20 years, may not convert the land by ploughing or otherwise into agricultural land, nor may he carry out any other agricultural operations that are likely to affect its character, *unless*

(a) the county planning authority has given consent; *or*

(b) three months have elapsed within which time the county authority have neither given nor refused consent; *or*

(c) the county authority has refused consent and twelve months have elapsed (the point of this final condition is to give the authorities time to take appropriate action, such as to acquire the land or to persuade the owner to enter into a management agreement).

Orders made under (i), (ii) and (iv) above normally have immediate effect, but they must be notified to landowners and occupiers concerned. If any representations are made against an order, the Secretary of State must convene a local inquiry, and consider whether to make an amending or revoking order as a consequence of that inquiry. Alternatively any person aggrieved may within six weeks of the order coming into effect ask the High Court to quash the order on the ground that the order was not within the powers given by the Act, or that the specified procedural requirements had not been observed (1981 Act, Schedule 10).

This procedure whereby an order comes into force *before* the possibility of an inquiry into objections, is a novel one, but is justifiable on the grounds of the need to prevent action being taken by a landowner during the period while an order is under consideration.

5. Housing

Local authorities are given wide powers to improve and acquire land in built up areas under the Housing Acts of 1957, 1969, 1974 and 1980, which will be considered in Chapter 19.

6. Highways

Under the Highways Act 1980, the appropriate central and local government authorities have extensive powers to provide new highways and (a power less extensively used) to close or divert existing highways.[21]

The Minister for Transport has power to designate land as the site for a 'special road' (commonly, but not in the statute, known as a 'motorway') and for the necessary access link roads and ancillary purposes, such as service stations. The designation order gives power to the Minister to acquire the land so required, either compulsorily or by agreement; in modern practice,[22] the designation order and the necessary compulsory purchase orders are made at the same time. The Act lays down a procedure for persons affected by these orders to object, and provides that any such objections that are not withdrawn, must be heard at a local inquiry conducted on behalf of the Minister, much in the same manner as a local planning inquiry.[23] The Minister must consider the report of any such inquiry before deciding whether to confirm his own orders, and there is then a right of appeal to the courts against the orders, on a point of law alone.[24]

The meaning of highways in relation to land use is considered further in Chapter 19.

7. Development Plans

The development plan, which outlines a local planning authority's proposals for the future land uses of their area, may be regarded as a vital part of positive planning. In the development plan local, regional and national development should be forecast, and the optimum land use of the area predicted, having regard to the anticipated resources of the public authorities concerned. The development plan is also a guide to the authorities in exercising development control — their *restrictive* planning powers. The contents of these plans and the procedures governing their making is discussed in the next chapter.

However, a development plan in itself can achieve nothing; it is merely a blueprint for the future. As an instrument of positive planning, it needs to be implemented by sensitive operation of development control and by positive intervention by the public authorities. Such intervention may take the form (by use of the special legislation designed for the purpose) of establishing a new town, by designating a national park or a motorway, or by designing and constructing a new housing estate.[25] In order to achieve any of these objectives, however, the appropriate authority will need to acquire land, either by agreement or compulsorily. Legal powers to acquire land for a vast variety of public purposes are contained in many statutes. The procedure that Parliament has prescribed (principally in the interests of those whose land is being taken against their wishes) is generally uniform, and will be described in Chapter 20. Powers also exist which enable local authorities to acquire land solely so as to ensure that desirable development is carried out either by public authority or by private enterprise, and this must now be explained.

8. The Acquisition of Land for Planning Purposes

For many years the most important land acquisition power was that conferred on district councils by section 112 of the 1971 Act and the corresponding provisions in earlier legislation. This section, as strengthened by section 91 of the 1980 Act, enables land to be acquired (compulsorily if necessary) for, *inter alia,* 'the proper planning of the area'. Much wider powers than this it would be difficult to conceive. A court of law would be extremely hard pressed to find that a particular proposed acquisition under this section would *not* be for the 'proper planning' of the area. When is planning 'proper' and when is it improper? An answer to that question could be given only by the planning authority who are themselves proposing to acquire the land.

Closely allied to this wide acquisition power is the power contained in section 123 of the 1971 Act permitting local authorities to dispose of land so acquired, either by sale or by long lease. These sections go back historically to the Town and Country Planning Act 1944, designed to deal with the reconstruction of land and premises damaged or adversely affected by enemy action. These powers, of land purchase and subsequent disposition, were widely used in many urban areas, such as Coventry, Exeter, Plymouth, Portsmouth, and of course in London. Some cities, such as Birmingham, were not content with these general powers, and obtained even wider ones by persuading Parliament to pass a local Act in their favour.

The Town and Country Planning Act 1959 and the Local Authorities (Land) Act 1963 went further down the road of allowing local authorities to act as major landowners and developers; under the 1959 Act they could appropriate land acquired for specific purposes, as land for development and grant long leases for the purpose; these powers are now replaced by corresponding sections in the Local Government Act 1972.

The 1947 Act had established a special public corporation, the Central Land Board, which had the primary task of collecting development charges.[26] They were also given the duty of acquiring land (at existing use value) that was ripe for development, but which was not in fact being developed. This power was highly unpopular, and was not often used, but some 15 years after the demise of the Central Land Board in 1952, a new corporation (the Land Commission) was given much the same powers.[27] This second corporation also was unpopular, and its land acquisition powers seemed to some to conflict with the functions of local authorities. The Land Commission, like its predecessor, was killed off in 1970.[28] When Parliament once more tackled the problem of ensuring that development was actually carried out where thought to be desirable in the public interest, the powers of acquisition and disposal were this time given to local authorities. In the Community Land Act 1975, it was provided that on a 'second appointed day',[29] no development (subject to a few minor exceptions) could take place otherwise than on land which had passed through public ownership. All development land was to be purchased (at existing use value) by the appropriate local authority,[30] and the authority would then arrange for the desired development to be carried out. This would be done either by the authority themselves, or by the authority selling the land to a developer. In the latter case, sale would take place at development value, the profit then accruing to the 'community' i.e. to the local authority concerned. Special arrangements were made in Wales, as the Act of 1975 had once more established a public corporation, the Land Authority for Wales. Somewhat strangely, in spite of the experience of the Central Land Board and the Land Commission, the Land Authority for Wales proved to be successful and reasonably popular with Welsh local government.[31] Consequently when it became the turn of the Community Land Act to receive its quietus at the hands of a Conservative Government, the Land Authority for Wales was left alive, in a revised form.[32]

As the law now stands, therefore, local authorities (outside Wales) have wide land acquisition and disposal powers, which can be used, if the authority concerned is so disposed, to ensure that development thought to be desirable, would be carried out, in the *right* place. 'Right', that is, according to the value judgment of the local planners. Potentially, the powers of positive planning are absolute, and it is perhaps difficult to understand why it was thought desirable to supplement section 112 of the 1971 Act by the 'revolutionary' provisions of first the Land Commission Act and then the Community Land Act. The Act of 1975 was seen, however, as a positive spur to local authorities to act, and to provide the 'carrot' of the financial profit which would have come into the municipal treasure chests as a consequence of the procedure of the Act being implemented. In practice this profit might well have been comparatively small, and in any event would have been long delayed.[33] If a second appointed day had ever arrived, local authorities would have been compelled to take into public ownership all land suitable for large-scale development.

Having acquired land for planning purposes (for example, for major town centre redevelopment), the local authority may carry out the desired development themselves. More commonly they will decide to arrange for at least part of the development to be carried out by private enterprise. This they may do by a variety of different arrangements. Thus, they may:[34]

(a) employ a contractor to carry out the work while retaining ownership of the freehold in their own hands;

(b) grant a lease, perhaps for 99 years, to a developer, subject to payment of a ground rent and to conditions as to the development to be carried out. This procedure is popular, as it enables the authority to retain detailed control;

(c) sell the freehold to a developer, while imposing restrictive covenants as to how the land is to be used. This may be attractive to the authority who wish to obtain a return of their capital;

(d) in some cases it may be appropriate to enter into a planning agreement under section 52 of the 1971 Act,[35] having first sold off the freehold.

Under the 1980 Act,[36] new provisions are included to prevent local and public authorities from hoarding land. Local authorities may be directed by the Secretary of State to dispose of land they have acquired and public bodies listed in Schedule 16[37] to the Act may be required to provide information as to their land holdings, so that the Secretary of State may maintain a register, and in specified areas the Secretary of State may then require the disposal of any land on this register.

Notes

1. Little can be achieved positively except through the ownership — and therefore the fullest control — over the land to be 'planned'. Local authorities are able to hire staff, obtain offices and buy stationery, etc., by virtue of the powers given to them as local authorities by the Local Government Act 1972 (see, in particular, section 112 thereof).

2. They will prepare a detailed plan for the town in consultation with the local planning authority; they will not need to obtain express planning permission for their project, as this will be covered by the Town and Country Planning (New Towns Special Development) Order 1963.

3. Subject to strict covenants as to design and lay-out, etc. The new town corporation will in this respect be in the position of a private landlord; see Chapter 3, p.35.

4. Subject to restrictive covenants which will normally be drafted so as to be enforceable against successive owners, ibid.

5. New Town Acts 1959 and 1977. The Act of 1965 was further amended in detail by the Act of 1980.

6. *Garden Cities of Tomorrow,* first published in 1902.

7. Earlier commercially based examples are to be seen in Saltaire (Yorkshire) and Bournville (near Birmingham).

8. Basingstoke and Andover in Hampshire, Droitwich in Worcestershire and Daventry in Northamptonshire.

9. Location of Offices Bureau Order 1963.

10. There are also some State Parks, established under State legislation.

11. Formerly the National Parks Commission, established under that name by the 1949 Act.

12. There are now 10 National Parks in different parts of the United Kingdom.

13. The Lake District and the Peak District. Some comparison may be made here, from an administrative point of view, with the new towns and the developing towns. As the new town corporations have shown drive and efficiency as compared with the strangling committee structure of the developing town, so the joint planning boards have achieved much more for their parks than have the joint planning committees, which have to refer back for many decisions to their parent bodies, on whom they are responsible for funding.

14. The area of the South Downs in Sussex has been so designated.

15. National Parks and Access to the Countryside Act 1949, section 87.

16. The 'countryside' includes woodlands and (with exceptions) rivers, canals and lakes: Countryside Act 1968, section 16.

17. Each local authority must have made a survey of the public access requirements in their area: 1949 Act, s.61.

18. National Parks and Access to the Countryside Act 1949, section 23; local authorities may establish 'nature reserves': ibid., s.21.

19. Either for local use or as part of a 'long-distance route'.

20. Highways Act 1959, section 28.

21. At common law the rule was 'once a highway, always a highway', but there are now a number of statutory procedures, enabling a court or (in some instances) a Minister, to order the closure of a public highway where this is no longer necessary, or where closure would be necessary for some desirable development, such as a new motorway.

22. Regularised by the Highways Act 1971.

23. The Highways (Inquiries Procedure) Rules 1976, will apply to such an inquiry. As to planning inquiries, see Chapter 14, p.144.

24. Government policy may not be called into question at such an inquiry: *Bushell* v. *Secretary of State* [1980] 2 All ER 608.

25. Powers to acquire land for housing are principally contained in the Housing Act 1957.

26. see Chapter 18, p.203.

27. Land Commission Act 1967.

28. Land Commission (Dissolution) Act 1970.

29. Which day never in fact arrived, as the 1975 Act was repealed before an order appointing such a day had been made.

30. Usually the district council, but the Act contemplated that the respective functions of a county and its district councils should be settled by a 'land acquisition management scheme'.

31. No doubt in part because of the linking membership of the governing body of the Authority with the Welsh local authorities.

32. Local Government, Land and Planning Act 1980, Part XII.

33. See article in [1980] JPL, p. 78.

34. Adequate powers are contained in sections of the 1980 Act. All these processes may be followed also by the new town development corporations.

35. Chapter 12, p.139.
36. 1980 Act, Part X.
37. This list includes the statutory undertakers and the National Coal Board.

7   Development Plans

1. Introduction

The concept of a development plan, introduced by the Act of 1947 to replace the interim and operative planning schemes of the 1932 Act, purports to meet two objectives, namely (a) to indicate what, in the opinion of the planning authority, is the optimum use for the future of the land in their area, and (b) to provide guidance to themselves and potential developers in the exercise of development control. The development plan is thus of importance in positive *and* in restrictive planning. In its positive aspects the plan should outline the policy of the planning authority for the foreseeable future, taking into consideration the existing land uses and the resources that it is anticipated will in due course be available to achieve those objectives. In its restrictive and more strictly legal aspects the plan can be no more than a guide. For instance, the fact that the plan may show that an area of land is reserved for predominantly residential use, does not mean of necessity that planning permission will be granted for residential use of a particular plot within that area; nor, indeed, that permission will necessarily or probably, be refused for any other use. Designation of a particular use in a development plan provides merely a persuasive argument that the land in question *should* be so used.

Under the 1947 and 1962 Acts development plans were somewhat precisely divided into county and town maps, and each map had to be programmed, indicating what development was proposed for the first 5 years of the plan period, what was proposed for the next 15 years, and finally the development that it was contemplated would not be achieved in less than 20 years. These plans became somewhat rigid, and the Act of 1968 introduced[1] a new kind of development plan, intended to be more flexible and to emphasise the resources actually expected to be available to achieve the development forecast. The requirement to prepare these new plans was introduced by degrees, and the operative sections of the 1968 Act and subsequently the corresponding sections of the 1971 Act, are applied piecemeal to separate areas of the country by order of the Secretary of State. These orders were made as and when the Secretary of State was satisfied that the local authority had the staff and other resources adequate to supervise these new style development plans. These plans are now (1980) in course of preparation in most areas of the country, and in some areas the procedure has been completed and the plans are legally in force.

2. The Modern Development Plans

Preparatory to the making of the plan itself the local planning authority must carry out a detailed survey of the existing land uses in their areas,[2] with the principal purpose of identifying the special local characteristics and any deficiencies and particular needs. A report on the survey must be prepared, made public, and a copy sent to the Secretary of State. Having completed the survey it then becomes the duty of the local planning authority to proceed with the making of proposals for a 'structure plan' (or plans) for their area.

The objectives of a development plan, both the structure plan and the several local plans, should include the following:

(i) the preservation of green belts round urban areas, and the prevention of sprawl into the countryside;
(ii) the safeguarding of the social and physical environment, including wooded areas, the protection of agriculture and areas of special amenity value;
(iii) the maintenance of the economy, the siting of industry and improvement of communications;
(iv) adequate facilities for leisure activities.

Ecological considerations should be taken into account, as should anticipated demographic changes, and economic and other resources must be realistically assessed.

A development plan will consist of two quite distinct elements; the structure plan, and one or more local plans. The structure plan, prepared by the county authority, will cover the entire area being dealt with under the single development plan. This will normally be the whole of the administrative county, but a structure plan may cover more than one county (by agreement between the county authorities), or it may be decided to prepare more than one structure plan for a single county. A structure plan is not really a plan at all; it is a written statement, in considerable detail, of the county's policy for the area. A structure plan is therefore usually a quite substantial document, perhaps of some 200 or more pages, supported by illustrative maps and diagrams as necessary.[3]

Local plans are very different; they will cover much smaller areas and may be of three different kinds:

(a) 'ordinary' local plans, which normally will cover a single urban area within the area of the structure plan. There will probably be several of these within that area, but together they will not necessarily cover the whole of the area covered by the structure plan;

(b) formerly these were action area plans; these covered comparatively small areas where it is considered that substantial comprehensive development or redevelopment is likely to, or should, take place within a period of 10 years;[4]

(c) subject local plans; these will be concerned with particularly sensitive problems within a defined local area, such as caravan sites at a holiday resort.[5]

The county planning authority, in consultation with the district councils in the county, will prepare a development plan scheme,[6] which will determine what local plans are to be prepared, by which authority (normally by the appropriate district planning authority), and within what period of time. The local plans will go into much more detail[7] than the structure plans, and will be concerned with the land use of individual parcels. The local plans will take the form of maps and diagrams supported by written statements, the emphasis being the exact opposite of the format of the structure plan.

3. Development Plan Procedure

(A) Structure Plans

It is an outstanding feature of the modern procedure regulating the making of the development plan (in both stages) that there should be ample opportunity for public participation in the planning process.

Consequently, the report on the survey must be made available for public inspection.[8] The structure plan itself must then be prepared in draft and made available for public inspection.[9] The authority is expected to publish and explain its proposals to the general public throughout the area, by means of advertisements, lectures, hand-outs, and also by town'forums'; a report must be made to the Secretary of State on the action taken to inform public opinion.[10] Any observations made by members of the public, or by public bodies (other local authorities, the water authority and the Department of Transport, etc.) with whom the planning authority are required to consult, must be duly considered.[11] Having made any modifications considered desirable as a consequence of this process, the county authority must then prepare their draft structure plan which will be a revised version of their original proposals. This they will submit to the Secretary of State for his confirmation.[12] Before he decides whether to confirm the plan, however, opportunity must have been given for objections and representations to be made (either for or against the proposals in the plan) by any members of the public, and consequently the submission to the Secretary of State must have been advertised. These objections and representations are then referred to a special kind of inquiry known as an 'examination in public', a procedure new to planning administration, which was introduced by the Town and Country Planning (Amendment) Act 1972 (which added new sections to the 1971 Act).[13] The examination in public, convened by the Secretary of State, is thought of rather as a round table discussion than an adversarial court-like 'hearing'.

When it is decided that an examination in public is necessary, the Secretary of State will appoint three persons to conduct it. One of these will be an ordinary member of the planning inspectorate of the Department of the Environment, one will be a regional officer of the same Department, and the chairman will be an independent person, perhaps a practising barrister or solicitor, perhaps a retired civil servant or local government officer. This panel will be told by the Secretary of State what the issues are that are to be considered, and whom of the objectors should be permitted to give evidence on each issue, although the chairman may, if he thinks fit, add to these lists. Issues not on the list will not be examined, nor will objectors or other persons not so listed be permitted to take part in the examination in public, although any person will be entitled to attend. The panel will then hold a preliminary sitting, and arrange the order of the items and witnesses to be examined. When the examination itself commences, the chairman of the panel will call on one or more of the objectors (so chosen in advance) to make points relating to a pre-selected issue. The local planning authority and other public bodies concerned will be allowed to take part in the discussion and then the panel will proceed to the next issue.

Members of the public, in spite of the name of the procedure, will not be allowed to speak, however relevant may be their observations.

When all the issues that have been pre-selected have been so considered, the examination in public will be terminated and the panel will submit a report to the Secretary of State, who will then decide whether to confirm, quash or modify the structure plan. The Secretary of State makes a commencement order, which has the effect of repealing the former provisions about development plans (contained in the 1962 Act) in relation to the area covered by the structure plan he has just approved. The structure plan together with the local plans then becomes the development plan (as defined in section 20 of the 1971 Act). The development plan is subject to questioning as to its validity before the High Court (see below). In keeping with the general requirement in this procedure, the approval of the plan by the Secretary of State must be advertised in the locality.[14] Copies of the plan (at both draft and final form) must also be made available on sale at a reasonable charge.[15]

(B) Local Plans

Local plans are normally prepared by the appropriate district council in accordance with the development plan scheme, but exceptionally, a local plan may be prepared by a county council. A formal survey is not necessary prior to the preparation of a local plan, but there must be consultation with the county (or district) authority. The same kind of procedure, giving opportunities for public participation must be followed in relation to each local plan (of all kinds) as that which applies to structure plan procedure.[16] But the final stage, after the draft plan has been revised and representation and objections have been received to the draft plan, these objections and representations must be considered, not at an examination in public, but before a local inquiry. This is convened by the local (district) planning authority, which has prepared the plan. The inquiry will be presided over by an inspector appointed by the Secretary of State and will follow the normal adversarial procedure of inquiries on a planning appeal.[17]

The inspector's report on the inquiry must be considered by the district council, and they will then adopt (or reject) their own plan with or without modifications. They must have sent a report to the Secretary of State on the measures they have taken to ensure that members of the public are aware of the proposals in the plan, and if he is not satisfied that there have been sufficient opportunities given for public participation, he may give the council directions accordingly.[18] Similarly, although a local plan does not normally have to be confirmed by the Secretary of State, the district council must send a copy to him, and he may decide to call it in for consideration and confirmation by him in lieu of the district council.[19]

A local plan must not contain proposals contrary to those contained in the structure plan, and normally it cannot become law until the structure plan has come into effect, but under the Act of 1980, this need not always be the case. But even in such a case, there must not be any conflict with the provisions of the structure plan when this comes finally into effect.[20]

(C) Alterations, etc.

If the Secretary of State decides to modify or alter the provisions of a structure plan, he may convene a new examination in public, but he is not obliged to do so. At any time after the approval of a structure plan the county authority may submit proposals (together with a detailed report) to the Secretary of State for its alteration. A district council may make proposals for the alteration of a local plan (and may be directed to do so by the Secretary of State) and the provisions about objections and inquiries referred to above will then apply.[21]

(D) Subsquent Proceedings

The structure plan and the several local plans together applicable to areas within that covered by the structure plan (for there need not be a local plan for the whole of the structure plan area) in law constitute the development plan. Any person aggrieved as a consequence of some substantial error of procedure in the course of making either the structure plan or a local plan, or any alteration, etc., thereof, or if he contends that the plan is not within the powers conferred by the 1971 Act, may make an application to the High Court. Any such application must be made within a period of six weeks from the date of the first publication of a notice saying that the Secretary of State has approved the structure plan, or that the local authority has adopted the local plan.[22]

On such an application the High Court may make an interim order suspending the operation of the plan insofar as it affects the property of the applicant, or the Court may quash the plan wholly or in part, either generally or only in so far as it affects the applicant's property. In practice applications to the Court under this provision are likely to be extremely rare; it would be difficult to argue that any plan was outside the powers of the Act, and procedural errors of substance are very uncommon. Indeed, there was no reported case in the courts under the corresponding provisions of the 1947 Act or 1962 Act; nor has there been one under the 1971 Act to date.

4. Public Participation

The procedure outlined above makes extensive provisions for the public to be made aware of the proposed (and actual) contents of a structure and a local plan, and to make observations and objections at all stages of the process. The examination in public of a structure plan is certainly limited, in that only selected topics are examined, and those persons who are permitted to take part also are limited, but there are no such limitations on the participation of members of the public at an inquiry into a local plan. The Skeffington Report[23] had recommended that authorities should undertake elaborate exercises in informing members of the public, so that they could effectively take part in the plan preparation process, and these recommendations have been adopted by many authorities.

In addition to public participation in the strict sense, local authorities are required, at both the structure plan and the local plan stage, to consult with other public bodies that will be interested. These would include electricity and gas boards, the water authorities and other public utility undertakings, and also the Minister for Transport as highway authority for trunk and special (motorways) roads in the area.

5. The Effect of the Development Plan

Once the structure plan has been approved by the Secretary of State and a local plan has been adopted by the local authority, these plans will have legal effect as the development plan for the area.[24] This in practice means little.

When the planning authority take some 'planning action', such as the consideration of an application for planning permission or whether to serve an enforcement notice, they are required by law 'to have regard to the provisions of the development plan and other material considerations'. If they propose to grant planning permission for some development that will conflict with the provisions of the development plan, they must advertise their proposals and allow an opportunity for objections.[25] But this does not mean that they must abide strictly by the terms of the plan. Having had regard to its provisions, the authority may decide to depart from those provisions, provided they observe the special procedure.[26]

Therefore, a prospective developer or landowner cannot rely completely on the plan. Even if he proposes to carry out some development on his land which accords with the provisions of the plan, he will still need to obtain planning permission. If eventually he is refused such permission, he will of course be entitled to appeal, and on such appeal he can (and almost certainly will) use the argument of the plan. But even then the Secretary of State is entitled to dismiss the appeal and refuse permission.

Nevertheless, a purchaser of property in a neighbourhood unknown to him would be well advised to inspect the plan before he commits himself to the purchase. Not only will the plan give him some indication of the types of development for which he is likely to be able to obtain permission, but also it will give him a forecast of the type of development, public or private, that is likely in the neighbourhood in the near future. He may, for instance, be interested to know if new schools are planned, if a major road is proposed, or if a housing or industrial estate is likely to be developed in the vicinity. The plan will certainly indicate any major proposed development by public authorities, such as motorways, new towns, airports, etc.

The development plan is thus a guide for development control, a blueprint for positive planning for the future, and an advance warning — or promise — for landowners. Although it has a clear status in law, that status is of only minor legal importance.

Notes

1. As a consequence of the report of a working party (known as the 'Planning Action Group', or PAG) within the former Ministry of Housing and Local Government, which reported in 1965.

2. Act of 1971, section 6 (as amended by the 1980 Act). The matters to be taken into account in the survey are listed in s.6(3) and include the principal physical and economic characteristics of the area. These matters are to be 'kept under review' (by what means is not precisely specified).

3. The required contents of a structure plan are specified (in very general terms) in s.7(3) of the 1971 Act. The plan must be accompanied by a statement of the reasons justifying the policy and general proposals of the plan: 1971 Act, s.7(6A) added by Sched. 14 to the Act of 1980.

4. Action areas should be identified in the structure plan: s.7(5). The requirement to prepare a special local plan for an action area was contained in section 11(6). The procedure is specified in detail in the Town and Country Planning (Structure and Local Plans) Regulations 1974, SI 1974 No. 1486 (hereafter in this Chapter referred to as 'the Regulations'). These provisions have been repealed by the Act of 1980.

5. There is no statutory obligation to prepare subject local plans, but they are relatively popular among planners.

6. 1971 Act, section 10(c), added by the Local Government Act 1972, and amended by the Act of 1980.

7. As to the amount of detail required, see 1971 Act, section 11(3).

8. Section 8(1)(a) of the Act, and reg.4 of the Regulations.

9. 1971 Act, s.8(2).

10. Ibid., s.8(3).

11. Ibid., s.18; Regulations, reg.6

12. Ibid., s.8, as amended by the Act of 1980.

13. Ibid., s.9, as amended by the 1972 Act.

14. Regulation 26, and form 6 in the Schedule to the Regulations.

15. Regulation 41.

16. 1971 Act, ss.11-13.

17. Chapter 13, p.144.

18. 1971 Act, s.12(4).

19. Ibid., s.14(3).

20. There are provisions for conciliation of contradictions between structure plans and local plans in Part XI (regs. 46-49) of the Regulations. The relevant provision in the 1980 Act is section 88, inserting a new section (15A) in the 1971 Act.

21. 1971 Act, s.10 (structure plans); ibid., s.15 (local plans), as amended by Sched. 14 to the 1980 Act.

22. Ibid., s.244.

23. 'People and Planning', published 1969. The whole subject of public participation is considered in Chapter 12.

24. The approval (or adoption) also must have been duly advertised in the local public press.

25. Chapter 10, p.115.

26. See, for example, *Simpson* v. *Corporation of Edinburgh* [1961] SLT 17.

8 Development and the Need for Planning Permission

1. Introduction

Restrictive planning operates principally by controlling development, although there are subsidiary controls in the planning legislation, as will be explained later.[1] Development control itself depends on the following key sections in the 1971 Act:

(a) Section 23, which provides that, subject to the GDO and a few other comparatively trivial exceptions, planning permission is required for the carrying out of any development on land;

(b) Section 22, which then defines 'development', in very wide terms, as the carrying out of specified 'operations', on land and also the making of a material change of use of any land (or buildings) (see Appendix, p.236);

(c) Section 29, which, read with the GDO, explains how planning permission is to be applied for and the action a planning authority must take on an application; and

(d) Section 87, and subsequent sections, which details the procedure for the enforcement of development control. Without these enforcement provisions, the preceding sections would be of little practical significance.

It is now necessary in the Chapters that follow, to examine these key sections in some detail.

2. The Need to Obtain Permission (s.23)

Permission is required for development, as a general principle: but it is not made a criminal offence, normally, to carry out development without first obtaining permission. Criminality follows only if the terms of an enforcement notice (served when there has been a contravention of planning control) are not obeyed; and it does not necessarily follow that an enforcement notice will be served everytime development is carried out without planning permission first being obtained.[2] Nevertheless, it is clear that development without permission is an illegal transaction,[3] which could have the effect of avoiding a contract, such as a conveyance or lease between two private individuals.[4] Even if some activity clearly amounts to development as defined in section 22, planning permission is not required in a few exceptional cases, and in other cases it is to be 'deemed' to have been granted, making any application for permission unnecessasry. These two situations are distinct and should be considered separately.

(A) Permission Not Required

(i) Where land was temporarily used for a use on 1 July 1948,[5] the resumption of the normal use, provided that resumption took place before 6 December 1968, did not need permission.[6]

(ii) Where land was used on 1 July 1948 for one purpose, and was also used occasionally for another purpose, permission is not required for that other purpose on similar occasions, provided the land had been so used since 1948 and before 1968.[7]

(iii) Where land was unoccupied on 1 July 1948 permission was not required for the resumption before 1968 of a use to which the land had been put before 1948 and after 7 January 1937.[8]

(iv) Where permission has been given for the use of land for a limited period of time, permission is not required for the resumption of the former use, provided this use was not in breach of planning control.[9]

(v) If an enforcement notice is served under s.87[10] permission is not required for the use of the land for any purpose for which the land could *lawfully* have been used if the development that was the subject matter of the enforcement notice had not been carried out (section 23(9)). 'Lawfully' in this context was explained by the Court of Appeal in *L.T.S.S. Print and Supply Services Ltd.* v. *Hackney LB,*[11] as referring to any use that was in accordance with development control. If planning permission had not been obtained for a change of use that had resulted in the use in question, then that use would not be a lawful one for the present (or any other, presumably) purpose. In the *L.T.S.S. case* there had been a change of use from use A to use B, without obtaining planning permission. There was then another change again without planning permission from use B to use C. An enforcement notice was served requiring the cessation of use C, and this was compiled with. Nevertheless, there could be no resumption of use B, as this was not a *lawful* use, and section 23(9) did not apply.

(B) Permission Deemed to have been Granted

Permission does not have to be applied for if the case is covered by a Development Order made by the Secretary of State under section 24 of the 1971 Act. In these cases the Order has the effect of granting planning permission for any development covered by its terms, normally subject to specified conditions. A Development Order may be made specially, limited to specified types of development, or particular areas, such as New Towns,[12] or Ironstone Areas,[13] or it may be of general application, as in the General Development Orders, the latest of which is that of 1977.[14] The current General Development Order covers no less than 23 types of development, for which planning permission is to be deemed to have been granted.

Perhaps the most important of these types or 'classes' are to be found in Class I, which covers certain types of development within the curtilage of a dwelling house (including, for example, the use of such buildings as hen houses, etc., and alterations or extensions to existing buildings of limited size), and Class IV, temporary buildings and uses covering a use of land for any purpose for not more than 28 days in any one calendar year). Class XXII covers the use of land as a caravan site, subject to licensing control under the Act of 1960.[15] There are also classes covering development carried out by highway authorities, by local authorities and by public utility undertakings, such as British Rail, gas and electricity boards and water authorities.

Particular types (either generally or in individual cases only) of development may be excluded from the list of development permitted in the General Development Order, by special *directions* made by the local planning authority under Article 4 of the GDO. Any such directions have to be advertised in the locality, and the directions will not have legal effect unless and until they have been confirmed by the Secretary of State; if there are objections he will order a local inquiry. If there are no objections and the directions are confined to Classes I-IV of the Schedule, the Secretary of State's approval will generally not be required. This procedure can be of considerable value where it is desired to exclude the concession of the GDO in relation to a particular parcel of land; for example, where by reason of the nature of the subsoil, the use of the site for caravans (even for a short time only) would be undesirable on public health grounds.

(C) Local Authorities, Statutory Undertakers, etc.

There is a further special type of case provided for in the Town and

Country Planning General Regulations 1976 (S.I. 1976 No. 1419). These Regulations detail a special procedure whereby a local authority may obtain 'deemed' planning permission in respect of development they propose to carry out themselves on their own land (Reg.4), or development to be carried out on the local authority's own land by some private person, such as a development company carrying out a redevelopment scheme in a city centre under an agreement with the local authority.

Development carried out by statutory undertakings is regulated by special rules contained in Part XII of the 1971 Act. First it is important to note the wide definition of this expression in section 290; it includes such bodies as British Rail, the gas and electricity boards, harbour authorities and the regional water authorities, etc.

Many types of development by statutory undertakers are covered by one or other of the classes of the GDO (above). In other cases, applications for planning permission must be made to the local authority in the ordinary way; many of the more important of these will be called in for decision by the Secretary of State and the appropriate Minister concerned with the particular undertaking (section 224), under section 225.

If the land is 'operational land', the undertakers will be entitled to compensation from the local planning authority under section 237, if an unfavourable decision is given on an application for planning permission. Operational land is defined in section 222, primarily as land used for the purposes of the undertaking, but not including land held simply for investment purposes. If some important task of the undertakers has been rendered impracticable by reason of a planning decision the appropriate Minister may, on representations made by the undertakers, overrule the decision of the planning authority (section 235) but an opportunity must be given for objections to be lodged against any such order.

3. The Meaning of Development (s.22)

Section 22(1) defines 'development' to mean any operation or change of use that falls within either of the two 'limbs' of the subsection; the remainder of section 22 then sets out a number of detailed exceptions, or exemptions, from the general definition. The two limbs of section 22(1), which should be engraved firmly on any student's memory, will be dealt with separately.

Both limbs of the definition refer only to operations or changes of use in, on, over or under land, but 'land' includes a building (1971 Act, section 290(1)), and also land covered by water; therefore the permanent mooring of craft in a river may (for example), amount to development.

(A) 'Building, Mining, Engineering or other Operations'

These words do not call for much elucidation. 'Building operations' are explained in section 290(1) as including any operations normally carried out by a builder, and 'engineering operations', by the same definition section, includes the formation or laying out of means of access to a highway. 'Mining operations' as such is not defined, but there is an explanation of 'mining' in the same section and it includes the mining and working of minerals, such as limestone, sand and gravel. 'Each shovelful or each cut by the bulldozer is a separate act of development', said Lord Widgery, CJ.[16] 'Other operations' is not to be construed *ejusdem generis* with 'building, mining, or engineering operations', as the House of Lords has said that those three expressions do not form a *class* within the *ejusdem generis* rule of interpretation. 'Other operations' is, on the other hand, to be understood as referring to operations having a *planning* significance, and therefore the demolition of a building, for instance, is not of itself an 'other operation' within the definition, unless the particular demolition in question seriously affects the amenities of the neighbourhood.[17]

Demolition of a building therefore does not amount to development for which planning permission is required, *unless:*

(a) the demolition is part of a scheme of redevelopment on the site,[18] or
(b) the demolition, as said above, is of planning significance.

Apart from this point about demolition, the 'operations' limb of the subsection does not cause much difficulty in practice.

(B) 'Material Change of Use'

When we consider this part of the definition of development, there is much more to be said and many decided cases to be considered. In the first place, there must be a *change* of use. For example, if premises used as a house are subsequently used as offices, and then used again as a house (when the original house use had been abandoned),[19] planning permission will normally be necessary for the use of the premises as a house, as this constitutes a *change* of use. In the second place, the change must be a *material* change, and it is this requirement that causes the most difficulty in practice. In an early Circular[20] the then Minister suggested that 'material' meant 'substantial', but this has never been adopted expressly by a court. It is reasonably clear that 'material' means material from a *planning* point of view, and also that the question what is material in any particular instance is 'a matter of fact and degree'.[21]

It is also reasonably clear that in a disputed case, it is a matter of *law* (ultimately) for the courts to decide whether a particular change is *capable* of being material, and it is a matter for the planning authority (and the Secretary of State if an appeal is made to him) to decide whether the change in question *is* material to the planning of the neighbourhood. Thus, in *Bendles Motors* v. *Bristol Corpn.*,[22] where the question at issue was whether the bringing of a (movable) egg vending machine onto a petrol filling station forecourt amounted to development, the court had to decide whether this was capable of being a material change of use, while the 'planners' had to say whether it was in fact material. In this case the court answered the first question in the affirmative, and whereas the court would probably have formed the view that this particular change was not material, they would not interfere with the decision of the planning authority (and the Minister) to the contrary. In *R* v. *Birmingham Corpn ex parte Habib Ullah*,[23] the Minister had decided that the accommodation of seven separate families in a single large house, without any physical alterations to the premises, was not capable of being a material change of use, because the house was still being used for residential purposes. The court, however, disagreed; there was a substantial difference between a house being used as a dwelling for a single family and one so used by as many as seven separate families. The court therefore sent the case back to the Minister so that he could consider whether this *change* of use was a material one from a planning point of view. No doubt he decided that question in the affirmative, but there is of course, no reference to this in the report of the case.

We must now consider a number of special situations which assist in explaining the meaning of this difficult expression 'material change of use'.

(i) Intensification of Use. If a use continues, but more intensively, can the intensification in itself amount to a change of use? Yes, said the court in the *Birmingham case* referred to above. The court has given the same answer in relation to an intensification of the use of a caravan site.[24] The difficulty here is how considerable must be the

intensification for it to amount to a change of use? The answer can only turn on the facts. Intensification of a use may grow imperceptibly. For example, a caravan site may be occupied by, say, six caravans. When does the intensification become considerable enough to amount to a *change* of use? When one more caravan comes on the site — when three more come — when 20 more come? The answers in practice to questions of this kind are not easy to give; the size of the site, the means of access, the facilities provided, the proximity of the site to other development, all these and other factors may be material points that should be taken into consideration.

(ii) Abandonment. If a use of land has ceased, and the land is either not used at all, or some other use is introduced, does the resumption of the original use amount to a material change? The answer here depends on whether the original use has been abandoned, and this itself can be determined only by establishing the *fact* of abandonment and proof of circumstances that show an *intention* on the part of the occupier to abandon that use. Obviously it will be easier to establish an intention to abandon if there has been some other use made of the land in the intervening period, as contrasted with the case where *no* use at all has been made of the land.

In *Fyson* v. *Buckinghamshire CC*,[25] land and buildings had been used for storage purposes for many years until they were requisitioned by central government in 1943. The buildings were used for several government purposes other than storage during the War and until 1950. When the property was finally released from requisition, it was unused for a time and then used again for storage. The court held that there was no need to obtain planning permission to resume the storage use as no development was involved. Although the land and buildings had not been used for storage purposes for some ten years, it was clear that there had been no intention to abandon the storage use; the government uses were carried on in spite of the wishes of the owners, under special legislation.

In *Hartley* v. *Minister of Housing and Local Government*,[26] on the other hand, the circumstances were sufficient for the court to infer an intention of abandonment. In this case a garage and adjoining land had been used for many years for ordinary garage purposes and the land was also used for the sale of second-hand cars. When the owner died in 1961, the business was carried on for some four years by his widow and son, but during this period no effort was made to deal in second-hand cars and the land was not used at all, although one or two sales probably took place. When the premises were sold in 1965, the new owner started using the land for sales of second-hand cars to a considerable extent. The court held that this amounted to development for which planning permission was necessary, as the original use of the land for this purpose had been abandoned between 1961 and 1965.

(iii) Multiple Uses. It is clear that more than one lawful use may attach to any property at the same time. In *Webber* v. *Minister of Housing and Local Government,*[27] a piece of land was used for the playing of football in the winter and for the grazing of donkeys in the summer. It was held that planning permission was not required for the change of use twice each year from football to grazing or vice versa. Both uses were established for the purposes of planning control.

(iv) Inconsistent Uses. There is no legal reason why a landowner should not make several applications for permission to carry out different types (or even the same) of development on his land, and there may in consequence be more than one planning permission in force for the same land at any one time. However, if development is actually carried out in accordance with a valid permission which is inconsistent with the development authorised by a different permission this will have the effect of nullifying the other permission, so that the developer could not (for instance) go back to it and act on it by developing part of the site in accordance with that other permission.[28] The fact that a landowner has applied for permission and been refused or has received permission subject to unacceptable conditions, does not prevent him in law from ignoring the unfavourable planning permission and relying on some earlier permission (express or implied) allowing him to do what he wants. An unnecessary application does not prejudice his position.[29]

(v) The Planning Unit. When considering whether some particular change of use is material, it is important to look at the 'planning unit', as a whole. Thus, the use of a small piece of farmland fronting on a road for the sale of fruit and vegetables, is a change of use, but it is not necessarily a *material* change of the 'planning unit', i.e. all the land in the occupation of the farmer.[30] When a shed adjoining a house and scrap yard was first used for the sale of new motor-car accessories (instead of the sale of parts pirated from the scrapped vehicles), this was not necessarily a material change of the unit, consisting of the house, the scrap yard and the shed,[31] and so, possibly, no development was involved. By considering the change in use of the shed alone, the planning authority had erred in law; they should have considered the whole planning unit. Sometimes development may have the effect of

destroying a planning unit and creating a new unit. When a building was erected, Courboisier-like on 'stilts', over part of the former Petticoat Lane second-hand street market, the market use of the roadway under the new building was nullified, because the erection of the building had the effect of creating a new planning unit.[32] Therefore planning permission was necessary for the resumption of the market use, although there was insufficient evidence of any abandonment.

(vi) Miscellaneous Points. If there is no change of use, there will be no development unless there has been some physical change in the property amounting to an 'operation'. Therefore, when a large coal-hopper, some 16-20 feet high, running on wheels, was introduced into a coal yard, planning permission was not required,[33] but the contrary is the case if new *fixed* equipment is introduced.[34] Even bringing land within the curtilage of a dwellinghouse, by moving a fence, may amount to a material change of use,[35] as may the use of the flat roof of a building as a landing pad for a helicopter.

4. Statutory Extensions and Exclusions of the Definition

Section 22(1) of the 1971 Act provides the main definition of the term 'development', but the following subsections of section 22 extend that definition in certain respects, and provide exceptions from the definition in other respects. The use of land for agriculture (an expression widely defined in s.290(1)) or for forestry is exempted from the definition, and therefore a change of use from (for example) arable to pasture is not development, but the removal of topsoil from agricultural land is development and is the only example of an act amounting to development which if carried out without permission is made a criminal offence, by a special statute, the Agricultural Land (Removal of Top Soil) Act 1953.

Works of alteration, maintenance or improvement of an existing building which are confined to the interior of the building, or which do not materially affect the external appearance of the building, are exempt from the definition; but this does not include work carried out to make good war damage, or works for the provision of underground additions (in either case if carried out after 1968). Alterations that affect the fenestration of a building, or where different coloured tiles are used in a re-roofing operation, or (even) a change in the colour of the paint on the outside of the front door are therefore within the definition, but development of this kind would not need planning permission, because they would fall within Class I of the General Development Order as amended.[36]

Works of maintenance or improvement carried out by a highway authority to an existing road also are not within the definition, provided such works are kept within the boundary of the road. 'Road' here is not defined, and it is therefore probably meant to be confined to the carriageway and does not include a grass verge, although that verge may form part of the highway.

The use of land within the curtilage [i.e. the immediate surroundings] of a dwellinghouse for any purpose incidental to the use of the dwellinghouse as such, cannot be a material change of use amounting to development within the definition. Thus, the parking of a holiday caravan in the garden of a dwellinghouse is not development, but it may amount to development if the caravan is used as an independent dwelling for mother-in-law or a lodger.

It is made clear by the Act itself that the conversion (whether building operations are involved or not) of a single private dwelling into two or more separate dwellings[37] is development for which planning permission is required, and the extension laterally or horizontally of an existing waste tip is also expressly declared to amount to a material change of use (section 22(3)).

By subsection (2)(f) of section 22, the Secretary of State is empowered to make an order declaring that particular changes of use shall not amount to development for the purposes of the Act. The Town and Country Planning (Use Classes) Order 1972[38] has been made under this subsection. This gives a list of classes of uses of land and buildings, and the effect of the Order is that a change of use falling *within* any one class shall not amount to development. Thus, a change in the use of a wholesale warehouse formerly used for the storage of (for example) flour, to the storage of boots and shoes, is not development, but a change in the use of a wholesale warehouse (Class X) for the storage of flour, to the sale of flour by retail (Class I) will amount to development, *provided* the change can be shown to be a 'material' one.

These Use Classes can lead to highly technical arguments; for example in a case that went to the House of Lords in 1980[39] over the meaning of the word 'depository' (Class X). Lord Denning in the Court of Appeal was quite sure that he knew what the word meant, but the members of the House of Lords were equally certain that the word meant something quite different.

The effect of the Use Classes Order must be clearly distinguished from the effect of the GDO. If a change of use (and the Use Classes

Order does not refer to 'operations') falls within a Class, then that change cannot be 'material', as it is not development. If a change of use — or an operation — falls within one of the Classes of the GDO (and complies with any relevant specified conditions), the change of use or operation is still development, but development of a kind in respect of which planning permission is to be deemed to have been granted.

5. Preliminary Applications

Enough has been said about the definition of development and the exceptions for it to be understood why in practice a landowner and his advisers may not always be quite certain whether what he is proposing to do on his land amounts to development, or indeed whether he will need to obtain planning permission. When in doubt of this kind, the prospective developer can ask the local authority to tell him the answer to the twin questions; development or not, planning permission required or unnecessary? This he may do formally under section 53 of the 1971 Act. Such a formal application should be made in writing and if the applicant does not agree with the planning authority's decision, he may appeal to the Secretary of State,[40] whose decision on the matter will be 'final';[41] but even then the decision may be questioned in the courts on an application for a declaration if the Secretary of State has made an error of law.

The decision of the authority on such an application should be in writing and is irrevocable, but apparently a letter which in effect answers the application under s.53 need not refer to the application or expressly describe itself as a determination under section 53.[42]

This formal procedure is not often used in practice and it often seems pointless, for if the decision is to the effect that planning permission is required, an application will have to be made, which could have been done in the first instance. Advice is on the other hand often asked for informally of the local planning authority's officials; the extent to which the authority are bound by advice so given will be discussed later.[43]

6. Crown Land

In accordance with the ordinary rules of the English common law, the planning legislation does not apply to land owned or occupied by or on behalf of the Crown, except in so far as it may expressly be applied to such land. Section 266 of the 1971 Act permits proposals to be made in a development plan in respect of Crown land, and buildings on Crown land may be listed under section 54, but Crown land may not be made the subject of a purchase notice. Planning permission is not required for development on Crown land, but there is no reason why there should not be an agreement between the Crown and the planning authority as to the future use of Crown land; express provision is made for such agreements under section 267 of the 1971 Act.

In practice government departments commonly consult with the local planning authority as to proposals for the development of Crown land within their area, although they are not obliged to do so.

Notes

1. See Chapter 15, p.163.

2. The planning authority have a discretion whether or not to serve an enforcement notice: see s. 87(1) of the 1971 Act.

3. *L.T.S.S. Print and Supplies Ltd* v. *Hackney LB* [1976] 1 All ER 311.

4. *Best* v. *Glenville* [1960] 3 All ER 478. In this case, a lease that expressly provided for premises to be used for a purpose that needed planning permission that was not in fact obtained was not avoided, because on the facts it was clearly contemplated by both parties that such permission was to be obtained. Similar questions may arise as between vendor and purchaser; see, for example, *Richard West and Partners Ltd* v. *Dick* [1969] 1 All ER 289.

5. The 'appointed day' on which the 1947 Act came into operation. This was of course an all-important day when effective development control commenced.

6. 1971 Act, s.23(1); but the temporary use may not be a use of land as a caravan site, unless the land was used on at least one occasion for that purpose between 1958 and 1960; section 23(7).

7. Ibid., s. 23(2)

8. This date was 10 years before the date when the Bill that became the 1947 Act was introduced in the House of Commons: 1971 Act, s.23(4).

9. Ibid., s.23(5) and (6).

10. See Chapter 16, p.181.

11. [1976] 1 All ER 311.

12. Town and Country Planning (New Towns) Special Development Order 1977 (SI 1977 No. 665).

13. Town and Country Planning (Ironstone Areas Special Development) Order 1950 (SI 1950 No. 1177), and see also the Town and Country Planning (Landscape Areas Special Development) Order 1950 (SI 1950 No. 729).

14. SI 1977 No. 289, as amended by SI 1981, No. 245, which in particular extends the concessions of Class I (below).

15. See Chapter 15, p.175.

16. *Thomas David (Porthcawl) Ltd* v. *Pery-Bont RDC* [1972] 1 All ER 733.

18. *LCC* v. *Marks & Spencer Ltd* [1953] AC 535.

19. As to abandonment of a use, see below.

20. Circular 67 of the Ministry of Town and Country Planning.

21. See e.g. *Marshall* v. *Nottingham Corpn* [1960] 1 All ER 659.

22. [1963] 1 All ER 578.

23. [1963] 3 All ER 668.

24. *James* v. *Secretary of State* [1966] 3 All ER 964, and see *per* Lord Widgery, CJ, in *Jones* v. *Secretary of State* (1974) 28 P & CR 362.

25. [1958] 2 All ER 286.

26. [1969] 3 All ER 1658.

27. [1967] 3 All ER 981. *Hartley* is another example of the same point.

28. See, for example, *Pilkington* v. *Secretary of State* [1974] 1 All ER 283.

29. *Newbury DC* v. *Secretary of State* [1980] 1 All ER 731.

30. *Percy Trentham Ltd* v. *Gloucestershire CC* [1966] 1 All ER 701.

31. *Burdle* v. *Secretary of State* [1972] 3 All ER 240.

32. *Petticoat Lane Rentals Ltd* v. *Secretary of State* [1972] 3 All ER 240.

33. *Cheshire CC* v. *Woodward* [1962] 1 All ER 517.

34. *Barvis* v. *Secretary of State* (1971) 22 P & CR 710.

35. This seems to follow from the early decision in *Sampson's Executors* v. *Nottinghamshire CC* [1949] 2 KB 439.

36. Above, p.95.

37. *Ealing Corporation* v. *Ryan* [1965] 1 All ER 137.

38. SI 1972 No. 1385.

39. *Newbury D.C.* v. *Secretary of State* [1980] 1 All ER 731.

40. 1971 Act, s.36, applied by s.53(2).

41. Ibid., s.36(6) *Pyx Granite Co.* v. *Ministry of Housing and Local Government* [1960] AC 260. A decision under section 53 to the effect that planning permission was not necessary, was held to be valid even when the terms of the Use Classes Order (on which the s.53 decision had been based) were changed before the development had been carried out: *English Speaking Union of the Commonwealth* v. *Westminster LB* [1973] JPL 29.

42. *Wells* v. *Minister of Housing and Local Government* [1967] 2 All ER 1041.

43. Chapter 10, p.115.

9 How to Make an Application

1. Introduction

Every application for planning permission must be prepared in writing, on a form[1] to be obtained from the district council, and normally prepared in quadruplicate.[2] The form should be supported by a plan showing the site of the application, with any necessary certificates and when the form is complete it must be sent (or handed) to the district planning authority. The appropriate fee also must be paid on the application.[3]

Sometimes it may not be clear to a prospective developer whether he needs to obtain planning permission, perhaps because he cannot decide whether his proposal amounts to 'development', or because he may not be clear as to the effect of some existing planning permission. Informally, of course, he can ask the staff at the local planning offices for advice. If they give him such advice, he may see fit to rely on it, but if the advice should subsequently turn out to have been false, he will not be able to insist on the planning authority standing by that advice. An authority is given a discretion by the statute, and it will not be bound to exercise the discretion in a particular way in consequence of something said by one of its officials, *unless*[4] (a) it was in clear terms amounting to a decision on an application, in circumstances where the official concerned was expressly authorised by the council to act on their behalf,[5] *or* (b) the circumstances were such that by its previous conduct, the local authority had caused the developer to understand that the council would accept responsibility for the advice.[6]

Apart from these instances, and it is by no means clear on the case law how far the second extends, the local authority cannot prevent itself from repudiating advice or information given by an official as to whether or not planning permission is required in a particular instance.

However, if an official does give false information or advice which the recipient has relied on to his disadvantage, and it can be established that the false information or advice must have been given carelessly, the person suffering loss in consequence may be able to recover damages in the tort of negligence.[7] Any such action will lie in the first instance against the official concerned, but as he will have been acting (presumably) in the course of his duties as a council employee, the council also will be vicariously liable for his action, and damages will be recoverable against them.

Parliament has also provided a formal procedure whereby a determination may be obtained from the district planning authority as to whether a proposal amounts to development and/or whether planning permission is required therefore.[8] No special form has been devised for such a preliminary application, but it is usual for the authority to require it to be in writing and clearly to identify the property, by plan or otherwise. There is a right of appeal to the Secretary of State if the landowner gets a reply he does not like or did not expect,[9] and there is then a further right to appeal against the Secretary of State's decision on a point of law.

The fact that the statute makes provision for such a procedure does not legally prevent a landowner from taking proceedings for a declaration in the courts to establish a claim, for example, that planning permission is not required in particular circumstances.[10]

2. Outline Applications

Having decided that planning permission is in law necessary for his project, the landowner should then consider whether to make an outline application in the first instance.[11] This is possible only where the application relates to the erection of a building or part of a building, and does not apply to changes of use or mining or engineering operations. A full fee is payable on an outline application.

The advantage to the developer of making an outline application is that he need only put in a plan showing the site, and indicate the nature of the development proposed (e.g. construction of ten houses, building of a petrol filling station, etc.). The size of the building, design, access to roads, drainage system, etc., can all be left to be settled later, and therefore at this stage there is no need for the developer to employ an architect or to prepare detailed plans; the principle of land use only is to be determined at this stage. If permission is granted on the outline application, the planning authority will make their decision subject to 'reserved matters', which will be specified in the decision. The reserved matters will of course refer to all the outstanding details on which the planning authority would normally need to be informed, density, design, access to highways, drainage arrangements, etc.

Development could not be commenced on the authority of an outline planning permission alone; the developer will still need to obtain the approval of the authority on the reserved matters and he will have to make a formal application for that approval, and a further fee will then be payable. There is no reason why such approval should not be applied for piecemeal, for one or two reserved matters at a time, but it is of course customary to apply for approval of all the reserved matters at one and the same time.

An outline permission is in law a planning permission, and therefore there is no need for the supporting certificates, etc., (under section 26 or 27, etc.[12]) to be prepared afresh on the application for approval of the reserved matters. Moreover, the planning authority cannot go back on their original decision when considering the reserved matters; by granting outline permission (e.g. for residential development) on the application, they have made their decision in principle, and they could not refuse approval of a reserved matter because they have changed their minds on the land use question; they are confined to considering the reserved matters alone.[13] However, the application for approval of the reserved matters must be made within a period of three years (section 42).

3. Certificates and Advertisements

In a number of different instances, the application for planning permission must be accompanied by a supporting certificate, or there must be some advertisement of the application before it is considered by the planning authority. Thus:

(a) The developer must certify *either* that he is the sole owner of all interests in the land that is the subject matter of the application, *or* that he has given a notice to all persons who were owners of any interest in the land at a time 21 days previous to the making of the application *or* that he has posted an appropriate notice on the land.[14]

If this certificate is not included in the application, the application is not 'to be entertained' by the planning authority. The meaning of this expression 'not to be entertained' is not entirely clear. Is the application — and any decision subsequently made thereon — void if the provisions of the section are ignored? The section does not clearly so provide, whereas a clear provision to that effect is included if an application relating to industrial development is not accompanied by a development certificate.[15] Perhaps the provision is directory only (not mandatory) and the validity of a decision would not be affected if this requirement had been ignored. Where the section is complied with, the local authority must consider any observations made by an owner of the property.

(b) If the application relates to a 'noxious use' of the land, a certificate must be included in the application to the effect that a notice of the application in the prescribed form[16] has been posted on the site.[17] 'Noxious use' is not a term of art in this context, but it is a convenient expression to signify the classes of development concerned, which are specified in art.8 of the GDO, and include a variety of matters, such as the construction of public conveniences, a sewage pumping station, a slaughter-house, a cinema or a Turkish bath, or the use of land for the disposal of refuse or as a cemetery, or the construction of any building to a height in excess of 20 metres.

Once again an application to which the section applies is not to be entertained by the planning authority unless it is accompanied by an appropriate certificate, and the authority may not determine the application for a period of 21 days from the date of the application so as to allow time for members of the public to make representations on the case.[18]

(c) If in the opinion of the planning authority an application would affect the character or appearance of a conservation area,[19] or the setting of a listed building,[20] the planning authority (*not,* in this case, the developer) must cause the application to be advertised in a local newspaper and a notice thereof to be posted on the site, and they must then allow a period of 21 days to pass before they determine the application, so as to allow members of the public to make representations on the case.[21]

(d) If the application relates to the erection of an industrial building,[22] the extension of such a building, or the change of use of a building from some other use to use as an industrial building, the application will be of no effect unless it is accompanied by an industrial development certificate (IDC). Such a certificate has to be obtained from the Department of Trade and Industry, and the issue or refusal of a certificate is entirely at the discretion of that Secretary of State (not the Secretary of State for the Environment). No legal procedure or form of application is laid down regulating applications for certificates, and the applicant who is refused a certificate has no right to appeal to a court or elsewhere, and has no remedy, except to exert political pressure on the Secretary of State through his Member of Parliament.

An IDC will be granted or refused in respect of the establishment of a new industry in a particular area, and not necessarily in relation to a specific site. Grant or refusal will be influenced by questions of 'the proper distribution of industry' and employment rather than by land use policy, and priority consideration will normally be given to the level of unemployment in the district.

The control applies to all industrial buildings, but there are exemptions from the control in respect of small buildings, varying in detail in different parts of the country.[23]

(e) Formerly[24] there was a similar control over the construction on and use of land for offices, but this has been abolished.[25] The Location of Offices Bureau, which had been established principally to assist firms to find office premises outside the London area and elsewhere, has also been abolished.[26]

(f) If the application relates to the construction of an oil refinery with a capacity of more than a million tons a year, or for a comparable extension, the application will be of no effect unless it is accompanied by an authorisation from the Secretary of State for Energy under the Petroleum and Submarine Pipe-Lines Act 1975, sections 34, 35, 36.

(g) If it is considered that the development proposed would conflict with the provisions of the development plan, it is perhaps unlikely that permission will be granted, but there is no special procedure to be followed by the applicant in such a case, although the application when received must be advertised by the authority before it is approved.

4. Time Limits

The Act of 1971 makes a number of provisions as to time limits in various circumstances as follows:[27]

(i) Development authorised by a planning permission must be begun[28] within a period of not more than five years from the date when the planning permission comes into effect,[29] unless the planning authority specify some other period.[30] In the case of an outline application, an application for approval of the reserved matters must be made within a period of three years from the date of coming into effect of the outline application,[31] and the development itself must be begun within a period of a further two years.[32] If these periods are not observed, the planning permission ceases to have effect and any subsequent development would be in breach of planning control.

(ii) If the planning authority consider it expedient to do so, they may require a developer to complete any development for which planning permission has been granted within a specified time, giving him at least 12 months to comply, and if he fails to complete within the time so specified, the planning permission previously granted will cease to have effect.[33]

(iii) The planning authority must come to a decision on an application for planning permission within a specified time and within that time they must notify the applicant accordingly in writing. In any ordinary case, this time will be a period of eight weeks from the date of receipt of the application,[34] but an extended period may be agreed in writing between the applicant and the planning authority, (usually at the instigation of the latter). If no decision has been notified to him within the time limit, the applicant may forthwith appeal to the Secretary of State on that ground.[35]

However, if a notice of a decision is given *after* the specified time, this does not necessarily mean that the decision is invalid. In particular, if such a notice has been acted upon by the developer, he cannot subsequently dispute its validity and argue (for example) that he is not bound by any conditions attached to the permission: *James* v. *Secretary of State for Wales.*[36]

5. Building Regulations

In any case where the development in question involves the erection, alteration or extension of a building (or in some cases of a material change of use[37]), the application for planning permission will be considered by the district council also as an application for consent under the Building Regulations 1976, made by the Secretary of State under the Public Health Acts 1936 and 1961. A further fee, in addition to that payable on the planning application, will be payable in respect of any application under the Regulations.[38]

This is not the place to consider the detailed provisions of the Building Regulations; suffice it here to say that the control imposed under the Regulations is very different in nature from that imposed under the town and country planning legislation. In particular:

(a) the Regulations are extremely detailed and, with a very few exceptions,[39] they leave very little discretion to the local authority, who must approve the plans if they comply with the regulations, and reject the plans if they do not so comply;

(b) appeals against refusals of consent lie not to the Secretary of State, but to the local magistrates,[40] and similarly, enforcement of any failure to comply with the provisions of the regulations is by way of criminal proceedings taken before the magistrates;[41]

(c) if the local authority fails to give a decision on an application for consent within the prescribed period of five weeks, the building owner may proceed with the development on the assumption that consent has been given, provided he otherwise complies with the Regulations.[42]

There is further discussion of this topic in Chapter 19.

Notes

1. There is no form prescribed in the legislation, but the application must be made on a form obtained from the local planning authority: 1971 Act, s.25, and GDO, art.5. A model form was scheduled to Ministry Circular 45/48, which is now quite out of date.

2. Four copies are usually required — one for the district council, one for the county council (or in some cases the highway authority), and two for the purposes of control under the Building Regulations (see para.5 of this Chapter). The authority are not permitted by the GDO to ask for more copies.

3. Local Government, Land and Planning Act 1980, s.87; Town and Country Planning (Fees for Applications and Deemed Applications) Regulations, 1981 (SI, 1981, No. 369).

4. See *Western Fish Products Ltd* v. *Penwith District Council* (1978) 122 Sol.Jo. 471, and p.118.

5. Under powers delegated to the official by virtue of s.101 of the Local Government Act 1972.

6. As in *Lever (Finance) Ltd* v. *Westminster Corpn* [1970] 3 All ER 496.

7. Unless such liability is expressly excluded: *Hedley Byrne & Co. Ltd* v. *Heller & Partners Ltd* [1964] AC 465.

8. 1971 Act, s.53, and Chapter 8, above.

9. Ibid., s.53(2), applying s.36, ibid. As to appeals, see Chapter 13.

10. *Pyx Granite Co Ltd* v. *Minister of Housing and Local Government* [1959] 3 All ER 1.

11. Under art.5(2) of the GDO, and s.42 of the 1971 Act.

12. See below, para. 3, of this Chapter.

13. *Hamilton* v. *West Sussex CC* [1958] 2 QB 286.

14. 1971 Act, section 27, 'Owner' in this context means any person owning the freehold or a leasehold interest of which at least seven years are unexpired; section 27(7), and Community Land Act 1975, section 6.

15. See below, sub. para. (d).

16. 1971 Act, section 26 and GDO, Sched. 3.

17. Unless the developer has certified that he is unable to comply with this provision because he has no rights of access to the land: but see also subs. (5) of s.26.

18. 1971 Act, s.26(7).

19. As to conservation areas, see Chapter 15, p.165

20. As to listed buildings, see Chapter 15, p.166.

21. 1971 Act, s.28(3).

22. 1971 Act, s.67 'Industrial building' is widely defined in section 66, ibid. The

control is expressed to apply only to industrial buildings of one of the 'prescribed classes' (s.67(1)), but *all* classes of industrial buildings have been prescribed for the purpose: Town and Country Planning (Erection of Industrial Buildings) Regulations 1966 (SI 1966 No. 1034).

23. 1971 Act, section 68; Town and Country Planning (Industrial Development Certificate) Regulations 1979, (SI 1979 No. 838); the exemptions are made by reference to employment office areas.

24. Originally introduced by the Control of Offices and Industrial Development Act 1965; the control operated in a manner very similar to that relating to industrial development.

25. The relevant sctions of the 1971 Act (ss.73-85) ceased to have effect as from 6 August 1979, by virtue of SI 1979 No. 908, made under s.86(1) of the 1971 Act.

26. Location of Offices Bureau (Revocation) Order 1980, SI 1980 No. 560.

27. Time limits are also prescribed within which appeals may be made against refusals, etc., of planning permission within which an enforcement notice may be served, within which such notices will come into effect, and within which appeals against enforcement notices may be lodged, but these are dealt with in appropriate Chapters later in this volume.

28. Development is to be taken as 'begun' for this purpose on the earliest date on which any specified operation comprised in the development is carried out, and 'specified operation' is itself also defined: see 1971 Act, section 43(1) and (2).

29. This will be the date of the decision, or when an appeal against a refusal of permission is determined.

30. 1971 Act, section 41; every grant of planning permission is to be deemed to have been granted subject to a condition to this effect.

31. 1971 Act, s. 42; the planning authority may substitute a period of five years for the period of three years and some other period for the subsequent period of two years: ibid. Note that these periods relate to times within which applications must be submitted; not times within which approvals must be obtained. Conditions to the latter effect were held to be void as being unreasonable, in *Kingsway Investments Ltd* v. *Kent CC* [1970] 1 All ER 70.

32. Ibid., s.42.

33. 1971 Act, section 44.

34. Ibid., s.31; GDO, art.7(6).

35. Ibid., s.36, applied by s.37, ibid. For appeal, see Chapter 13.

36. [1966] 3 All ER 964.

37. 'Material change of use' here does not mean the same thing as it does under s.22 of the 1971 Act, but means such a change in the use of the building as would bring into operation provisions of the Regulations that would not apply to the building in its existing use.

38. Building (Prescribed Fes) Regulations 1980, SI 1980 No. 286.

39. Public Health Act 1936, s.64, and Chapter 19, p.210.

40. Public Health Act 1936, s.65 and Chapter 19, p.210.

41. Ibid., s.65(4); Public Health Act 1961, s.10(2).

42. Public Health Act 1961, s.10(2).

10 Action on an Application

1. Introduction

When an application for planning permission, properly made out as described in the last Chapter, is received in a district council (or national park planning board) offices, it first has to be processed, and is then referred to the appropriate body to make a decision. The 'appropriate body' may be the chief planning officer (or his deputy) in a case where the power to make the decision has been delegated to him by his authority, or it may be a committee (or perhaps a sub-committee) of the district authority. Alternatively, it may be the county council where a county matter, such as an application for mineral working is involved, or exceptionally it may be the Secretary of State. We will deal with these stages separately.

2. Processing an application

On receipt of the application it must be checked to ensure that it is prima facie in order (signed by the applicant, clearly indicates what development is involved, includes a plan, etc.). If not, it must be returned to the applicant. The application cannot be received unless the appropriate fee accompanies it, except in a few cases where there may be no fee payable. In the case of an application for approval of matters reserved on an outline application, a further full fee is payable. Then the application must be numbered and recorded in the register of planning applications[1] and an acknowledgement in the form set out in Part I of Schedule 2 to the GDO must be sent to the applicant. The application must then be checked in detail; if it relates to a 'noxious use', the processing officer will have to ensure that the applicant has served the necessary advertisement under section 26,[2] and in any case there must be a certificate as to ownership.[3] If the officer considers that the proposed development is likely to affect the character of a conservation area or the setting of a listed building, he will have to arrange for the necessary advertising to be made in order to comply with section 28 of the 1971 Act. In such a case, according to local practice, it may be necessary to refer the application to a conservation area advisory committee.[4] The need to preserve trees on the site or to impose tree-planting conditions (see s.59) may also be relevant. The application will also have to be advertised locally, and a period of 21 days allowed for objections, if the proposal is not likely to be rejected and it will conflict with the provisions of the development plan.

The officer concerned will then have to consider the effect of the proposed development. The applicant may be requested to provide evidence to enable the authority's officer to verify any information (such as to ownership) relating to an application, as is allowed by art.5(4) of the GDO. If the application relates to industrial development the necessary certificate must have been obtained (unless the case is exempt). Also, the officer must decide whether the case is one within the delegated power (if any) of the chief, or other officer,[5] whether there is any potential conflict with the provisions of the development plan,[6] whether a 'county matter' is involved and what other material considerations are to be taken into account.

In any case he will also have to consider what consultations with other authorities will be necessary; if the proposed development will affect a main road, a copy of the application should be sent to the highway authority. If a trunk or special road is concerned the highway authority will be the Department of Transport. The regional water authority and/or an internal drainage board may have to be consulted; British Rail, the National Coal Board, the local gas or electricity authority and the Ministry of Agriculture are other bodies that may be concerned in particular cases.[7] The particular authority may have a practice of consulting such bodies as the local civic society. Some local authorities also make a practice of referring particular applications having a design content to panels of architects before the case is considered by the committee.

If the application refers to proposed development that may affect land within a parish, (or community in Wales) and the parish council has informed the district council under para.20 of Schedule 16 to the LGA 1972 that they wish to be informed of such applications, the officer will have to ensure that the parish council are duly informed. At least 14 days must then be allowed for the parish council to make observations on the case before the application is considered by the district [or county] authority.

Then the officer should consider whether there is some particular member of the public who may be affected by the proposed development, and who should therefore be advised, as a matter of good relations, although not as a strict legal requirement. In recent times intervention by the Commissioner for Local Administration[8] (the Ombudsman) has caused authorities to be particularly careful in this respect.

Planning authorities — and this means in practice planning officers — have often been advised in Departmental Circulars to discuss the details of an application with the applicant. This is obviously desirable and important, for it may be possible to persuade the applicant to make minor variations in his proposals, to discuss with him conditions that he may be prepared to accept, or even on occasion to persuade him that the application is completely impracticable or unacceptable and so encourage him to withdraw. By these means recommendation to the deciding authority to refuse the application or to impose conditions that are distasteful to the applicant may be avoided. It may further have the result of avoiding a potentially expensive and time-consuming appeal to the Secretary of State.

In some circumstances, such discussions may result in an agreement under section 52 of the 1971 Act. Such a planning agreement, the provisions of which will be enforceable against not only the developer but also subsequent owners of the land, may stipulate for the developer to observe certain restrictions in return for a promise of planning permission by the authority. Under section 126 of the Housing Act 1974, a similar agreement may go further and impose positive obligations on the developer, such as requiring the provision of land for a car park for the use of persons resorting to the building to be erected. It has even been suggested and has become fairly common practice with some planning authorities, that advantages (from the planning authority's or public's point of view) can be secured by means of a planning agreement that it would not be lawful to obtain by the means of a condition in a planning permission, such as the provision of a *public* car park, a children's playground or an open space.[9] The validity of such clauses in a planning agreement, which can come near to administrative blackmail, has not yet been tested in the courts, but some writers argue that the wording of section 52 and section 126 is wide enough to cover such devices.[10]

Planning officers conducting discussions with prospective developers must be careful not to make false or misleading statements about the legal position, and indeed they should not make promises as to the action their authority will take (unless, in the latter case, they are acting within the scope of authority delegated to them). In the first case, false or misleading statements (for example, 'you do not need planning permission for that type of development'), although the authority will not in any way be bound by such a statement[11] the officer concerned may be liable in damages in respect of any harm caused to the developer, and his authority also would be vicariously liable in respect of their officer-employee's negligence.[12]

In the second case, where a promise or statement is made about the authority's *future* conduct (for example, 'if you do this or that, you will get planning permission') the law is not so clear. The better view seems to be that the authority will not be *estopped,* or bound by such a statement made by an officer, unless he was acting within his delegated powers.[13] Although the authority may thus be able to avoid being held to their officer's statement, such a state of affairs is, to say the least, bad for public relations.

Having carried out all relevant consultations, made any necessary advertising and inspected the site, the officer should then prepare a report on the application, setting out all material considerations,[14] including the effect of the development plan, and come to a reasoned conclusion recommending either approval or refusal of the application, and probably suggesting (in a case of approval) relevant conditions to be imposed.[15] This report, often accompanied by a report on the plan under the Building Regulations,[16] will then be sent forward to the deciding body. If the application is an outline one, the officer should keep a record of outstanding reserved matters and check that applications for consent are made in due time. The identity of the decision-making body will vary as described in the following paragraphs.

3. Decision Made By Officer

Having received the report of his subordinate and satisfied himself as to its accuracy on the facts, and also that the case falls within the powers delegated to him by the council,[17] the deciding officer will then make up his own mind on the case and cause a decision to be issued on behalf of the authority, often after consultation with the authority's solicitor.

Finally, all officers dealing with development control should appreciate that time may mean money to the developer, and that he should not be kept waiting for a decision on his application unnecessarily. Obviously the proper processes must be gone through, but these should be organised efficiently so as to obviate wasted time. It is the duty of the elected representatives to ensure that adequate staff and other resources are available and officers should make representations accordingly.

4. Decision Made By Committee

Normally the district council will have delegated all its powers to make decisions on planning applications to its planning committee (or possibly to a plans sub-committee) under section 101 of the LGA 1972, except so far as those powers may have been delegated to one of the council's officers. Exceptionally, the council may have reserved to itself the power to take decisions on particular applications; but even in those cases the application will be considered first by the planning committee so that they may make a recommendation to the council as to the action to be taken.

In either case, whether the committee has power to act on behalf of the council, or whether it can only make a recommendation, the committee (meeting perhaps monthly or fortnightly) will receive a report on each application from the officers as described above.

The committee will consist of a limited number of members of the council, perhaps only 7 or 8, perhaps as many as 30, and will be presided over by one of their number as chairman, usually chosen from the majority political group on the Council. The committee will meet in public,[18] but a sub-committee may meet in private, unless it resolves otherwise. Nevertheless a committee (or the council) may resolve to exclude the press and public from the meeting while a particular matter is under consideration, if this is considered for some special reason to be in the public interest. In any case officers of the council will be present to give advice on each application — these will include the chief planning officer, the director of technical services, the solicitor and perhaps the financial officer, or their respective representatives. There will also be a committee clerk present who will take a record of the proceedings and prepare the minutes afterwards.

After hearing the officers and deliberating on the application, the committee will come to a decision. Although applicants and interested third parties may possibly be present at the meeting as members of the public, they will not be entitled to speak.

5. Decision Made By the County Council

If the application involves a 'county matter',[19] i.e. mineral development, or a matter which the district council chooses to refer as a county matter because of its concern with general county policy (perhaps because it conflicts with the provisions of the development plan), the application will have to be decided by the county council, normally of course by their planning committee to whom powers will have been delegated. The application will, however, in most cases[20] first be placed before the district council's committee for them to express an opinion on the case. The application together with the district council's opinion, will then be forwarded to the county council, where much the same committee procedure will be followed as explained in the last preceding paragraph. The applicant must be informed accordingly.

Some counties have divided their areas into sectors, each with a specially constituted area or divisional sub-committee, to which applications concerned with county matters will be referred either with delegated powers, or powers only to recommend. In some counties representatives of district councils are invited to serve as co-opted members on these area or divisional sub-committees, and in other counties they are invited to attend as observers only.

6. Decision Made By the Secretary of State

The Secretary of State may decide, under section 35 of the 1971 Act, to call in for decision by himself, *any* application for planning permission. He will, however, do this only on rare occasions, often in response to pressure from local amenity groups or individuals. However, he will more frequently call in an application involving the demolition of a listed building (see Chapter 15), and also applications for development of the operational land of statutory undertakers (see Chapter 8, p.96). In recent years successive Secretaries of State have let it be known that in other cases they will exercise the powers of the section only where some development of national or considerable regional importance is involved. The advantage of the procedure, from the point of view of a potential objector to the proposed development, is that the Secretary of State will not decide a case himself until a public inquiry has been held, at which objectors would be entitled to appear and make their views known.

7. The Decision: Generally

Regardless of the identity of the decision-maker, a decision must be made within eight weeks from the date when the application was lodged with the local authority,[21] but this time may be extended by agreement in writing between the applicant and the planning authority. Therefore, in cases where it seems that consideration of the case is likely to take some considerable time, the officer concerned should endeavour to obtain the applicant's agreement to an extension of time. If the prescribed (or extended) time is exceeded, the applicant may appeal to the Secretary of State on the grounds of no determination, but a decision given out of time is not void, especially if it is acted upon.[22]

Notice in writing of the decision must be given to the applicant,[23] and this notice, in any case where permission is refused or granted subject to conditions, must state the reasons for the authority's decision.[24]

When making the decision, the authority (committee, council or officer) must take into account:

(a) any representations made to them under section 26 (noxious uses) or section 28 (conservation areas and listed buildings);
(b) any observations made by a parish or community council under para. 16 of Sched. 20 to the LGA 1972;
(c) the provisions of the development plan, although if they consider it proper to do so and make the proper consultations, they may depart from the plan;[25]
(d) any other *material* considerations (see Chapter 11, p.129).

It should also be remembered that the authority cannot grant permission for industrial development (except in the exempted cases) unless the application is accompanied with a valid industrial development certificate,[26] and if the case concerns a caravan site, they must consult with the site licensing authority.[27]

A decision may be a refusal, a conditional permission, or an outright unconditional permission. If the application is for outline permission only any permission granted will be subject to approval of the reserved matters.[28] Apart from material considerations, other technical points arising on decisions will be left to the next Chapter.

The notice of the decision is not itself the decision; it is quite clear from the wording of the GDO that the decision is made by or on behalf of the authority, and the notice is served subsequently.[29] As previously stated the development must be commenced within the time stated (normally five years) and if it is not completed within a reasonable time, the planning authority may serve a completion notice under section 44. This notice may give the developer a time not less than 12 months from the service of the notice, within which he must complete the development. If this time is not observed, the planning authority can treat the case as one where development has been carried out in breach of planning control and serve an enforcement notice (Chapter 16), as the planning permission then ceases to take effect. The completion notice is, however, subject to a right of appeal to the Secretary of State, and even if he confirms the notice his order is then subject to a further right to apply to the High Court under ss. 242(3) and 245(3) of the 1971 Act to quash his order.

8. Environmental Impact Statements

In some cases, it may be desirable that there should be a thoroughgoing analysis of the impact that some major proposed development may have on the environment. Led by the United States of America,[30] many countries[31] in the world now require, as a part of their land use control legislation, such an analysis to be carried out and 'an environmental impact statement' prepared, and made available for public comment, before the project can be allowed to proceed. The statement, in most countries, must examine the effects on the physical and social environment, on the quality of human life, and on the flora and fauna of the site. The advantages and disadvantages of the project must be examined and weighed against each other. No such requirement is at present part of any of the laws of the United Kingdom, but from a legislative point of view (if the political motivation were present) it would be a comparatively simple matter to fit it in to the development control machinery. In practice, environmental impact analysis, under considerable public pressure, was to some extent undertaken in respect of the extension of the Windscale nuclear reactor (1978-9) and the proposals for the Vale of Belvoir coalfield (1980).

   If this legislation were introduced, it would have to deal with the following:

(a) should a statement be required for development by private enterprise or should the requirement be confined to development in the public sector;

(b) should a monitoring agency be established such as the Environmental Protection Agency in the USA;

(c) to what types of project should the requirement apply.

The EEC have issued a draft directive requiring Member States to legislate on the subject, but this has not yet (1981) been finally approved by the Council of Ministers.

9. Opposing an Application for Development

So far we have considered the action to be taken by the planning authority on receipt of an application. What advice can be given to local residents or others anxious to prevent some development taking place that is considered detrimental, either to their own property interest, or to the local environment generally? First, it is suggested that a careful watch should be kept on the register of planning applications so that the potential objectors may be fully apprised of what is proposed.

Having found that an 'undesirable' application has been made, a campaign should be launched without delay. This should include:

(1) a formal letter of objection, fully reasoned, to the local planning authority. This may of course achieve its object, but it is here assumed that the authority are minded to grant permission.

(2) Pressure should then be put on the authority by lobbying councillors (district and county), writing to the Press, seeking the support of the local Member of Parliament, obtaining as many signatures as possible to a petition, etc. The support of national amenity societies such as the Council for the Protection of Rural England, the Ramblers' Association, the Georgian Group, etc., as may be appropriate, should be sought.

(3) Consideration should be given to asking the Secretary of State to call in the application under section 35; however, he is unlikely to do this unless the matter can be shown to be of national or regional importance. If the matter is called in, the Secretary of State will convene a local inquiry, and this is of course an interim purpose of the objectors.

(4) If a local inquiry is to be convened, the objectors will then need to collect a 'fighting fund' so as to be able to employ solicitors and perhaps counsel, and expert witnesses. As many local residents as

possible should be recruited to give evidence in opposition to the proposed development.

Notes

1. Maintained under section 34 of the 1971 Act and para. 21 of the General Development Order 1977. Registration must be effected within 14 days of receipt of the application.

2. Chapter 9, p.110.

3. Under section 27, Chapter 9, p.109.

4. Note that this procedure applies to development that may *affect* a conservation area, and not only to development *within* such an area. The decision as to whether advertisement is necessary is strictly a matter for the authority, but in practice this is always taken by officers as a matter of procedure. As to conservation areas generally, and advisory committees in particular, see Chapter 15, p.165.

5. He will normally be the chief planning officer or his deputy, as named by the authority under s.101 of the LGA 1972.

6. Consultations must take place in that event under the GDO, para. 15.

7. Some of these bodies are required to be consulted by articles 11, 12 and 15 of the GDO; in other cases the DoE has recommended consultation (see Circular 23/77). In all these cases it has been agreed that the standard Consultation Code will be observed, supervised by the National Development Control Forum, an informal body established by DoE.

8. As to the Commissioners, see Chapter 4, p.55.

9. As to conditions, see Chapter 11, p.129. For an interesting discussion of this problem, see article by Sir Desmond Heap and A.J. Ward at [1980] JPL 631. In the United States of America subdivision control, which has long been held to be constitutional under the 'police power' is used to enable the local municipality to require a developer to provide space for schools, fire stations, public parks, etc., as part of his development layout. Much the same result is achieved in France and Belgium by the control known as 'lotissement'.

10. The opening words of section 52(1) are very wide, and section 52(3) makes it reasonably clear that the terms of an agreement are not to be read as in any way fettering the discretion of a local authority in advance: compare the general principle discussed in Chapter 11, p.130.

11. *Southend-on-Sea Corpn* v. *Hodgson* [1961] 2 All ER 46.

12. *Hedley Byrne & Co Ltd* v. *Heller & Partners Ltd* [1963] 2 All ER 575.

13. *Western Fish Products Ltd* v. *Penwith DC* (1978) 122 Sol.Jo. 471; and see Chapter 9, p.107.

14. As to this expression, see Chapter 11, p.129.

15. 1971 Act, section 29(1).

16. Chapter 19, p.210.

17. Under section 101 of the LGA 1972. Delegation to an officer is used sparingly by most local planning authorities, it being confined to comparatively simple cases, such as extensions to existing buildings or the erection of a single dwelling-house. The officer acting under delegated powers will normally be required to report his action taken to a subsequent meeting of the relevant committee.

18. Public Bodies (Admission to Meetings) Act 1960, as amended by LGA, 1972, s.100.

19. 'County matter' is defined in para. 19 of Sched. 16 to the 1972 Act as amended by

s.86 of the 1980 Act, and is in practice confined almost exclusively to matters concerned with mineral workings and the disposal of waste.

20. This will depend on the detailed arrangements for such cases agreed between the two councils.

21. Where there is a reference to the Secretary of State, this reference has to be made within the time limit, and there is no further prescribed time limit for the Secretary's decision: GDO, art.6(6).

22. Thus, conditions attached to a permission given out of time can still be enforced, at least if the development permitted has been carried out: *James* v. *Minister of Housing and Local Government* [1966] 1 WLR 135.

23. GDO, art.6(6).

24. GDO, art.6(7): see Chapter 11, p.132.

25. *Simpson* v. *Edinburgh Corpn* [1961] SLT 17.

26. 1971 Act, s.67 and Chapter 9, p.110.

27. Ibid, s.29(5); as the licensing authority (under the Caravan Sites and Control of Development Act 1960) is the district council, this will be of consequence only when the planning decision is being given by the county council. As to caravan sites, see Chapter 15, p.175.

28. Chapter 9, p.108.

29. *Norfolk CC* v. *Secretary of State* [1973] 3 All ER 673. The 1946 GDO, made under the 1932 Act, provided that the decision was to be sent to the applicant: in s.31 of the 1971 Act the expression used is 'such notice as may be prescribed [by the GDO] as to the manner in which his application has been dealt with'.

30. See a lecture by the present author given to the Cambridge Institute of Land Economy, and an article at [1979] JPL 142.

31. Notably Canada, Australia, Eire, France and the Netherlands.

11   The Result of an Application

1. Introduction

When a valid application for planning permission[1] has been received and processed as described in the previous chapter, a decision will then have to be taken, by the planning authority (the district or the county council) or more commonly on their behalf by one of their committees to which the power to make a decision has been delegated, or, possibly by an officer.[2] The authority has a wide discretion given by section 29 of the 1971 Act, to refuse permission or to grant either unconditionally or subject to such conditions 'as they think fit'. In coming to their decision the section provides that the authority must have regard to the provisions of the development plan[3] and any other 'material considerations'. They must also take into account any representations made in response to action taken under sections 26, 27 or 28.[4] There are also a number of provisions about conditions which are explained later in this Chapter, but otherwise the statute appears to leave the decision very much to their discretion. But the courts in applying the statutory provisions have imposed considerable restrictions on that discretion.

2. Restrictions on the Discretion of Authorities

In the first place, it is clear that the authority (or their delegate) must *exercise* the discretion entrusted to them by Parliament; they have a *duty* to decide any valid application brought without being tied by any decision of principle they may have made in advance. Obviously they must take notice of any general policy laid down in the development plan, so far as this may be relevant, and they should be consistent in their decisions, but each application must be considered on its merits. Therefore, when a district council refused planning permission for residential development within four miles of the Jodrell Bank telescope, because they had previously entered into an agreement with Manchester University (the owners of the telescope) to the effect that they would never permit any development within the proximity of the telescope, they were held by the court to be acting unlawfully.[5] They had no power to enter into such an agreement that would have the effect of tying their hands for the future, and they should have considered the application on its merits. Nevertheless, when the case went on appeal to the Minister, it was held by the court that the Minister was legally correct when he refused permission for the development, on the planning merits of the case.

Similarly, a planning authority cannot by their own prior acts, or the acts or statements of their officials, prejudge the issue, or prevent themselves from acting in a particular way. Thus, a developer had discussed with the planning authority's officials the details of his proposal to erect a fish processing plant in a Cornish fishing village. The officials assured the developer that if he accepted their suggestions, planning permission would be granted. When he complied with the suggestions but was refused planning permission, he took proceedings for a declaration to the effect that he was entitled to a permission. The Court of Appeal refused to grant the declaration. The planning authority could only be bound by the promises of their officials if the circumstances had been such that the officials had been acting under delegated powers and could therefore have been found to have actually granted permission on behalf of the authority. There was no such delegation in this case. Therefore in the present case the authority were entitled to ignore their officials' promises and refuse permission.[6]

In coming to their decision, the authority must have regard to any relevant provisions in the development plan, but this does not mean that they must slavishly follow its provisions. Having had regard to the development plan, they may in a proper case depart from its provisions.[7] In a case where they do in fact decide to depart from the development plan in a material particular, they must follow the special procedure laid down in the Town and Country Planning (Development Plans) Direction 1975, made under the GDO.

This Direction provides that if a district council propose to approve an application which in their opinion would conflict with or prejudice the implementation of the development plan, they must advertise the proposal locally and allow 21 days to elapse within which members of the public may make representations, before they decide on the application. If no county matter is concerned but the proposal conflicts with some modification of a local plan made by the Secretary of State, they must first notify the Secretary of State and abide by his directions, (if any). Otherwise, provided conditions are imposed which would in the planning authority's opinion safeguard the development plan, the application may be approved. In any event, the district council must under art. 15 of the GDO consult with the county council in such a case.

The authority is also bound to have regard to any other 'material considerations', so far as may be relevant. It is reasonably clear that these considerations must relate to town and country planning — to land use matters — as the authority are operating within the terms of a planning statute and their discretion has been conferred on them for planning purposes. The courts have interpreted this to mean also that the authority may not have regard to — or be guided by — considerations that are not 'material' in this sense.

What then are material considerations for this purpose? The word 'material' is to be understood much in the same sense as it is when used in the phrase 'material change of use', which forms part of the definition of development, which we have already considered.[8] The question is also linked to the type of conditions that may properly be attached to a grant of planning permission issued under the section, which will be considered later.

Whether adequate utility services, such as water, electricity, and gas, or even schools, will be available for the development proposed is clearly a material consideration.[9] The availability of a mains sewer for an individual house is probably not a planning consideration, as this can be controlled under the public health legislation and the Building Regulations, but the lack of any proper sewerage systems for a large housing estate would be relevant, as such development could properly be regarded as premature. Traffic and highway considerations are clearly material to planning, and so are matters of national importance, such as the operation of a radio telescope[10] or the siting of a new airfield.[11] The general availability of housing accommodation in the area will be relevant when considering an application for a change of use from residential accommodation to offices.[12] The cost of the proposed development, and the fact that the development could be carried out more cheaply on some alternative site, is not, however, a material consideration,[13] nor is any question as to who may occupy the houses to be built on a residential development;[14] the social mix of people living on an estate is not, apparently, a 'planning' matter.

3. Conditions

Very similar questions have to be considered in connection with the kinds of conditions that may lawfully be imposed on a grant of planning permission. Although section 29(1) says that the planning authority may impose such conditions as they think fit, it is clear that those conditions must have reference exclusively to planning matters, and may not (for example) purport to impose a system of rent control on a caravan site; a matter that is in no way concerned with planning.[15] Conditions must fairly and reasonably relate to the development for which permission is sought,[16] although an authority may impose conditions so as to exercise some land use control over adjoining land, provided it is under the control of the applicant.[17]

Conditions must not be unreasonable in effect; thus, a condition requiring the construction of an estate road to serve adjoining property in addition to and other than that which was the subject matter of the application, was struck down as being unreasonable.[18] Such a condition amounted to requiring the construction of a public highway at the developer's expense. A condition must not be unintelligible or unworkable,[19] and it must not normally operate so as to deprive a developer of his existing user rights without compensation,[20] although when granting permission for some specific use, a condition may be imposed restricting future changes of use that would otherwise have not amounted to development, being changes within the same use class under the Use Classes Order.[21]

Some conditions are expressly authorised by the legislation:

(a) as to the preservation of trees and the re-planting of trees on the site (s.59 of the 1971 Act);

(b) those which regulate the development of land which is not the subject matter of the application, but which is under the control of the applicant: s.30(1)(a), ibid.;

(c) requiring the renovation of works at the end of a specified period: s.30(1)(b), ibid.;

(d) requiring the development to be commenced within a specified period of time: s.30(3), ibid;

(e) limiting the planning permission to enure only for the benefit of a named person or persons: s.33(1). In practice such a condition, though legally sound, may be difficult to justify on planning grounds on an appeal to the Secretary of State;

(f) granting planning permission retrospectively, and so preventing enforcement action being taken against some development that was initially carried out without permission: s.32, ibid;

(g) as to time limits, providing that the work is to be begun within a specified time: ibid., s.41. Every permission is deemed to be subject to a condition that the development shall be commenced within a period of five years or such other period as may be expressly stated. In the case of a use of land for the mining or working of minerals this period is ten years (Minerals Regulations 1971, regs. 6 and 7).

As these conditions are all expressly provided for, their *legality* cannot be called into question, but they may be open to challenge on *planning* grounds. The conditions considered in the opening of this paragraph may be liable to challenge on legal *or* planning grounds.

4. Effect of a 'Void' Condition

It would seem reasonably simple to strike out from the planning permission a condition that was found, for one reason or another, to be void for illegality (not just 'bad planning'). This is not, however, the attitude that has been taken by the courts who have held[22] that in any case where the condition is an important one, such that it is clear that the planning authority would not have granted planning permission at all had they realised they had no legal power to impose that particular condition, the illegality of the condition will then bring down with it the whole permission. In some circumstances, therefore, it may not suit a developer to argue that a condition is illegal because the result may well be that he is in an even worse position, as he would have no valid permission at all.

This attitude to conditions also may not suit the planning authority. They may take action to enforce the condition; it is then, after argument, held that the condition was illegal. The authority will then have to commence their enforcement proceedings again *de novo,* this time arguing that development has been undertaken without planning permission; by this time the four-year limitation period[23] may have expired.

5. Conditions Generally

Conditions should not be imposed lightly and in particular conditions should not be inserted in a permission if enforcement is impracticable. Contempt of planning control is only too common and this is exacerbated by conditions that are ignored by developers and planning enforcement officers alike.

Particular care must be taken over the drafting of conditions; they must not be unreasonable, as we have said, but they must also be precise and readily intelligible. When dealing with special types of development, other legislation must be borne in mind; this is of particular relevance to caravan sites[24] and waste tips or disposal sites.[25]

6. Reasons for a Decision

In any case where the planning authority have refused planning permission or imposed conditions on a grant of planning permission, they are required by the GDO[26] to give the reasons for their decision. If they fail to comply with this provision, and give no reasons, the remedy of the developer is to take proceedings for a *mandamus,* requiring the authority to obey the law and state their reasons;[27] the absence of reasons does not invalidate the decision.

On the other hand, incoherent or unintelligible reasons may constitute adequate grounds for a court to quash the decision.[28] The distinction is of course based on the argument that if the authority has purported to formulate some reasons, and those reasons do not logically support the decision, then the decision itself must be a bad one.

In practice the reasons given for an 'adverse' planning decision often amount to little more than a formal incantation, such as for example, 'the development proposed would be detrimental to the amenities of the locality'. It is difficult to challenge such reasons on any legal grounds, but they may on occasion provide fuel for an argument on an appeal to the Secretary of State under s.36 of the 1971 Act.[29]

Notes

1. Much the same considerations apply to an application for listed building consent, for approval to the display of an advertisement, or for consent to fell a tree subject to a tree preservation order. See Chapter 15, p.163.

2. Under section 101 of the Local Government Act 1972. As the power to take a decision on the application has been conferred by Parliament on the planning authority, the power to delegate the decision process must itself be conferred by Parliament, and therefore there can be no delegation outside the terms of section 101, and the exercise of the decision power must itself be strictly within any delegation made by the authority under section 101.

3. This means the development plan (structure plan *plus* any relevant local plan(s)) currently in force.

4. Persons who make representations under any of these sections (as to which see Chapter 9, p.109) are known in the statute as 'section 29 parties'.

5. *Stringer* v. *Minister of Housing and Local Government* [1971] 1 All ER 65.

6. *Western Fish Products Ltd* v. *Penwith DC* (1979) 77 LGR 185. The authority cannot estop themselves by their conduct from exercising their discretion freely: *see* also *Southend-on-Sea Corpn* v. *Hodgson (Wickford) Ltd* [1961] 2 All ER 46, but there are suggestions *(obiter)* to the contrary in *Norfolk CC* v. *Secretary of State* [1973] 3 All ER 673.

7. *Simpson* v. *Corpn of Edinburgh* [1961] SLT 17 (a Scots case).

8. Chapter 8, p.97.

9. *Esdell Caravan Park* v. *Hemel Hempstead RDC* [1965] 3 All ER 737.

10. *Stringer,* note 5, *supra.*

11. *Rhodes* v. *Minister of Housing and Local Government* [1963] 1 All ER 300.

12. *Clyde & Co* v. *Secretary of State* [1977] 3 All ER 1123.

13. *Murphy* v. *Secretary of State* [1973] 2 All ER 26.

14. *R* v. *Hillingdon MBC, ex parte Royco Homes Ltd* [1974] 2 All ER 643.

15. *Chertsey UDC* v. *Mixnam's Properties Ltd* [1964] 2 All ER 627.

16. *Pyx Granite* v. *Minister of Housing and Local Government* [1959] 3 All ER 1.

17. Whether or not in his *ownership;* 1971 Act, s.30(1).

18. *Hall & Co* v. *Shoreham-by-Sea U.D.C.* [1964] 1 All ER 1.

19. *Fawcett Properties Ltd* v. *Buckinghamshire CC* [1960] 3 All ER 503.

20. But see *Kingston-upon-Thames LBC* v. *Secretary of State* [1974] 1 All ER 193.

21. *City of London Corpn* v. *Secretary of State* (1973) 71 LGR 28.

22. *Hall & Co* v. *Shoreham-by-Sea UDC* (note 18, *supra); Kent CC* v. *Kingsway Investments (Kent) Ltd.* [1970] 1 All ER 70; *Newbury BC* v. *Secretary of State* [1980] 1 All ER 731.

23. Chapter 16, p.183.

24. Chapter 19, p.175.

25. Chapter 19, p.174.

26. GDO, art 7(7).

27. *Britt* v. *Buckingham CC* [1963] 2 All ER 176.

28. *Givaudan* v. *Minister of Housing and Local Government* [1966] 3 All ER 696.

29. Chapter 13, p.143.

12 Public Participation in Planning Procedures

1. Introduction

Public participation in the planning process was the subject matter of an important Departmental Report *People and Planning,*[1] issued by the then Ministry of Housing and Local Government in 1969. In this Report the need to involve public opinion in the formation of planning policy and in decisions of development control were emphasised. Professor McAuslan in his recent book[2] has suggested that it is a major role of planning law to ensure public participation, as against the two other 'ideologies' of the law, the protection of private property in land and the protection of public interest. It is not the opinion of the present writer that public participation can be identified as a major purpose of the law, but it has certainly become one of the objectives of the planning legislation in recent years, although the euphoria of the early 1970s has abated somewhat. In this chapter we will endeavour to bring together the various legal provisions, some of which were the result of recommendations made in that Report. They can be discussed under the two headings of development plans and development control.[3]

2. Development Plans

The machinery, devised originally by the 1968 Act, was considerably influenced by the ideas of the Skeffington Report and a Departmental Report issued in 1965 (the Planning Advisory Group, sometimes known as the PAG Report). If members of the public are to be expected to participate intelligently in the process of development plan making, they must be fully advised of the planning authority's proposals, and educated in planning theory. Therefore the legislation, now contained in the 1971 Act (as amended in 1972) makes provision for two stages in the preparation of a plan. After the making of the survey (which must itself be published) adequate publicity in the area must be given to the proposals (1971 Act, s.8 as amended by the 1980 Act). *People and Planning* and subsequent Circulars[4] of the Department of the

135

Environment then recommended that the planning authority should not only make copies of the plan available (as is required by the statute[5]) but they should also arrange for exhibitions on vehicles and in shopping centres, etc, and convene meetings (or 'forums') at which planning officials and elected representatives would attend, explain the proposals, answer questions made by members of the public, and consider any relevant objections or representations.

After the proposed structure plan has been reconsidered in the light of any such observations or representations, a draft plan is prepared and again made available to the public, so that they may send any further objections or representations to the Secretary of State. After this the practice of public participation tends to break down, as it is only those topics that are considered sufficiently important by the Secretary of State (or possibly by the Chairman of the panel), that will be considered at the examination in public.[6]

The procedure on the making of a local plan (of any kind, including an action area plan) follows much the same pattern, except that there are wider opportunities for participation by individual members of the public at the final stage, as there are no restrictions (except the discretion of the inspector) on what issues may be raised, or who may speak, at the public inquiry convened by the district council responsible for the plan. Once again the authority must report to the Secretary of State on the action they have taken to ensure adequate publicity.[7]

Public participation in making the local plan is therefore more likely to be effective than it is in relation to the structure plan. Indeed, the procedure regulating the examination in public, which is an attempt to get away from the more usual adversarial approach to planning procedures, runs counter to the ideas of *People and Planning*. Ample opportunity has been afforded at examinations in public for the well-organised civic societies and similar pressure groups to have their say, but the individual landowner and certainly the ordinary member of the public, is much less likely to be allowed to express his views.

3. Development Control

In the process of development control, the law makes considerable provision for publicity, and for public participation in some measure; as participation depends on foreknowledge, so eternal vigilance by interested persons is an essential factor. The amenity society or individual who is concerned about particular planning proposals in his locality must use the tools afforded him by the law, especially those designed to help him to inform himself.

(a) The Register

The register of planning applications[8] and its partner, the register of advertisement applications,[9] is the most important means of informing individuals as to current development applications, and should be consulted regularly by members of parish councils, amenity societies, etc. These registers are available to public inspection free of charge, at the district council offices at all reasonable hours. The registers will give details, not only of the application itself and any accompanying plans, but also will record decisions taken on each application, the result of any appeal and of resultant enforcement action.

(b) Other Documents

The structure plan and local plan(s) must be placed on deposit at district and county council offices and must be made available for public inspection, and copies may be put on sale at reasonable prices.[10] Copies of compulsory purchase orders, public path orders, access orders and other similar documents also must be made available for public inspection.

(c) Notices

Public notices must be displayed on the site of applications for planning permission for any development that in the opinion of the authority may affect the character of a conservation area or the setting of a listed building,[11] and the applicant for permission must advertise any application for a 'noxious' use of his land.[12] He also must ensure that the owner of any interest in the land that is the subject of an application is made aware of the application.[13] The owners of all interests in any land which is the subject of a compulsory purchase or similar order must be served with notice of the making of the order.[14]

(d) Parishes

Parish or (in Wales) community councils which have informed their district council that they wish to be informed, must be sent a copy of any application for planning permission that may affect the parish or community; the parish council will then have 14 days within which to advise the district planning authority of any views they may have on the application, and they must be advised of the eventual decision taken on the application.[15]

(e) Enforcement

There is no provision for members of the public to participate in enforcement action. A planning authority cannot be compelled to serve an enforcement notice and there is no express provision in the 1971 Act or any other legislation for a citizen to sue for an injunction to prevent or abate a breach of planning control, comparable with the 'citizen's suits' of the Clean Air legislation in the United States. Perhaps an individual who had suffered loss as a consequence of a breach of statutory *duty* (e.g. failing to take all material considerations into account) could sue a planning authority for damages, but the 'loss' would have to be clearly established.

(f) Generally

In all these cases where provision is made for notice of an application for planning permission to be served, the planning authority are under a statutory duty to allow a specified time (usually 21 days but 14 in the case of parishes) within which members of the public, landowners or others, may make observations; and any observations so received must be considered by the district (or county, in the case of a 'county matter'[16]) council before they come to a decision on the application.

(g) Inquiries

Members of the public may attend and will normally be allowed to speak at inquiries into appeals against the refusal of planning permission. If the authority propose to grant planning permission, there will be no inquiry and consequently no opportunity for members of the public to have their say, unless they can persuade the Secretary of State to call in the application under section 35 of the 1971 Act.

(h) Minutes

In addition, the minutes of the proceedings of a local authority must be made available to members of the public, and they are entitled to take extracts from the minutes; some councils sell copies of their minutes.[17] Unfortunately, a member of the public is not entitled as of right to inspect the minutes of a committee of a local authority, not even if the committee is acting under fully delegated powers; this is because, although such a committee is acting on behalf of the council, the minutes of the committee are not themselves minutes of the council, to which the provisions of the statute are confined.[18] It is however the practice of most councils to allow publication of the minutes of their committees acting under delegated powers, such as the planning committees.

4. Other Forms of Participation

In many instances local planning authorities are advised by DoE to consult with other bodies, and in some instances are required to do so by law. Consultation with other authorities, the Department of Transport and statutory undertakers is mandatory when they are preparing a structure plan or a local plan (1971 Act, Part I), and art. 15 of the GDO lists a considerable number of consultations that must take place on the receipt of certain applications for planning permission. Authorities have been advised to consult regional water authorities and the Countryside Commission in appropriate cases, and they should consult with local amenity societies when considering applications for listed building consent. Consultation, however, is public participation only in a restricted sense, owing to the nature of the process and the limited persons who are consulted.

Co-option of members of amenity societies, etc., to membership of advisory committees for conservation areas, goes a little further, and this is now a common practice by local authorities.[19] Some authorities advertise all the important applications for permission as they are received, whether the authority is required to do so, as above explained, or not. Mobile units and shop window displays are used to advertise draft plans; in fact many authorities go far beyond their statutory obligations to inform the public. The Housing Acts of 1969, 1974 and 1980 require elaborate publicity to be given to the declarations of general improvement areas and housing action areas,[20] so the public can rarely complain about lack of information, except in the case of planning by agreement, to be discussed in the next paragraph.

5. Secret Planning

Very much planning goes on behind closed doors, in spite of the legal provisions described above. Local authorities have been advised on numerous occasions by the Department of the Environment to discuss development projects with the developers concerned, and in particular to endeavour to resolve pending appeals against planning decisions by discussion, with a view to reaching a compromise. These discussions naturally are carried on inside planning offices and the general public will be aware only of the outcome, by which time it is often too late to object or influence the eventual decision.

A special example of planning behind closed doors is what is sometimes known as 'consensual planning'. Under section 52 of the Act of 1971, the planning authority may enter into an agreement with a prospective developer, whereby he agrees to accept specified restrictions on the use of his land, which restrictions will then be enforceable against the other party to the agreement and successive owners of the land affected as if they imposed enforceable restrictive covenants.[21] In return, it is then understood either implicitly or by specific provision in the agreement, that the developer will obtain planning permission for his project subject to the restrictions. The practice has been made more popular since the passing of the Housing Act 1974, section 126 of which enables positive obligations to be imposed on a developer (and his successors in title) by a similar type of agreement.[22]

By means of an agreement under one of these sections, the planning authority may be able to extract concessions from a developer, such as the provision of a public car park or recreation ground within the development and at the developer's expense, which they could not lawfully obtain by the insertion of appropriate conditions in a grant of planning permission.[23]

Once such an agreement has been entered into, the planning authority (and of course the developer) will be bound by its terms; there is no question of the authority being able to dishonour its promises on the ground that the agreement had fettered its discretion,[24] because of the express terms to the contrary in section 52(3) of the 1971 Act. Members of the public, amenity societies and the like, will therefore have no opportunity of influencing the terms of the agreement. The agreement is not itself a planning permission, and the agreement would have to be followed by an application and a decision under section 29 in the ordinary way, but that decision would be a foregone conclusion, by virtue of the terms of the agreement. The other party would presumably be entitled to an order from the court if the authority refused to grant permission. Some planning authorities may decide to involve persons who are obviously interested in the discussions leading to a section 52 or section 126 agreement, but there is no statutory requirement that they should do so, and an authority may not always be able to identify those persons who are — or will be — interested in a particular development. Those persons may not even be aware of the significance of the project in issue even if they were informed of the proposed agreement. Consensual planning of this kind, which has obvious advantages in the public interest by reason of the concessions that may be obtained from the developer, may thus amount to a denial of any form of public participation in the decision process.

6. Challenging a Decision

Can a private individual, or an interest group, challenge the legal validity of a planning decision once given? If the decision is fundamentally unsound in *law,* such a plaintiff may be able to establish sufficient interest[25] for him to be able to apply to the High Court for judicial review by way of a declaration or an order of *certiorari,* or he may be able to persuade the Secretary of State to use his default powers under section 276 and order the planning authority to revoke the planning permission under section 45 of the 1971 Act.

Notes

1. Sometimes known as the 'Skeffington Report'.
2. *The Ideologies of Planning Law* (1980) by P. McAuslan.
3. For a detailed discussion of the subject, see a series of articles in the Town Planning Review, Autumn 1979.
4. See, e.g. DoE Circular 71/73.
5. 1971 Act, s.8(1). The authority must report to the Secretary of State on the steps they have taken to secure publicity, s.8(3).
6. Chapter 6, p.86.
7. 1971 Act, section 12.
8. Ibid., s.34; GDO 1977, art. 21.
9. Art 21, Town and Country Planning (Control of Advertisements) Regulations 1969.
10. Town and Country Planning (Structure and Local Plans) Regulations 1974, Part VIII.
11. 1971 Act, section 28.
12. As defined in the GDO; see Chapter 9, p.110, and 1971 Act, s.26.
13. Ibid., section 27.
14. Acquisition of Land (Authorisation Procedure) Act 1946.
15. Local Government Act 1972, Sched. 16, para. 20.
16. See Chapter 10, p.120.
17. Local Government Act 1972, s.228.
18. *Wilson* v. *Evans* [1962] 1 All ER 247.

19. Circular 23/77, para. 44 of the DoE.

20. Chapter 19, p.214.

21. Chapter 3, p.37. The agreement should be registered as a local land charge under the Local Land Charges Act 1975.

22. This agreement also will be registrable as a local land charge.

23. See, e.g. *Hall* v. *Shoreham on Sea UDC* [1964] 1 All ER 1 and p.130; and see the comment in Chapter 10, p.115.

24. As in *Stringer* v. *Minister of Housing and Local Government* [1971] 1 All ER 65; see Chapter 11, p.127.

25. A landowner whose property rights are affected will have a sufficient interest, but otherwise there may be considerable difficulties on this point: see *Gregory* v *Camden LBC* [1966] 2 All ER 196. But this may be avoided if the Attorney-General will agree to a relator action: see *Att.-Gen. ex rel. Co-operative Retail Services Ltd* v. *Taff-Ely BC* [1979] JPL 466.

13 Appeals to the Secretary of State

1. Introduction

In any case where an application for planning permission is refused by or on behalf of the planning authority, or where conditions have been imposed on a grant of permission, an aggrieved applicant may appeal to the Secretary of State.[1] He will have a similar right of appeal if he is not notified of the authority's decision within the prescribed period (usually eight weeks).[2] Any such appeal is initiated by notice in writing served within six months (or such extended time as within that six months the Secretary of State may allow).[3]

On receipt of the notice, the Secretary of State is required to convene a hearing before a person (usually called an inspector) appointed by him, unless the appellant and the planning authority agree that the case may be heard without a hearing, 'on the papers'. The Secretary of State must give both the appellant and the authority at least 42 days advance notice of the time and place (usually in the vicinity of the site) where an inquiry will be held.[4] Then not less than 28 days before the date fixed for the hearing the authority must send to the applicant and the Secretary of State a 'Rule 6 Statement', setting out the principal grounds on which they are relying for their decision, and the planning authority may require the applicant to send to them a similar outline statement of his case. The authority's statement should amplify the reasons originally given in the notice of the decision served on the developer, and may, indeed, introduce fresh reasons. The Rule 6 statement should be accompanied by a list of plans and documents on which the planning authority intend to rely. However, if the authority subsequently use arguments in support of their case at the hearing which were not included in the authority's Rule 6 statement, the appellant will be entitled to ask for an adjournment of the hearing to enable him to consider these fresh arguments, and he may ask the inspector to order his extra costs caused by any such adjournment to be paid by the authority.[5]

2. The Hearing

The inquiry will be conducted by an inspector, who is a civil servant, on the staff of the Department of the Environment, and who is normally a qualified planner, surveyor or architect (or perhaps a lawyer) according to the nature of the issues likely to be raised. At its commencement the inspector must announce whether this is a case in which the decision will be made by him on behalf of the Secretary of State (see para. 5 below). The inquiry will be held in some convenient building in the locality of the appeal site, and the Department will normally have required the local authority to publish notices about the inquiry in the neighbourhood, and the inquiry will usually be open to the press and the public. The procedure to be followed is basically at the discretion of the inspector, provided he observes the Inquiries Procedure Rules 1974 and the common law rules of natural justice (see below).

After the formal opening of the inquiry by the inspector, the appellant will be invited by him to open his case, which he may do personally or by counsel or by a solicitor engaged for the purpose. The appellant will then call his witnesses (who will often speak to a prepared statement), and they will be subject to cross-examination by the planning authority's representative and any other interested parties. The appellant will then have a right to re-examine his own witness, but questions in re-examination must be confined to the issues raised in cross-examination.

Evidence will not be given on oath, and the inspector has a discretion to allow hearsay or indeed any evidence that he considers relevant.[6] Representatives of a government department may be called as witnesses by either the appellant or the planning authority, but they cannot be compelled to answer questions on matters relating to Government policy.[7] With that exception, it might be treated as a breach of natural justice if the inspector refuses to allow a party the opportunity of cross-examining a witness, unless in the circumstances such a refusal is not 'unfair'.[8] 'Natural justice' is a common law concept, which can therefore be modified by statute law, but basically all it means is that the appellant is entitled to a fair trial, subject of course to any provision in regulations made under statutory authority.

When the appellant has concluded his case, the planning authority will open their case and call witnesses who will be subject to cross-examination by the appellant and any other interested parties, and the planning authority will have a right to re-examine their witnesses (as above).

3. Evidence at the Hearing

The strict legal rules of evidence do not apply to planning inquiries, and the inspector will normally admit any evidence that he considers to be relevant to the issues before him. The planning authority will normally put in evidence, at an early stage of the hearing (sometimes even before the appellant has opened his case), the provisions of the development plan in so far as they are relevant.

The planning officer in charge of the case will almost certainly be a key witness for the planning authority. His position may at times be delicate, if he does not agree with the decision made by his authority. Perhaps the officer has advised the planning committee that permission should be granted on the application, but the committee has decided to refuse the application and the applicant has appealed. What kind of evidence should the planning officer give in these circumstances?

It is suggested that he should confine himself to formalities — the development plan, the receipt of the application, the authority's decision and their official reasons therefor. If he is asked in cross-examination what advice he gave the committee, or what are his personal views, he should refuse to answer. As a qualified planner he clearly cannot give opinions contrary to his own professional conscience and he cannot tell lies to the inquiry; on the other hand, he is an employee of the authority, and he should not give evidence directly counter to their views. In such circumstances it is suggested that the chairman of the committee or some other elected representative should be called as a witness to justify the planning authority's decision.

4. Conclusion of the Hearing

After the appellant and the planning authority have concluded their case, the inspector will then normally allow any interested persons present to make statements and (if they wish) to give evidence. In particular 'section 29 parties' (those whose representation under ss.26, 27 or 28 of the 1971 Act are required to be taken into account by the planning authority when making their decision under s.29), are entitled to be heard. The appellant will then have a right to make a closing speech summing up his case and answering any points raised against him.

The inspector will close the inquiry, but will often arrange a visit to the site, at which he will give an opportunity for the planning authority, the appellant and other interested parties to be present. At this visit anyone may point out salient features on the site, the view, density of traffic, etc, but no fresh arguments can be raised at this stage.

5. After the Inquiry

The inspector will then go away to prepare his report, which will conclude with three passages, findings of fact, conclusions on the facts, and recommendations as to the action to be taken. In a majority of cases,[9] the inspector will have been authorised to make a final decision on behalf of the Secretary of State, and in that event his recommendations will be in the form of a decision.

Where this is not the case, the inspector's report will be considered by officials in the Department, and a decision letter will be issued in the name of the Secretary of State. Decisions often take a considerable time, perhaps as long as nine months or a year, and this procedure is open to the criticism that the eventual decision is in fact taken by a 'faceless' official who has not heard the appellant's case. In most instances the decision, although made in the name of the Secretary of State, does not reach the desk of any political Minister in the Department. Copies of the inspector's report must be made available to any party who appeared at the inquiry and had then asked to be supplied with a copy.

If it is proposed to differ from the findings of fact arrived at by the inspector, the Secretary of State must inform all parties who appeared at the inquiry and give them an opportunity of asking within 21 days for the inquiry to be re-convened. Similar action must be taken if it is proposed to take into consideration fresh facts that were not before the parties at the inquiry.

6. Written Representations

Where the parties agree, and they are customarily encouraged to do so by the Secretary of State, there is no oral hearing. In such a case the appellant is invited to make written representations, in response to written observations by the planning authority. Copies of the representations are sent by the DoE to the planning authority, who may reply. Replies and (possibly) further replies are exchanged, until all parties are satisfied. An inspector is appointed and he will carry out a site inspection, at which all parties are invited to attend. After this the inspector makes his report to the Secretary of State or (more frequently) issues a decision letter on the Secretary of State's behalf. This procedure is popular, and is almost invariably used on advertisement appeals. (75 per cent of all appeals are so dealt with).

7. Further Action

If the decision is not to the liking of the parties (including, the local planning authority), any party aggrieved[10] has a right of appeal to the High Court, exercisable within a period of six weeks from the date of issue of the decision letter.[11] This right of appeal must allege *either* that there has been an error of law, *or* that there has been some substantial error of procedure.

(a) Error of Law

This may raise the question whether the proposed project amounts to development, or whether planning permission is required in the particular circumstances.

(b) Error of Procedure

The error here must be of sufficient substance that it can be shown that the plaintiff has been prejudiced thereby. If, for example, a section 29 party was not notified of the time and place of the inquiry, but he was in fact present, having heard about it from a neighbour, he cannot claim to have been prejudiced although there will have been a technical breach of the rules.

The commonest form of error of procedure is to show that the Inquiry Procedure Rules have not been observed in some material particular, or perhaps that there has been some breach of the principles of natural justice. In *Nicholson*[12] the decision on a compulsory purchase order was quashed on appeal because the inspector had now allowed the plaintiff to cross-examine a material witness.

Sometimes the appellant, or some other party, may be dissatisfied with the conduct of the inquiry, but does not have a complaint of sufficient substance to justify an appeal to the court. Perhaps he considers the inspector was not adequately qualified or (as was alleged on one occasion) he was too deaf to hear the witnesses properly. In such a case, the complainant may complain to the Council on Tribunals. They will investigate the complaint and issue a report, but they cannot affect the decision of the Secretary of State in that case. Similarly, if the complaint relates to the conduct of the Secretary of State (perhaps the inquiry was not adequately advertised, or the decision of the Secretary of State was unreasonably delayed, etc.), the complainant can ask a Member of Parliament to refer the case to the Parliamentary Commissioner for Administration for a full investigation. Again this cannot affect directly the final decision of the Secretary of State, which can be set aside only by an order of the court.

8. Unusual Inquiries

Sections 47-49 of the Act of 1971 provide that the Secretary of State may refer certain matters to a Planning Inquiry Commission instead of being heard by an inspector in the ordinary manner. The more important of the matters that may be so referred are an appeal to the Secretary of State under section 36, or an application for planning permission that the Secretary of State has directed should be determined by him under section 35 of the Act. The type of matter that may be referred to a Commission is one of national or regional importance, where a special inquiry is considered necessary, or cases where the technical or scientific aspects of the proposed development are of so unfamiliar a character as to jeopardise a proper determination of the question unless there is a special inquiry (see s.48(2)). A separate Commission is specially constituted by the Secretary of State for each case, and it will consist of a chairman and not less than two other members; the qualifications of the members are not specified in the legislation, but the Secretary of State is likely to choose a senior lawyer (perhaps a judge) as chairman and appropriately qualified scientists or industrialists as members, according to the type of questions to be investigated. A Commission has power to regulate its own procedure, and there are no regulations applying thereto, but the proceedings are subject to the general supervision of the Council on Tribunals (s.49).

It is perhaps somewhat strange that the procedure of the Planning Inquiry Commission has not been used since it was first introduced in the Act of 1968. Since then there have been at least two major inquiries[13] that would have seemed appropriate for this procedure.

In the first, which was an application by British Nuclear Fuels Ltd for an extension of their nuclear plant at Windscale in Cumberland, the Secretary of State first called in the application for planning permission under section 35 and then refused permission. Next he convened a local inquiry under his general power contained in s.282 of the 1971 Act, to consider whether permission should be granted. This inquiry was held before Mr Justice Parker (a High Court judge), assisted by a scientist and an industrialist, and the proceedings lasted several months, as the proposed development was strongly opposed. After the close of the inquiry the Secretary of State made a development order under s.24 of the Act of 1971 granting planning permission, but providing that this order was not to come into force unless and until it had been approved by resolution of the House of Commons. In due course, after a lengthy debate, that resolution was passed. By this means the Windscale affair was subjected to the widest national scrutiny, but it is by no means clear that this could not have been achieved by the procedure of a Planning Inquiry Commission.

When the National Coal Board applied for planning permission to open a new coal field in the Vale of Belvoir in Leicestershire, the Secretary of State agreed, after local and nationwide pressure, to call in the application and to convene a local inquiry. This was conducted by a specially appointed inspector, Mr Maurice Mann, QC (an eminent barrister) assisted by two officers from the Department of the Environment. The inquiry in this case lasted 80 days, and again it is not clear why the Commission procedure was not used. The choice of a special inquiry was certainly not made so as to avoid the supervision of the Council on Tribunals, as members of the Council attended several sittings of the inquiry, and the proceedings were conducted in a thoroughly satisfactory manner.

The question that is most disturbing about these major inquiries relates to the type of issues that may be raised. Essentially, the question before the inquiry is one of land use; should planning permission be granted for the development proposed, in that location? Problems of national policy are strictly not relevant. Should the nation seek new sources of coal, should existing coalfields be fully exploited before new fields are opened, should nuclear energy be developed, are new motorways essential to the national interest,[14] what *is* the national interest, industrial and economic 'growth', or preservation of the environment, and are such questions inconsistent anyway? Such matters were allowed to be ventilated at both Windscale and Belvoir, but they are not really relevant to a land use inquiry. Perhaps in time some new form of inquiry for this 'large scale' type of development will be devised. Section 50 of the 1971 Act, which provided for the possibility of appeals lying to an independent tribunal (but which also has never been used), was repealed by the Local Government Land and Planning Act 1980, otherwise this procedure might have been the answer to our questions.

Another possible solution to this kind of problem is to require the preparation of an environmental impact statement[15] before an application for planning permission is made in major projects of this kind.

9. Conclusion

The normal inquiry procedure outlined above in paragraphs 1-7, applies in general to all appeals to the Secretary of State under the 1971 Act, except to the examination in public procedure of the structure plan, but the Inquiries Procedure Rules do not always apply; in particular, they do not apply to appeals against enforcement notices.

Notes

1. 1971 Act, section 36.
2. Ibid., section 37; as to the prescribed period see GDO, art. 7(6).
3. GDO, art. 20.
4. Town and Country Planning (Inquiries Procedure) Rules 1974 (SI 1974 No. 419), made under s. 11 of the Tribunals and Inquiries Act 1971; see rule 5. These rules apply to inquiries held into appeals under section 36, to cases referred to the Secretary of State under section 35, to inquiries in connection with listed buildings and (formerly) under tree preservation orders, and on appeals against a refusal of consent to display an advertisement. As tree preservation orders are no longer subject to confirmation by the Secretary of State, the rules do not apply to them (see SI, 1981, No. 14). The rules do not however apply to inquiries into appeals against enforcement notices or in respect of purchase or blight notices.
5. Rule 10(5) of the Inquiries Procedure Rules.
6. *Miller (T.A.) Ltd* v. *Minister of Housing and Local Government* [1968] 2 All ER 633.
7. Inquiries Procedure Rules, rule 8.
8. *Nicholson* v. *Secretary of State* [1978] JPL 39. In *Bushell* v. *Secretary of State* [1980] 3 WLR 22, the House of Lords had to consider the extent of an inspector's duty to allow cross-examination of government witnesses at a highway inquiry (which is conducted in manner similar to a planning inquiry). The court upheld the inspector's refusal to allow cross-examination as to the reliability of the methods of traffic prediction used by the Department; this was a matter of government policy. The procedure must be fair, but what is 'fair' is to be determined in the light of the matter to be determined.
9. Where the case falls within the Town and Country Planning (Determination of

Appeals by appointed persons) (Prescribed Classes) Regulations 1972 (SI 1972 No. 1652), as amended in 1977, made under s.287 and schedule 9 of the 1971 Act. Where this procedure applies the decision of the inspector is for all legal purposes a decision of the Secretary of State, and there is consequently a further right of appeal to the courts. A special set of procedure rules applies in these cases Town and Country Planning (Determination by Appointed Persons) (Inquiries Procedure) Rules 1974 (SI 1974 No. 420). An appellant may object, before the inquiry starts, to being dealt with under this procedure, and the case then is left for the Secretary of State to make the decision.

10. As to who may appeal, see Chapter 14, p.154.

11. See Chapter 14.

12. Note 8 above.

13. The inquiry into the Third London Airport, which lasted over a period of more than two years and was presided over by a High Court Judge (Lord Justice Roskill) was constituted before the passing of the 1968 Act. The inquiry into objections to the Greater London Development Plan, which also lasted for more than two years, commenced in early 1968. This was presided over by Frank Layfield QC.

14. National policy in relation to motorways was one of the matters the objectors had unsuccessfully attempted to raise in the course of the inquiry leading to the *Bushell case* (note 8 above).

15. Chapter 10, p.122.

14 Applications and Appeals to the Courts

1. Introduction

In this chapter it is proposed first to describe the various routes whereby a question of land use law may be brought before a court in this country, and then to discuss the functions of the courts in such a case, distinguishing them from the functions of the local planning authority and the Secretary of State. Such cases may arise by way of statutory appeals (those provided for in the 1971 Act itself), by direct challenges, on a prosecution, or incidentally in an ordinary action between private individuals.

2. Statutory Appeals

Sections 242-247 of the 1971 Act make provision for appeals and applications to be heard by the High Court from certain decisions of the Secretary of State.[1] These may be listed as follows (see s.246). Appeals against:

(a) an enforcement notice;
(b) a listed building enforcement notice; or
(c) an enforcement notice relating to the replacement etc. of trees (under section 103).

Strictly speaking, these are the only 'appeals' provided for in the legislation,[2] but in addition, section 245 permits a 'person aggrieved' to question before the High Court the validity of certain orders made by the Secretary of State, and these are commonly referred to as being 'appeals'. The more important orders that can be so questioned are listed in s.242(2) and (3) of the 1971 Act, and are as follows:

(d) a highway closure or diversion order made under Part X of the 1971 Act; the Highways Act 1980[3] makes similar provision for questioning the validity of trunk road and footpath diversion or stopping up orders made under that Act;

(e) orders requiring the discontinuance of an existing use, (s.51) and tree preservation orders;

(f) decisions of the Secretary of State on appeal to him under section 36 or on cases referred to him (s.35). This is of course the most important, and most frequently used, of the items in this list;

(g) decisions on consents to fell trees, to display advertisements, and to grant listed building consent, etc.

In all these cases it is provided that the validity of these orders cannot be called into question in any other proceedings whatsoever,[4] and the proceedings in the High Court must be commenced within a period of six weeks from the confirmation of the order or when the action was taken. If this short time limit is not observed, the proceedings cannot be brought.[5]

Proceedings under section 245 may be taken only by a 'person aggrieved', which means normally the person most closely affected by the order in question and certainly does not include a 'mere busybody',[6] The planning authority may not be a person aggrieved in this context, but they are allowed to apply under section 245(2).

(h) The validity of a structure plan or a local plan, or of orders made in respect thereof, also may be called into question by an aggrieved person by a similar procedure under section 244 of the 1971 Act. The grounds of such an application are the same as those for an application under section 245 (below).

3. Grounds for a Statutory Appeal

As these rights of appeal are conferred by statute, so the grounds on which the appeal may be based are limited to those listed in the statute. In the case of a 'true' appeal under s.246 ((a) — (c) above), *any* person on whom a notice was served, the appellant (to the Secretary of State) *or* the local planning authority may appeal on a point of law, or require the Secretary of State to state a case for the opinion of the High Court. 'Point of law' is not defined in the statute, but the expression obviously includes questions of interpretation of the statute (e.g. as to the meaning of 'development'), and also it may include questions such as whether there was any factual evidence available to support the decision, and errors of procedure (for example, a breach of the rules of natural justice) may also amount to a point of law.

If the case is brought under section 245, to question the validity of the order in question, the 'aggrieved' applicant must confine his argument to alleging *either:*

(a) that the order was not within the powers of the Act, *or*
(b) that some relevant requirement of the Act (as to procedure) has not been complied with.

The High Court may then suspend the operation of the order for a specified time, or, if satisfied with the soundness of the applicant's argument, quash the order or plan, totally or in part.

Several points arise under this section:

(i) If the argument is based on (a) above, to the effect that the Secretary of State's order was *ultra vires,* this is virtually the same thing as raising a point of law. If there is no evidence that supports the decision,[7] or if an appeal has been dismissed against a refusal of planning permission in a case where planning permission was not required in law, the Secretary of State's decision will have been *ultra vires,* and therefore should be quashed.

(ii) If the application turns on some error or deficiency in the procedural requirements (case (b) above) the applicant will be expected by the court to show that he has been prejudiced in consequence, and that the error was not a trivial one. The procedural requirements referred to include the requirements of any relevant Inquiries Procedure Rules made under the Tribunal and Inquiries Act 1971, discussed in Chapter 13.

4. Direct Challenges

Any person having a 'sufficient interest'[8] in the matter may apply to the High Court on an application for judicial review of a planning decision, and ask for an order known as a *certiorari* which, if granted, will quash the decision, or a declaration as to the effect of the law in a particular case; however, proceedings of this kind can be brought only in special circumstances, as follows:

(a) Proceedings to Quash a Decision of the Planning Authority

Proceedings for a *certiorari* have always been discretionary[9] (i.e. the court can at its discretion refuse to grant the remedy), and it has also always been a basic principle that the court's discretion would not be exercised in favour of an applicant if there is some other satisfactory course of action open to him. Under the terms of the Act, an applicant for planning permission can always appeal to the Secretary of State if he is refused planning permission by the local planning authority, and that would be his normal remedy. Nevertheless, it seems that he may be able to obtain a *certiorari* to quash their decision, if it can be shown to have been contrary to law (as contrasted with one made purely on bad planning grounds), provided the remedy from the court would be more expeditious and therefore more satisfactory than the remedy by way of appeal to the Secretary of State. The Secretary of State in any event, could not rule finally on the point of law.[10] It is much more difficult to obtain a *certiorari* to quash a grant of planning permission. Obviously only a third party, a neighbour, would want to do this and he would normally not be accepted by the court as a person having sufficient interest.[11]

(b) Proceedings for a Declaration Against the Planning Authority

Sometimes a developer or landowner may be in dispute with the planning authority about his legal position; he may, for example, consider that a project does not need planning permission, or perhaps that the planning authority would not be entitled in law to refuse planning permission in a particular case. In the two possibilities named, the developer's normal course of action would be to apply for a determination by the authority under section 53 of the 1971 Act and follow this through, if necessary with an appeal to the Secretary of State. Although the Secretary of State's decision on such a question is said in the section to be 'final', this does not prevent a developer from applying for a declaration as to the legal position, on an application for judicial review.[12]

In other circumstances, a landowner may seek a declaration from the court to the effect that a planning permission granted to a third party was not justified in law. It seems that as in the case of an application for a *certiorari* such a plaintiff may not have a sufficient interest in the proceedings for the court to be prepared to consider the case. Certainly this seems to be so if such a plaintiff is asking for a declaration by virtue of his position as the owner of neighbouring land, unless he can show that some property interest of his (such as a restrictive covenant that he was entitled to enforce) will be affected,[13] but apparently if he is asking for a *certiorari* to quash the decision, he may be successful even in such circumstances.[14]

(c) Proceedings Against an Order Made by the Secretary of State

Whatever the nature of the proceedings, whether the plaintiff is asking for a *certiorari* or a declaration, he would have to overcome the bar set by section 242(1) of the 1971 Act, to the effect that the validity of an order of the Secretary of State or of a structure or local plan, etc., may not, otherwise than as provided in sections 244-6 (as explained above) 'be questioned in any legal proceedings whatsoever'. This exclusion clause, as it is sometimes called, effectively shuts out any application for a *certiorari* to quash a decision of the Secretary of State or a structure plan, etc. However, an application for a declaration to the effect that such an order or plan was a nullity from the beginning — was made without jurisdiction — may still lie.[15] A purported order, based on a void decision of a planning authority, or one purported to have been made by the Secretary of State but which was made totally outside his authority, would be a nullity, and therefore can be treated as such, without any need for it to be quashed by a court order. The validity of the *order* is not being called into question as it is not really an order at all. If asked, the court may so declare on an application for judicial review. In planning practice such proceedings are of course extremely rare.

5. Prosecutions and Default Action

It is not normally a criminal offence, though it is unlawful,[16] for a landowner to carry out development without first obtaining planning permission. It is, however, criminal for such a developer to fail to comply with the terms of an enforcement notice consequently served on him by the planning authority. As explained in a subsequent chapter[17], the planning authority may in such a case take default action, but they may also, or alternatively, prosecute the offending landowner for a criminal offence.[18]

If the authority take default action they may for example pull down a building erected without planning permission where the developer has failed to comply with an enforcement notice. They will then be entitled to recover their expenses from the person so in default.[19]

In either type of these proceedings, the defendant may not question the validity of the enforcement notice on any of the grounds that he could have used on an appeal against the notice to the Secretary of State under section 88(1) (b) to (e) of the 1971 Act.[20] This leaves it open for the defendant in any such proceedings to argue by way of defence only that:

(i) the steps required to be taken by the enforcement notice exceeded what was necessary (s.88(1)(f)), *or* the time given for compliance with the requirements of the notice was insufficient — (ss.88(1)(g)).

(ii) the notice was a nullity because it was not served on the instructions of the planning authority,[21] or was served by the wrong planning authority,[22] or was otherwise void *ab initio* (above).

(iii) if the defendant in proceedings taken in respect of a breach of an enforcement notice relating to a contravening change of use, was not served with a copy of the enforcement notice, he will not be restricted as to the grounds he may raise in defence. He will be able to use any of those listed in section 88, provided he was not aware of the existence of the enforcement notice and held an interest in the land at the time when the notice was served (section 245(1) and section 89(5)).

6. Incidental Proceedings

The validity of some forms of planning action may exceptionally be called into question in proceedings between two private individuals. For example, in a contract for the sale of an interest in land, it may be stipulated that the purchaser is to be entitled to cancel the contract if he is prohibited under planning legislation from carrying out a project of development, or if he is unable to obtain planning permission. Controversy may subsequently arise between the parties as to whether planning permission is necessary in the circumstances; a court may then have to resolve the question in proceedings for breach of contract or on a vendor and purchaser summons. The effect of carrying out development without planning permission might arise in proceedings for the recovery of rent under a lease.[23]

Disputes as to the effect or enforceability of restrictive covenants and building schemes are determined by a reference (by either party) to the Lands Tribunal, a special administrative tribunal which also has jurisdiction to determine disputed compensation claims (on compulsory acquisition or for planning restrictions) discussed in a later chapter. An appeal lies from the Lands Tribunal to the Court of Appeal.

7. The Functions of the Courts

In all these cases it is the function of a court, having found the facts, to rule upon, or to declare, the law on those facts. When a prospective developer appeals against a refusal of planning permission to the Secretary of State under section 36 of the 1971 Act, the Secretary of State stands in the shoes of the local planning authority. He can do anything they could do, and he decides the case not only according to law, but also according to what he considers to be the planning merits of the case. On the other hand, when the developer appeals from the Secretary of State to the High Court, the court is confined to questions of law, and is not concerned with the planning merits — or de-merits.

Thus, in the familiar case of *Birmingham Corpn* v. *Minister of Housing and Local Government, ex parte Habib Ullah,*[24] the Minister had held that the use of a large house as a residence for seven families could not amount to a material change of use or development, as the house was still being used as a residence. On further appeal, the court held that as a matter of law such an event was *capable* of being a change of use; whether it was in fact a *material* change was a planning question for the planning authority (and the Minister on appeal), and not one for the court. So the appeal was allowed and the question of materiality was referred back to the Minister. Similarly, in *Bendles Motors Ltd* v. *Bristol Corpn*[25] the planning authority and the Minister on appeal had decided that the act of bringing an egg vending machine (a movable object) onto a petrol filling station forecourt was a material change of use of the forecourt,[26] presumably because of the additional traffic that such a machine could be expected to generate. The court refused to interfere with this decision; there was here a *change* of use. Whereas the members of the court may not have thought the change was significant enough to be material, this was not a question for them to decide. Whether or not a change of use is *material* is a planning question for the planning authority and the Minister, not a point of law for the courts. Judges have described this kind of question as being one of 'fact and degree', which can be settled only on the planning merits of the case.[27]

Therefore it is hopeless for the developer who is unsuccessful on an appeal to the Secretary of State to appeal to the court on grounds that are essentially planning questions. Law and planning merits at times get confused; for example, if a decision is not supported by the facts in the case, the court may find that the decision was bad in law.[28] Substantial errors of procedure also may at times lead the court to interfering with a decision in a manner which could appear to be deciding the case on planning merits. The logical distinction between law and planning policy is clear but it is not always easy to draw in practice.

Notes

1. Apart from the exceptional case where a direct challenge may be possible (para. 4 below) the law makes no provision for appeals to lie to the courts from decisions of a local authority, with the solitary exception of an appeal against a waste land enforcement notice under section 105 of the 1971 Act.

2. Apart from section 105 (note 1 above).

3. And its predecessor of 1959.

4. Section 242(1); but see para. 3, below.

5. *Smith* v. *East Elloe RDC* [1956] 1 All ER 855.

6. *Att.-Gen. of Gambia* v. *N'Jie* [1961] 2 All ER 504.

7. *Coleen Properties Ltd* v. *Minister of Housing and Local Government* [1971] 1 All ER 1049.

8. This is the expression used in Order 53 of the Rules of the Supreme Court, under which an application for judicial review may be brought. Its exact meaning is by no means clear, and perhaps never could be precise. It is also not clear whether different criteria as to its meaning are to be applied in relation to each of the different remedies of an order of *certiorari,* a declaration, etc.

9. A *certiorari* is an order of the High Court, requiring the record of a decision made by an inferior court or administrative body to be brought before the High Court, so that it may be examined and if some illegality of substance or procedure is found the decision will be quashed. Historically this procedure originated in the jurisdiction of the Courts at Westminster, acting in the name of the Sovereign to ensure that the lower courts were observing the law.

10. *R* v. *Hillingdon LBC, ex parte Royco Homes Ltd* [1974] 2 All ER 643.

11. Unless, apparently, he can show that the decision was void in law and that it affected him in some way: *R* v. *Hendon RDC, ex parte Chorley* [1933] 2 KB 696.

12. *Pyx Granite Co Ltd* v. *Minister of Housing and Local Government* [1959] 3 All ER 1.

13. *Gregory* v. *Camden LBC* [1966] 2 All ER 166, where the allegation in proceedings for a declaration was to the effect that the planning authority had not had regard to all material considerations in coming to their decision, as required by section 29(1) of the Act. The plaintiff, a neighbouring landowner who argued that the value of his property would be affected by a planning decision permitting the erection of a nurses' home at the end of his garden, was not allowed to pursue the case, on the ground that he did not have a sufficient interest in the subject matter.

14. In *Chorley's case* (note 11 *supra,* a landowner was allowed to take proceedings for · *certiorari* to quash a decision of the planning authority permitting the erection of a block of flats on adjoining land, when he was able to prove that an estate agent acting for the developers had been a member of the committee that had made the decision. This was a breach of the principles of natural justice because the 'judge' in the matter was not unbiased.

15. See the argument in *Anisminic* v. *Foreign Compensation Commission* [1969] 1 All ER 208.

16. Chapter 8, p.94 but there may be an offence if agricultural top soil is removed; see the Act of 153.

17. Chapter 16, p.181.

18. 1971 Act, section 89.

19. 1971 Act, s.91. Establishment expenses were added to the amount so claimed: Local Government Act 1974, s.36.

20. 1971 Act, s.243(1) (a). Note also the special provisions about listed building enforcement notices and waste land notices under ss.65 and 105 respectively.

21. As in *Norfolk CC* v. *Secretary of State* [1973] 1 WLR 1400, where the notice as to a planning decision was wrong.

22. The notice may, for example, have been served on the instructions of the district planning authority in a case where, as a 'county matter', was involved, it should have been considered by the county authority. As another example, an officer may have acted in excess of his powers delegated to him by his authority.

23. This might have arisen in *Best* v. *Glanville* [1960] 3 All ER 478, and see *Turner* v. *Bell & Co* v. *Searles* (1977) 33 P & CR 208.

24. [1963] 3 All ER 668.

25. [1963] 1 All ER 578.

26. From use as a petrol filling station alone to use as a petrol filling station *and* for the sale of eggs from the machine.

27. See *Marshall* v. *Nottingham Corpn* [1960] 1 All ER 659.

28. See, for example, *Lord Luke of Pavenham* v. *Minister of Housing and Local Government* [1967] 2 All ER 1066.

15   Special Statutory Controls

1. Introduction

It might well be assumed that the control over land use imposed by the requirement to obtain planning permission for any development, especially in view of the all-embracing definition of development, would satisfy Parliament in its anxiety to control landowners and to preserve the environment, 'in the public interest'.[1] But this is not so. A number of subsidiary or specialised controls are imposed by the 1971 Act (and its predecessors) itself, and yet others are contained in other modern statutes. In this chapter we shall therefore discuss the controls over non-conforming uses, over building of special historic or architectural interest, over trees and advertisements, over waste land and the deposit of waste minerals generally, and over caravans. Statutory provisions designed to control pollution of the atmosphere, of inland waters, and the environment generally by noise, are outlined in a subsequent chapter, together with housing and highway controls. We are discussing non-conforming uses first, however, as these are most closely related to 'normal' planning control.

2. Non-conforming Uses

By a 'non-conforming use' is commonly meant a use of land that does not contravene planning control in law, but which does not conform with the predominant land use in the area. Examples may be the corner shop in a residential area or the small light industries that grew up among artisan dwellings in late Victorian Birmingham. Not all of these non-conforming uses are necessarily undesirable from an environmental or planning point of view — the corner shop often performs a most useful function and certainly need not offend against local amenities. Sometimes, however, it is essential to get rid of a non-conforming use in the interests of residents or others in the locality, but this may not be a simple matter.

A use that has become established[2] in planning law may be regarded as a valuable asset, and the law does not normally allow it to be taken

163

away without compensation being paid to the landowner.[3]
Consequently if it is proposed to require the discontinuance of an
existing use[4] or that any works or buildings should be altered or
removed, the planning authority must make an order under s.51 of the
1971 Act. When using this power the authority must have regard to the
development plan and any other material considerations, and they
may make the order only 'in the interests of the proper planning
[whatever that may mean!] of their area (including the interests of
amenity)'.

The order having been made, copies must be served on landowners,
and the order is subject to a right of appeal to the Secretary of State, and
it (whether appealed against or not) will not come into effect until it has
been confirmed by the Secretary of State. Any person aggrieved may
apply to the High Court for the order to be quashed on the grounds of
an error of law or a substantial error of procedure.[5]

Use of land contrary to the terms of a confirmed order under this
section amounts to an offence; in effect the order may be enforced in
the same manner as an enforcement notice.[6] Also any person who has
suffered 'damage' as a consequence of the order by depreciation of the
value of an interest in the land or by being disturbed in his enjoyment of
the land, can claim compensation from the local planning authority.[7]
He may also serve a purchase notice on the authority if his property is
no longer of any reasonably beneficial use.[8]

In somewhat different circumstances, the planning authority may
make an order under section 45 revoking or modifying an existing
planning permission (section 51 orders, it should be appreciated can be
made in cases where there never has been any planning permission).
Section 45 orders must be advertised, and will come into effect
automatically after a specified time unless there is an objection; in that
event the order does not come into force until such time as it has been
confirmed by the Secretary of State.[9] Again the order can be enforced
in manner similar to an enforcement notice,[10] and there is a right to
apply to the court for the order to be quashed on a point of law.[11]
Compensation is payable by the planning authority to any person who
has incurred abortive expenditure[12] or has sustained loss or damage
directly attributable to the revocation or modification.[13] Alternatively
a purchase notice may be served in an appropriate case.[14]

3. Conservation Areas

Before we consider the detailed control imposed by the 1971 Act over listed buildings, it is necessary to explain the concept of the conservation area, first introduced onto the statute book by the Civic Amenities Act 1967, now replaced by the 1971 Act, as strengthened by the Town and Country Amenities Act 1974 and the Act of 1980.

Under section 277 of the 1971 Act, as so amended, every local planning authority is required 'from time to time' [a meaningless expression!] to determine which parts of their area are areas of special architectural or historic interest, the character or appearance of which it is desirable to preserve or enhance'. The reference to architectural interest in the section is widely understood in practice as applying not only to buildings but also to features of landscape and attractive countryside. Any such area is then to be designated a 'conservation area'.

It is impossible to define exactly the type of area that may be so designated, but examples might include a cathedral close, the buildings and land around a village green, a group of colleges in a university city, an area of pleasant Georgian or Victorian buildings, or an area of parkland. The effects of designation have been considerably increased by the 1974 Act. They may be summarised as follows:

(1) The planning authority must advertise locally any application for planning permission for any development which in their opinion would affect the character or appearance of the area;[15] the authority must then allow a period of 21 days to elapse before considering the application and when they do so, take into account any observations or representations they may have received.[16]

(2) No building except listed buildings and classes of buildings specified by the Secretary of State,[17] within a conservation area may be demolished without the consent of the local planning authority.[18]

(3) It is the duty of the planning authority to formulate and publish proposals for the preservation and enhancement of the conservation areas in their locality, from time to time.[19] Also under s.277(8), a planning authority is required to pay special attention to the desirability of preserving and enhancing the character of a conservation area, when exercising any of their powers under the 1971 Act.

(4) No tree within a conservation area may be cut down, topped, lopped, uprooted or wilfully damaged without the consent of the

district planning authority[20] unless the landowner has given at least six weeks notice to the authority, within which time they could make a tree preservation order.[21]

(5) Special regulations may be made as to the display of advertisements in conservation areas, but this power has not yet been implemented.[22]

(6) Local authorities have been advised by the Secretary of State[23] to establish conservation area advisory committees, consisting mainly of persons who are not members of the authority. Suggestions for membership include local architects and members of local archaeological, historical and civic amenity societies. Applications for planning permission falling within section 28 of the Act could be referred for advice to the appropriate advisory committee (there may well be more than one such committee operating within an authority's district), although the actual decision would have to be taken by a committee or officer of the planning authority as decision-making powers cannot be delegated to a committee having a majority of non-council members. Most planning authorities have set up at least one advisory committee for one or more of their conservation areas.

The Secretary of State has special default powers in respect of conservation areas, and he may after consultation with the authority, himself designate an area as a conservation area.[25] Once a resolution designating a conservation area has been passed, the designation becomes effective; it does not have to be advertised, nor is there any right to object to the designation, although the resolution has to be registered in the local land charges register (if passed after 1974).

4. Buildings of Special Architectural or Historic Interest

A. Listing

Under section 54 of the 1971 Act the Secretary of State is required to compile a list, or to approve a list compiled by other persons or bodies,[26] of buildings of special architectural or historic interest for a local authority's area. 'Listing' is an important,[27] but simple process; the owner of the building and the local authority must be informed of the listing by the Secretary of State, but no one has any right to object or appeal against listing.

B. Effects of Listing

The effects of listing are as follows:

(1) The planning authority must advertise any application for development which in the opinion of the authority affect the setting of the building;[28]

(2) Any person who carries out any works for the demolition of a listed building or for its alteration or extension in any manner which affects its character as a building of special architectural or historic interest, is guilty of an offence, unless the works have been authorised under the Act.

(3) Any person doing an act which causes or is likely to cause damage to a listed building is guilty of an offence under section 57, unless his act is covered by a consent from the authority or the building is excepted under section 56 (below).

(4) If works have been or are being executed to a listed building, and the works amount to a contravention of section 55 (being carried out without consent) the local authority may serve an enforcement notice under section 96 of the 1971 Act.

(5) The owner of a building can in some cases circumvent the possible effects of listing. Under section 54(A) of the 1971 Act (added by Sched. 15 to the 1980 Act) a person who is applying or has already obtained, planning permission for development involving the alteration or demolition of a building, may apply to the Secretary of State for a certificate that he does not intend to list the building. If such a certificate is granted, the Secretary of State will not be able to list the building for a period of five years from the date of the certificate, nor will the local authority be entitled to serve a building preservation notice during that period. There is, of course, no procedure for any appeal against a refusal to give such a certificate, and it would not seem that the Secretary of State's decision could be questioned in any way. The certificate would not prevent the building from being included in a conservation area (and so protected against demolition).

C. What Buildings May be Listed

Before listing any building the Secretary of State must consult with such persons as he considers appropriate who have a special knowledge or interest in such buildings.[29] A building may be listed because of its intrinsic architectural merit or historic interest, or because of the contribution it makes to a group or row of buildings.[30] It need not necessarily be of great age if it is architecturally interesting, and it need not be of any great architectural merit, if it has historical associations (e.g. because it was the birth-place or home of some famous person). The building may be as large as Chatsworth or

Longleat, or it may be a country cottage (e.g. the house of the Brontë's at Haworth).

D. Authorised Works

Any owner of the building desirous of carrying out works covered by section 54 to alter or demolish the building, may apply to the local planning authority for 'listed building consent'. The procedure follows closely the pattern set for an application for planning permission, and if consent is refused, or conditions are imposed in the consent, the applicant may appeal to the Secretary of State, and there is then a further right of appeal to the High Court on a point of law. No consent is, however, necessary if the listed building is an ecclesiastical building within the meaning of section 56.

Under the Act of 1980, listed building consent when given, will take effect for a period of five years only, but consent may be given after works of alteration or demolition of the listed building have started.

E. Enforcement

Proceedings for an offence may be taken forthwith if there is a breach of the provisions of section 54 but in such a case it will be a defence (apart from cases falling within s.56) if the accused person can establish that the works were urgently needed in the interest of safety or health or for the preservation of the building (s.55(6)).

In a case of demolition, even a consent from the local authority will not be a defence to proceedings if facilities have not been made available, for at least a month, for the Royal Commission on Historical Monuments to record the building, if they wish to do so (s.55(3)).

Alternatively, an enforcement notice may be served under section 96; this will have much the same effect as an ordinary enforcement notice. There is a right of appeal against the notice to the Secretary of State on the grounds listed in section 97; there are penalties for non-compliance with a listed building enforcement notice (s.98); the local authority has power to act in default (s.99), and the Secretary of State has special default powers under s.100.

The local authority can take urgent action in cases where it is considered important to preserve the character of the building, on giving the owner seven days' notice, within which time he has a right of appeal to the Secretary of State. Subject to such an appeal the authority can then execute the necessary work (s.101).

Further, the local authority can acquire compulsorily a listed building that is in need of repair (s.114), provided they have first served on the owner a repairs notice (s.115) requiring him to carry out specified repairs, with which he has failed to comply. If the compulsory acquisition goes forward in these circumstances, the owner will be entitled by way of compensation the value of the building with the benefit of listed building consent (s.116), unless it can be shown that the building was deliberately allowed to fall into disrepair; in the latter case the compensation will be assessed on the basis of the site value, without the benefit of any listed building consent or planning permission for development or redevelopment (s.117).

In practice, this power to acquire at a low price, a listed building that has been allowed to fall into disrepair, is seldom used by local authorities. Once such a building had been acquired the authority would feel obliged to spend rate fund moneys on its repair and maintenance, and sums of this kind (usually very substantial) are rarely readily available.

F. Building Preservation Notices

If a building has not been listed, and it seems to the district authority that it is in danger of demolition or substantial alteration, etc., and they consider it is of a character that it ought to be listed, they may serve on the owner and occupier a building preservation notice under section 58. This holds the position, as it were, for six months and within that period the building is in the same position legally as if it had been listed, and it cannot lawfully be demolished or altered, etc. During that time the Secretary of State is asked to consider whether the building should be listed. If it is listed, well and good; if it is not listed the building is no longer protected. If the building is not listed, the authority may have to pay compensation in respect of any loss or damage sustained by the owner as a consequence of the service of the building preservation notice, which has by now turned out to have been abortive (s.173).

G. Listed Buildings Generally

When considering whether or not to grant listed building consent, the primary consideration of the authority should be to preserve the building but often difficult economic questions may arise. The building may be virtually useless in its present state, and the authority will then be entitled to consider whether renovation is an economic possibility. If faced with an application for demolition, it seems that the authority is entitled to consider the developer's proposal for a substitute building, but in that event they should also take into account other possible types of development. See on this difficult problem *Kent*

Messenger Ltd v. *Secretary of State* [1976] JPL 372 and *Richmond LBC* v. *Secretary of State* (1979) 37 P & CR 151, discussed in an article at [1980] JPL 715.

It should be appreciated that some works that need to be carried out on a listed building (but not all) may amount to development. In that case planning permission will be necessary as well as listed building consent; the grant of consent does not necessarily imply planning permission, and vice versa (1980 Act, Sched. 15, para. 7). However, in a case where planning permission is not required (or is deemed to have been granted under the GDO) and consent to alter or extend (*not* to demolish) a listed building is refused or is granted subject to an unacceptable condition, and there has been an unsuccessful appeal to the Secretary of State, the owner of any interest in the building who can prove that the value of his interest is less than it would have been if consent had been granted or the condition had not been imposed, is entitled to compensation from the local authority.[31] In some cases where listed building consent is refused it may be possible to serve a purchase notice.[32]

Listed buildings that are dwellinghouses but which are legally unfit for human habitation[33] cannot be the subject of a demolition order under the Housing Acts, and can merely be subject to a closing order.[34] If such a house is not in good repair, it may be made the subject of a notice under section 9 of the Housing Act 1957, which would require the person having control to carry out repairs so as to make the house fit a repairs grant may then be payable under the Housing Act 1980.

Grants for the maintenance of historic buildings may be made by the district council under the Local Authorities (Historic Buildings) Act 1962.

If a building is of sufficient national importance it may be acquired or taken into guardianship by the Secretary of State, or by the local authority under the Ancient Monuments and Archaeological Areas Act 1979.

5. Advertisements

The Town and Country Planning (Control of Advertisements) Regulations 1969,[35] made under what is now section 63 of the 1971 Act, contain a complete and separate code of control over the display of advertisements.

In principle, no advertisement may be displayed without the consent of the local planning authority, and consent must be applied for in manner precisely similar to the procedure applying to an application for planning permission. Consent may be withheld only in the interests of amenity and public safety;[36] every consent is deemed to have been granted (unless expressly otherwise provided) subject to the standard conditions as to tidiness and safety,[37] and a consent is also deemed to have been granted for a period of five years only, unless otherwise specified.[38]

'Advertisement' is extremely widely defined in the Regulations,[39] and it is made an offence to display any advertisement otherwise than in accordance with the Regulations,[40] although there is no power to serve an enforcement notice in relation to any contravention.[41] There is a right of appeal to the Secretary of State against a refusal of consent or the imposition of conditions[42] (the inquiry on such an appeal is often conducted on the papers, without a formal hearing), and subsequently there is a further right to apply to the High Court to quash the Secretary of State's decision on a point of law or procedure.[43]

However, the need to apply for consent to display an advertisement does not apply in the following cases:

(a) In cases where the Regulations do not apply. By Regulation 3, consent is not necessary if:
   (i) the advertisement is displayed on enclosed land and is not readily visible from any land to which the public have access;
   (ii) the advertisement is displayed within a building (but not if it is visible from outside: see Reg. 12) or in a vehicle or if it forms part of a building; *or*
   (iii) if the advertisement appears on an article displayed for sale.
(b) Election notices, statutory notices and traffic signs are exempt under regulation 9, and so are advertisements displayed by a planning authority (Reg. 10).
(c) 'Existing' advertisement (i.e. those displayed on 1 August 1948) may continue to be displayed, until 'challenged' by the local authority by notice under Reg. 16,[44] in which case an application for consent must be made in the normal manner (Reg. 11); after the expiration of any express consent under the five year rule, an advertisement may continue to be displayed until similarly challenged under Reg. 16 (Reg. 13).
(d) There are then six classes of exempt advertisements, all subject to very precise detailed rules as to size, illumination, etc., listed in Regulation 14. These include advertisements displayed on business

premises, notices advertising social, etc., events, and estate agent's or other notices about the sale or letting of houses or other property.

Any consent may subsequently be revoked or modified under Regulation 24, and compensation will be payable in respect of any expenditure, loss or damage occasioned in consequence (Regs. 24 and 25).

If the district authority considers that any part of their area should be defined as an area of 'special control', they may make an order to that effect under Reg. 26, and any such order must be reconsidered at least once every five years. The order must be duly advertised in accordance with the Second Schedule to the Regulations, and it will not come into force until it has been approved by the Secretary of State, who will first consider any objections and (if there are any objections) hold a public local inquiry.

In considering whether to define such an area, the district authority must consult other appropriate authorities (Reg. 26(3)). The nature of an area to be so defined is not described in the Regulations, but it is obviously intended that the area should have a special amenity value; perhaps the main street of an old city, the area around a cathedral or colleges in a university town, may qualify for consideration; indeed many of the kinds of area that may be designated as a conservation area are usually most appropriate for definition under the present Regulations. This is because the effect of such an order, when in force, is to preclude the authority from granting express consent for the display of many types of advertisements, while preserving the exemptions in Regulations 9 (election notices, etc.), 11 (existing advertisements) and 14 (the six exempted classes).

If an advertisement is displayed in accordance with the Regulations by reason of express consent having been obtained or consent not being required, planning permission is not also required for any development involved (s.64), although the display of advertisements on the external part of a building not normally used for that purpose amounts to a material change of use of that part of the building under section 22(4).

6. Trees and the Countryside

Special measures may be taken by the local authority to preserve particularly attractive areas of countryside by declaring conservation areas and supplementing these by defining areas of special control for advertisements. Also under section 11 of the Countryside Act 1968, every public body in the exercise of their functions are required to 'have regard to the desirability of conserving the natural beauty and amenity of the countryside'.

When it comes to the protection of trees, in the countryside or in urban areas, the Act of 1971 is somewhat more robust than the high-sounding but ineffective provisions of the Act of 1968.

There is first a general provision in section 59, which provides that the planning authority must ensure, when appropriate, that when granting planning permission, conditions are imposed for the preservation of trees, and also to consider whether the making of a tree preservation order is desirable.

Under section 60, power is given to make such an order in relation to a single tree, a group of trees or an area of woodland. A tree preservation order will have the effect of prohibiting, except with the consent of the authority, the cutting down, topping, lopping, uprooting, wilful damage or wilful destruction of any tree to which the order relates. The order when made must be duly advertised in accordance with the Regulations,[45] and if opposed, will not come into effect until confirmed (probably after a local inquiry) by the local authority (s.60(4) as amended by the 1980 Act).

The order will make provision for consents to fell, etc., any trees subject to the order, to be granted (or withheld) by the planning authority on application, and there is a right of appeal to the Secretary of State against a refusal of consent to fell, or against a condition imposed in such a consent. A person aggrieved may apply to the High Court to quash a decision by the Secretary of State on a point of law or procedure.[46] It is an offence to fail to comply with the terms of the preservation order, even if the offender is not aware of the terms of the order.[47]

A consent to fell may be issued subject to a condition requiring re-planting, and such a condition may be enforced by a notice served under section 103. Section 174 and the Regulations provide for compensation to be paid in certain cases where consent to fell is refused. The normal order limits this to cases where the refusal is on amenity grounds alone and not for reasons of good forestry.[48]

A tree preservation order cannot apply to a tree that is dead or dying or that has become dangerous, and consent to fell is not then necessary, or if the land is subject to a forestry dedication covenant; or if felling is in accordance with a plan approved by the Forestry Commission.[49]

Quite apart from tree preservation, a local authority has power to require the felling of a dangerous tree, and a neighbouring landowner can require the authority to take that action.[50]

7. Waste Land

If the local authority consider that the amenity of some part of their area is seriously injured by the condition of a 'garden, vacant site or other open land',[51] they may serve on the owner and occupier[52] of that land, a notice under section 65 requiring specified steps to be taken for abating the injury, and providing that the notice shall take effect on the expiration of a specified time, not less than 28 days[53] after the service of the notice.

If any person continues or aggravates the injury to the amenities, and any of the steps specified in the notice have not been complied with, he may be convicted of an offence under section 104. However, any person served with a section 65 notice may appeal, not to the Secretary of State, but to the local magistrates,[54] within the effective period, on any of the grounds specified in section 105. On such an appeal the magistrates may correct any informality, defect or error in the notice that is not material, or they may dismiss the appeal, quash the notice, or vary its terms in favour of the appellant.[55] There is then express provision for a further right of appeal from the magistrates to the Crown Court, on either law or fact (section 106).

Default action to enforce a waste land notice may also be taken by the local planning authority under section 107.[56]

There are also a number of provisions in other statutes enabling a local authority to require the tidying up of waste land, on grounds of public health, rather than amenity. Thus:

(a) If any premises is in such a condition as to be prejudicial to health or a nuisance,[57] action may be taken to secure the abatement of this statutory nuisance under ss.92-100 of the Public Health Act 1936.
(b) An accumulation of rubbish on any land in the open air which is seriously detrimental to the amenities of the neighbourhood may be made the subject of action by the local authority under section 34 of the Public Health Act 1961. This section gives the authority power to take steps to remove the rubbish, provided they have first given the owner and occupier of the land at least 28 days notice of their intention so to act. During that 28 days the owner or occupier may serve a counter-

notice saying he intends to take the steps himself, or he may appeal against the notice to the local magistrates.

(c) Under section 3 of the Control of Pollution Act 1974[58] it is unlawful for any 'controlled waste'[59] to be deposited on any land unless a disposal licence issued by the county council (in Wales, by the district council) is in force covering that operation. Moreover, no disposal licence may be issued for a use of land for which planning permission is required,[60] and no planning permission is in force. Penalties follow on non-compliance with the section, but there is a right of appeal to the Secretary of State against a refusal of a disposal licence.[61]

(d) The clearance of abandoned vehicles and other objects from land in the open is provided for in the Refuse Disposal (Amenity) Act 1978, and the Removal and Disposal of Vehicles Regulations 1968.[62]

(e) If any person throws down, drops or deposits any litter in any place in the open air to which the public have access, he is guilty of an offence under the Litter Acts 1958 and 1971: the maximum penalty is now a fine of £100.

8. Caravans

Cheap holidays for the family in a caravan and the 'permanent' caravan residence are prevalent features of post-war Europe. Control over both types of sites in England has, as elsewhere, been an important part of land use and public health legislation.

So far as the 1971 Act is concerned, the use of land for the parking of one or more caravans, as residences (temporary or permanent), for storage or for sale, constitutes a material (in most circumstances) change of use of the land amounting to development. The parking of a single, or possibly more than one, caravan within the curtilage of a dwelling house is, however, permitted development,[63] but if the caravan is used as an extra home for mother-in-law (or some other person), this is no longer a use 'incidental to the enjoyment of the dwellinghouse is, however, permitted development,[63] but if the The GDO also grants permission for the use of land as a caravan site for various purposes listed in the 1960 Act (below), including caravans on sites approved by organisations exempted by the Secretary of State (such as the Boy Scouts Association, the Caravan Club, etc.).[64]

Public health control is exercised through the Caravan Sites and Control of Development Act 1960, under which a site licence must be obtained from the local authority for any land on which there are caravans used for human habitation. There is also a separate but similar control over land on which tents used for human habitation are stationed under section 269 of the Public Health Act 1936. Conditions may be imposed under both these Acts and in the case of the 1960 Act, section 5 thereof provides for a model set of conditions to be issued by the DoE. There is a right of appeal to the local magistrates against any conditions or against a refusal of a site licence. No caravan licence may be granted unless the site is covered by a valid planning permission. The conditions under both statutes will relate to public health, hygiene and safety, not planning matters.

Sites for gypsy caravans are a problem in some areas;[65] under the Caravan Sites Act 1968, the Secretary of State can require a local authority to provide sites for gypsy caravans. A person living permanently in a caravan as his sole or principal residence has a degree of security of tenure and protection against arbitrary rent increases, under the Mobile Homes Act 1975.

9. Minerals

Unlike advertisements, historic buildings and trees, the special rules controlling the use of land for mining operations is not contained in a single code in either the 1971 Act or Regulations, but is to be found in several provisions and statutes.

In the first place 'mining operations' is within the definition of development in section 22(1) of the 1971 Act, and although these two words are not expressly defined it is clear that they include the mining and working (and exploring for) minerals, including sand, gravel and coal, etc. Express permission is not however necessary for

(1) ironstone workings in certain specified counties that was in progress on 1 July 1948;[66]
(2) certain operations reasonably required for the mining or working of minerals by mineral undertakers;[67]
(3) development by the National Coal Board.[68]

Further, the Town and Country Planning (Minerals) Regulations 1971[69] make certain modifications of the 1971 Act in relation to minerals. In particular, a planning permission will remain effective if development is begun within ten [not five as is normal] years from the date when mining operations begin to be carried out. Although each separate extraction of minerals is an act of development, an 'operation', an enforcement notice may be served in respect of a breach of a condition controlling the *use* of land for mining, and this may be served within a period not of four, but of ten years from the breach.

The Minerals Regulations do not apply to coal or other minerals vested in the National Coal Board, and special provisions[70] apply to the payment of compensation to the Board for planning decisions in relation to the underground working of coal.[71]

Mineral undertakers (and the National Coal Board) may apply to the High Court under the Mines (Working Facilities and Support) Act 1966, for facilities orders to let down the surface, explore for minerals, etc., but they would still need planning permission unless they can bring the case within the GDO (above).

Applications for planning permission in respect of mineral working are a 'county matter', which must therefore be referred by the district council receiving the application, to the county council for a decision (1980 Act, section 86(4)).

Notes

1. As Professor McAuslan would say in his *Ideologies of Planning Law,* (Chapter 2, *ante,* p.18).
2. Whether or not as the consequence of a certificate of established use.
3. Exceptionally, a condition to this effect may nonetheless be valid: *Kingston upon Thames BC* v. *Secretary of State* [1974] 1 All ER 193.
4. 'Use' must be distinguished from operations (s.290(1)), but a use that does not change the actual physical characteristics of the land, such as storage of scrap materials, is not an 'operation' but a use: *Parker* v. *Secretary of State* [1979] 1 All ER 211.
5. 1971 Act, sections 242 and 245.
6. Ibid., section 108.
7. Ibid., s.170, as to assessment, see s.178 and Chapter 17, p.198.
8. Ibid., s.189; as to purchase notices, see Chapter 17, p.194.
9. Ibid., s.46.
10. Ibid., s.108.
11. Ibid., ss.242 and 245.
12. Such as the making of plans: *Southern Olympia Ltd* v. *West Sussex CC* (1952) 3 P & CR 60.
13. 1971 Act, s.164, as to assessment, see section 178, and Chapter 17, p. 198.
14. Ibid., s.188.
15. Section 28; note that the section is not confined to proposed development *within* the area, but the test for compliance with the section is the subjective one of the opinion of the authority.
16. 1971 Act, s.29(4); Chapter 10, p.115.
17. Formerly the Secretary of State could give directions excepting specified types of buildings, but this power has been repealed by Sched. 15 of the 1980 Act.

18. 1971 Act, s.277A, added by the 1971 Act; the enforcement provisions of ss.96-99 apply (see below, para. 4).

19. Ibid., s.277B, as amended.

20. Ibid., s.61A.

21. See below, para. 6.

22. 1971 Act, s.63(3), as amended.

23. Circular 23/77, para. 44.

24. Or a committee or officer to whom the powers have been delegated. The decision-making power could not be delegated to the advisory committee as (having a majority of members who are not councillors) it is not a committee of the authority under s.101 of the LGA 1972.

25. 1971 Act, s.277(4).

26. This theoretically could mean anyone; in practice it is rare for a list to be approved and the only 'body' likely to possess the necessary expertise to prepare one is the local authority.

27. The value of a building in the East End of London, where vacant sites are rare, went *down* from £1,700,000 to £200,000 simply because the building had been listed and therefore could not be demolished: *Amalgamated Investment and Property Ltd* v. *John Walker & Sons Ltd* [1976] 3 All ER 509. The actual listing is done by inspectors of the DoE specially appointed, and lists are prepared for each planning authority's area. In recent years the DoE has delegated the preliminary work of preparing the lists to the county council in some areas.

28. 1971 Act, s.28(1) (b); the same procedure then follows as that applicable to a conservation area (para. 3 above).

29. If he knows there are such persons whom he considers 'appropriate', he must consult and it seems that his action in listing, if he fails so to consult, would be *ultra vires:* see *Agricultural, Horticultural and Forestry Industry Training Board* v. *Aylesbury Mushrooms Ltd* [1972] 1 All ER 280.

30. *Iveagh* v. *Minister of Housing and Local Government* [1964] 1 QB 395, relating to a row of Georgian houses in St. James Street in the West End of London.

31. 1971 Act, s.171, and Chapter 17, p.198.

32. Ibid., s.190, and Chapter 17, p.194.

33. Chapter 19, p.213.

34. Housing Act 1957, section 24.

35. SI 1969 No. 1532.

36. Regulations 5(1).

37. Regulation 7, and Schedule 1.

38. Regulation 20.

39. See Appendix, p.235 and Regulation 2(1); railway signals and memorials are expressly excluded from the definition, but it does include a hoarding.

40. Regulation 8.

41. The power to make provision for the service of an enforcement notice in respect of advertisements contained in section 109 of the 1971 Act has not been implemented in the Regulations.

42. Regulation 22.

43. Section 242(3) (e) and section 245(3) of the 1971 Act.

44. The person concerned will then be entitled to claim compensation from the planning authority for any expenses incurred over the removal, etc. of the advertisement: 1971 Act, section 176.

45. Town and Country Planning (Tree Preservation Orders) Regulations 1969 (SI 1969 No. 17) as amended by SI, 1981, No. 14 which sets out a model form of order.

46. Section 242(2) (c) and section 245(3).

47. 1971 Act, section 102, and *Maidstone BC* v. *Mortimer* [1980] 3 All ER 552.

48. Where a certificate has been given to that effect: see arts. 5 and 9 of the model order.

49. 1971 Act, section 60(6), (7) and (8).

50. Local Government (Miscellaneous Provisions) Act 1976, sections 23 and 24.

51. As to the meaning of this expression, which is essentially a question of fact, see *Stephens* v. *Cuckfield RDC* [1960] 2 QB 373.

52. The identity of the owner, and possibly of the occupier, is likely to be particularly difficult to trace in these circumstances, and it may be necessary to post a request for information notice on the land under sections 284 and 283 of the 1971 Act.

53. This effective period will be extended if there is an appeal against the notice.

54. Originally under the 1947 Act, all appeals against enforcement notices, lay to the magistrates, not the Secretary of State, but in all cases other than the present section this was changed by the Act of 1962.

55. Section 105(4) and (5).

56. Cf. default action in respect of an enforcement notice: Chapter 16, p.186.

57. 'Nuisance' here is to be understood in its ordinary common law sense, as involving at least two properties *(National Coal Board* v. *Neath BC* [1976] 2 All ER 478). It is not necessary to prove that the condition of the land is *both* prejudicial to health *and* a nuisance (the *Neath* case) but it is clear that if a nuisance is alleged there must be some threat to public health or hygiene: *Coventry City Council* v. *Cartwright* [1975] 2 All ER 99.

58. These sections of the Act of 1974 are in force.

59. Defined in section 30 of the 1974 Act, as meaning household, industrial and commercial waste, terms which are themselves elaborately defined in the same section.

60. It will be remembered that the deposit of refuse or waste material on land involves a material change of use, even if the land is already used for that purpose but the superficial area or height of the deposit is extended: 1971 Act, section 22(3) (b).

61. 1974 Act, section 10.

62. SI 1968 No. 43, originally made under the Civic Amenities Act 1967, since replaced by the 1978 Act.

63. GDO, Class i, para. 3. The caravan cannot be kept in the front garden under this provision.

64. GDO Class xxii; 1960 Act, Schedule 1, paragraphs 2-9.

65. It is an offence for an itinerant trader or gypsy to pitch a stall on a highway verge: Highways Act 1980, section 150, and see also Part XVII of the Local Government Land and Planning Act 1980.

66. Town and Country Planning (Ironstone Areas Special Development) Order 1950, SI 1971 No. 1177.

67. GDO, Sched. 2, Class xix.

68. GDO, ibid., class xx.

69. SI 1971 No. 756.

70. Town and Country Planning (National Coal Board) Regulations, 1974, SI 1974 No. 1006, made under section 273 of the 1971 Act.

71. All coal is vested in the Board under the Coal Industry Nationalisation Act 1946.

16 The Enforcement of Planning Control

1. Introduction

Even as land use planning without law becomes a mere drawing board exercise, so planning law itself without sanctions becomes a series of empty threats and promises. If the objectives or ideologies[1] of planning law in a given society are to be achieved, that law must include measures of enforcement in some form. The English system requires special steps to be taken before any sanctions can be enforced against persons contravening planning control. Although it is unlawful for a landowner to carry out development without first obtaining planning permission, and this may have indirect consequences,[2] the planning authority cannot at that stage take direct action by way of a criminal prosecution to penalise or prevent[3] any such contravention. Before effective sanctions can be brought to play, the authority must serve an enforcement notice; this itself may then, if it does not achieve its object of bringing the contravening use to an end or removing the offending building, be followed by sanctions. These may take the form of default action by the authority or a prosecution, or the authority may take both default action *and* prosecute. In an important case where it may be thought the offending landowner may prove to be contumacious, the enforcement notice may be reinforced by the more drastic stop notice. We will now consider the procedure in more detail.

2. Enforcement Notices

When the planning authority consider there has been a breach of planning control, they may serve an enforcement notice under section 87 of the 1971 Act. This is a power, not a duty, and the authority cannot be compelled by an aggrieved neighbour to the contravening development, or by anyone else, to take enforcement action. In exercising their discretion under the enabling section, the authority must have regard to any directions given by the Secretary of State, to the provisions of the operative development plan, and to any 'other material considerations', an expression the meaning of which has already been considered in another context.[4] As the power is a discretion conferred by statute, the authority cannot tie their hands to exercise or not to exercise that power in any particular manner.[5]

Enforcement notices, which may have a serious effect on the rights of a private landowner, have always been regarded by Parliament and the courts as important documents, subject to a number of detailed provisions, all of which must be observed if a notice is not to be found to be invalid. These may be listed as follows:

(i) A notice must be served on the owner and the occupier(s) of the land to which it relates, and on any other person having an interest in the land. 'Owner' is defined in section 290(1) of the 1971 Act, and the authority may (and in most cases should) obtain information as to ownership of interests in the property by serving a notice requesting that information, on the occupier or any person in receipt of rent from the land, under section 284 of the 1971 Act. Service of a notice may be effected by any method that can be proved, but service by one of the methods listed in section 283 of the 1971 Act will be deemed to have been effective unless the contrary is proved. Where the land in question is a caravan site, it seems that every owner of a caravan on the site is an 'occupier' for this purpose and is entitled to be served with a notice.[6]

(ii) The notice must be served on the orders of the authority or a committee or officer of the authority to whom the power to act under section 87 has been delegated by the planning authority under section 101 of the Local Government Act 1972.

(iii) The notice must specify the matters alleged to constitute a breach of planning control.[7] There is deemed to be such a breach if development has been carried out without planning permission either express or implied (for example by virtue of the GDO), or if any condition or limitation subject to which planning permission was granted has not been complied with.[8]

(iv) The notice must also specify the steps required to be taken in order to remedy the breach of planning control that is complained of, and these must not exceed the minimum necessary to achieve this purpose.[9]

(v) *Two* dates[10] must be specified in the notice; the period on the expiration of which the notice will become effective (the 'effective period') and the date within which the required steps must be taken (the 'compliance period'). The compliance period must be sufficient to allow a reasonable time to take the steps required after the expiration of the effective period.[11] The effective period must not be *less* than 28 days from the date of service of the notice. If the notice has to be served on a number of occupiers, and service therefore cannot be effected on all occupiers on the same day, care must be taken to ensure that the effective period is stated to be the same in all the notices.[12]

If an appeal is lodged with the Secretary of State within that 28 days the effective period will be extended until the final determination of that appeal and the expiry of a further six weeks, within which time an appeal may be made to the High Court. If there is an appeal to the court the effective period will be yet further extended until the final determination of such an appeal (allowing for the possibility of yet further appeals from the High Court to the Court of Appeal and possibly from there to the House of Lords).

(vi) There is a time limit of four years from the breach of planning control within which an enforcement notice may be served, in any case where the breach consists of the carrying out of building, mining, etc., operations, of a failure to comply with a condition or limitation as to such operations, or which amounts to a change of use without planning permission of a building *to* use a dwellinghouse. If the breach concerns any other type of material change of use or breach of conditions (including a change *from* a dwellinghouse to use as some other kind of building), the four-year time limit does not apply, provided that the change of use in question occurred after 1 January 1964. If it occurred *before* that date, no enforcement notice can be served in any case (section 88(1) (d)).

If these technical rules are not observed, an enforcement notice may be invalid. The remedy[13] may be, in cases covered by section 88(1) (below) to appeal to the Secretary of State, in others to resist proceedings taken on a prosecution or by default action, or it may be possible to obtain a declaration from the court.[14]

3. Appeals Against Enforcement Notices: the Grounds

The landowner or other person served with an enforcement notice (or any other person having an interest in the land to which the notice relates) may appeal in writing to the Secretary of State under section 88 of the 1971 Act. The same fee is chargeable as on a planning application, but this fee will be refunded if the appeal is withdrawn or is allowed on other than planning grounds (S.I., 1981, No. 369). The appeal must be lodged before the expiration of the effective period which cannot be extended by the Secretary of State. The notice of appeal need not be in any particular form, but should state the grounds on which the appellant intends to rely, and also give the facts that form the basis of those grounds, although the grounds and facts may be stated later or added to, before the hearing of the appeal.[15] The grounds of the appeal must be brought within one or more of those stated in section 88(1), which are as follows:

(a) that planning permission ought to be granted; this amounts to an appeal on the planning merits of the case. In some circumstances the appeal against the notice will be in fact an appeal against a refusal of planning permission, but in other cases there may never have been any application for permission. If the appeal is allowed, this will have the effect of a grant of permission, which the Secretary of State may direct is to have retrospective effect under section 32(1). It is in this type of case when the charge will *not* be refunded;

(b) that the matters alleged in the notice do not amount to a breach of planning control. This is the heading which puts the law in issue as well as the facts. It may be contended that the action of the appellant complained of in the notice did not amount to development, that planning permission had already been granted covering the development, that the conditions in question had in fact been complied with, or that they were *ultra vires* the planning authority, etc. It cannot, however, be argued that the notice was faulty because (for example) it did not specify two dates, or that the person signing the notice had not been properly authorised to do so by the local planning authority. Matters of this kind, or others, not listed in section 88(1) can only be raised in proceedings for a declaration or by way of a defence to a prosecution under section 89, or perhaps by resisting default action, but not on an appeal to the Secretary of State;[16]

(c) that the notice was served more than four years after the breach of planning control complained of, except in the case of those changes of use to which the four year time limit does not apply;[17]

(d) in cases to which (c) does not apply, that the breach of planning control occurred before 1 January 1964;[18]

(e) that the notice was not served in accordance with section 87(4); this is confined to a contention that the notice was not served on the correct persons, as the manner of service is immaterial provided it was effectual.[19] Errors in service may, however, be disregarded if neither the appellant nor any person who has not been served, has not been substantially prejudiced;

(f) that the steps required to be taken by the notice exceed what is necessary to remedy the breach of planning control. This will not in practice be frequently used, except possibly as a delaying tactic, as it does not raise any question of substance;

(g) that the time allowed for compliance with the terms of the notice (the 'compliance period') falls short of what should reasonably have been allowed; again a ground that does not raise any question of substance.

4. Appeals against Enforcement Notices: the Procedure

When a valid notice has been served, any recipient of the notice may appeal as above stated. The notice of appeal having been duly lodged, the Secretary of State will convene an inquiry before a person appointed by him, unless the parties have agreed that the appeal may be disposed of on the papers. The procedure at such an inquiry will follow closely that applicable to an appeal against a refusal of planning permission,[20] although technically the rules of procedure do not apply.[21] In some cases the inspector will himself give the decision on behalf of the Secretary of State;[22] in other cases he will make recommendations only, for the Secretary of State (or an official in the Department in his name) to decide. The inspector may be assisted at the inquiry by a legally qualified assessor from the Department, in any case where legal issues of any complexity are likely to be raised.

When deciding the appeal, the Secretary of State may dismiss the appeal and uphold the enforcement notice, or he may quash the notice. In addition he may:

(i) correct any informality, defect or error in the notice, provided he is satisfied that this is not material;[23]

(ii) disregard certain cases where the notice has not been properly served, as above mentioned;

(iii) vary the terms of the notice in favour (but not in a manner contrary to his interests) of the appellant;[24]

(iv) grant planning permission for any development to which the enforcement notice relates, or discharge any condition or limitation subject to which planning permission for that development had been granted. A decision to this effect may operate retrospectively under section 32(1);[25]

(v) determine any purpose for which the land may lawfully be used.[26]

To this extent the decision of the Secretary of State may go outside the actual issues raised by the enforcement notice itself.

5. Subsequent Action: Further Proceedings

What further action can be taken by the local planning authority if the terms of the enforcement notice are not observed once it has become effective by lapse of time, the determination of any appeal and the compliance period has expired? The authority can forthwith follow two normal lines of action provided for in the 1971 Act; prosecute and/or act in default. They may also have other action open to them.

A. Prosecution

An offence will be committed if the owner of land on whom an enforcement notice has been served fails to take 'any steps' required by the notice (other than discontinuing the use of land (section 89(1)), and it is also an offence for any person to use the land or to cause or permit[27] its use in any manner which contravenes the terms of the notice (section 89(5)).

Although mining operations can be treated as a use of the land, and an enforcement notice can be served requiring the discontinuance of such a use, a prosecution may be brought for failure to comply with such a notice (Minerals Regulations 1971, Reg. 3).

Maxmimum fines of £400 may be imposed for offences under this section, but prosecutions are not often taken by local authorities in respect of 'operations' as their main objective is to secure the demolition or removal of the offending building, and to secure this they can take default action. In the case of an offending *use,* however, the taking of proceedings is their only 'normal' remedy.

B. Default Action

Default action is provided for in section 91 of the 1971 Act. If 'steps', other than the discontinuance of a use, required by an enforcement notice have not been taken within the compliance period, the local authority can then instruct their staff to enter the premises (if necessary by force)[28] and take the steps required by the notice (i.e. demolish or take away the offending building or other works). Various provisions of the Public Health Act 1936 are applied to this procedure, including a power to sell any materials recovered by the authority from the demolition (section 91(4)). Expenses necessarily incurred by the authority in carrying out default action may be recovered from the owner of the premises concerned. A reasonable sum by way of establishment expenses may be added to the sums actually incurred;[29]

the money is recoverable by ordinary proceedings, normally in the county court.[30]

C. Injunction

Default action in respect of operations at least is likely to achieve its object in preventing any continuation of the contravention of planning control. A prosecution may theoretically lead to the imposition of a heavy fine,[31] but this is rare in practice. Some offenders are not deterred by comparatively small monetary penalties especially if the profit to be derived from the contravening development (e.g. the rents from a caravan site in a holiday area) is considerable. If it can be proved to the satisfaction of the court that the ordinary machinery of the law is inadequate to prevent further breaches of the statute, the planning authority may be able to obtain an injunction from the High Court, restraining the offender from continuing the contravening development. This is an efficient procedure, for any breach of the terms of the injunction will be treated by the court as a contempt and the offender will be promptly imprisoned until he has 'purged' his contempt, i.e. satisfied the court that he has complied with the injunction and does not intend to offend again. But this course of action can be resorted to only after the ordinary machinery (i.e. the prosecution before magistrates) has been resorted to on several occasions without deterring the offender.[32] Although the application to the High Court is likely to be heard quickly, it is an exceptional procedure and is not to be resorted to lightly, then probably only after considerable delay.[33]

D. Stop Notices

By 1968 it had become obvious that the existing machinery for following up on an enforcement notice was inadequate to prevent the obdurate offender from continuing to flout planning control. Many weeks could pass after the service of an enforcement notice before a prosecution could be brought to the magistrates, and the proceedings may be protracted still further if the offender appeals to the Secretary of State (even if he had no grounds whatsoever) against the enforcement notice. A further six or more months would then pass, during which time the offender would be able to continue to draw substantial rents from his unlawful caravan site or other contravening use of the land.

And so Parliament introduced, in the 1968 Act, the additional procedure of the 'stop notice', and this was revised and strengthened by the Town and Country Planning (Amendment) Act 1977.

Under section 90 of the 1971 Act as amended by the Act of 1977, the planning authority may at any time after an enforcement notice has been served, (but before it has come into effect) serve a stop notice on any person appearing to the authority to have an interest in the land or to be engaged in any activity prohibited by the enforcement notice. Such a notice may prohibit the carrying out of any specified activity alleged by the enforcement notice to be a breach of planning control. The stop notice need not necessarily refer to *all* the activities included in the enforcement notice, nor need it apply to the whole of the land affected by the enforcement notice, but it may not apply to any activity not included in the enforcement notice.

It is perhaps difficult to understand why the novel word 'activity' was used in the 1977 Act, without definition. The section in its original form in the 1968 and 1971 Acts referred to 'operations', which almost certainly did not include a change of use; presumably 'activity' is wide enough to embrace an operation, a change of use and a breach of a condition or limitation.

The service of a stop notice has the following effect:

(a) any person who has been served with the notice commits an offence if he fails to comply with the notice once it has come into effect. The notice operates as from a date specified in the notice, not less than three days and not more than 28 days from the first date of service.
(b) Also, *any* person who fails so to comply with the notice will be guilty of an offence if the notice has been posted on the site,[34] unless the person charged can prove that he could not reasonably have been expected to know of the existence of the stop notice.

Moreover, these offences will be committed regardless of any appeal pending against the enforcement notice, and the maximum penalty on conviction is a fine of £1,000.[35]

The stop notice will, however, cease to take effect if it is withdrawn by the local authority, if the enforcement notice is withdrawn or quashed, or if the compliance period for the enforcement notice has expired (so that the enforcement notice itself is enforceable). A stop notice also cannot apply to the use of a building as a dwellinghouse, the use of land as a site for a caravan occupied as a sole or main residence, nor to most activities that had commenced more than 12 months previously.[36]

Section 177 of the 1971 Act (as amended by the 1977 Act) provides that a person who has suffered loss as a consequence of the service of a stop notice may claim compensation from the planning authority if the enforcement notice is eventually quashed otherwise than by a grant of planning permission, or if it is varied in a material particular or if it is withdrawn by the authority. No compensation is payable under the section if the enforcement notice (or the stop notice) is declared to be invalid by a court, but is not 'quashed'. A developer seeking to invalidate an enforcement notice on grounds other than those specified in section 88(1) should therefore apply for a *certiorari* rather than a declaration on an application for judicial review.[37] This potential liability to pay compensation makes the stop notice procedure unpopular with many local authorities, and it is not often used in practice.

6. Other Proceedings

An enforcement notice may also be served in respect of the control over listed buildings (section 96), and the grounds on which an appeal against such a notice may be based are specified in section 97. Enforcement notices would not really be relevant in the case of trees, but there is power to require the replacement of trees, and this is enforceable within a period of four years by the service of a notice under section 103. The statute confers a power to make regulations for the service of an enforcement notice in respect of advertisements (section 109), but this power has not been implemented, and there is simply a provision in the Regulations (made under the same section), for the authority to serve a notice (Reg. 16), challenging the continued display of any advertisement. Orders requiring the discontinuance of an existing use are enforceable under section 108, and proceedings for a penalty may be taken under section 104 if a waste land notice is not complied with.

7. Established Use Certificates

When the 1968 Act removed the four-year time limit for enforcement action in the case of most contravening uses, Parliament was persuaded, by way of compensation, to provide a procedure whereby a landowner could establish once and for all the date when a use of his land had commenced. If that date could be shown to have been pre-1964 (four years *before* the passing of the 1968 Act), no enforcement action can be taken in respect of that use.[38]

Consequently a landowner can apply under section 94 of the 1971 Act to the local planning authority for an established use certificate. This he does in manner precisely similar to that for an application for planning permission, and if the certificate is refused, there is a right of appeal to the Secretary of State (which may result in a local inquiry) and the further possibility of an appeal to the High Court on a point of law.[39]

Sections 94(7) of the 1971 Act provides that an established use certificate is to be conclusive for the purposes of an appeal to the Secretary of State against an enforcement notice served in respect of any land to which the certificate relates, provided that notice was served *after* the date of the application for the established use certificate.

In other words a certificate acts as a complete answer to an enforcement notice served in respect of a contravening use, but it will be issued only where the use was begun before 1964 without planning permission; or was begun after 1963 as the result of a change of use not requiring planning permission.[40] As 1964 becomes more remote in time so applications for certificates, not common in practice today, will become even less frequent.

Notes

1. As suggested by Professor McAuslan; see Chapter 2, p.18.
2. *LTSS Print and Supply Services Ltd* v. *Hackney* [1976] 1 All ER 311, and *ante,* p.93. p.93.
3. Exceptionally if it can be shown that other remedies have been tried without satisfactory results, the authority may be able to obtain an injunction requiring a contravening developer to desist: see below, p.187.
4. Chapter 11, p.129.
5. Ibid., and only planning considerations may be taken into account.
6. *Banbury* v. *Hounslow LB* [1966] 2 QB 204.
7. Section 87(6) (a) of the 1971 Act.
8. Ibid., s.87(2).
9. Ibid., s. 87(6) (a), and see also the grounds for appeal, below.
10. *Burgess* v. *Jarvis and Sevenoaks RDC* [1952] 2 QB 41.
11. 1971 Act, s.87(6) (b) and (c).
12. *Stevens* v. *Bromley LB* [1972] 1 All ER 712.
13. 1971 Act, section 87(3). However an 'established use certificate' may act as a defence in some circumstances: see para. 7 below.
14. Chapter 14, p.156.

15. Section 88(2), and see *Howard* v. *Secretary of State* [1974] 1 All ER 644 where it was held that the requirement to state the grounds and the facts in the notice of appeal was not mandatory but directory only.

16. Chapter 14, p.156.

17. Above, para. 2, p.183.

18. This is the date when the four year time limit was originally relaxed in the case of most changes of use, by the Act of 1968. It is important that changes of use are recorded in the deeds relating to a property, otherwise the date of commencement of a use may in subsequent years be difficult to establish. The landowner may in some cases be advised to seek to obtain an 'establishment use certificate' for this purpose (see p.189 below).

19. Above, p.182.

20. Chapter 13, p.144.

21. Chapter 13, p.144.

22. Chapter 13, p.146.

23. Section 88(4) (a), and see *Miller-Mead* v. *Minister of Housing and Local Government* [1963] 1 All ER 459.

24. Ibid., s.88(5).

25. In such a case the Secretary of State must have regard to the provisions of the development plan so far as material to the subject matter, and to any other material considerations: s.88(5) and (6).

26. Sections 88(5) (b).

27. As to the meaning of this phrase, see Appendix 1, p.235.

28. Using the powers and procedure contained in section 280 of the 1971 Act.

29. Local Government Act 1974, section 36.

30. See Chapter 14, p.157.

31. If proceedings are taken on indictment, when the trial will normally be before the crown court with a jury, a fine of an unlimited amount may be imposed.

32. For an example, see *Att.-Gen.* v. *Bastow* [1957] 1 QB 514. It is no longer necessary for a local authority to join the Attorney General in such proceedings: Local Government Act 1972, section 222.

33. This is because the remedy by way of injunction is granted at the discretion of the court.

34. In accordance with s.90(5) of the 1971 Act.

35. Criminal Law Act 1977, section 28(2).

36. See section 90(2), ibid.

37. Chapter 14, p.155.

38. As the name suggests, established use certificates are of no relevance to contravening *operations*.

39. Under sections 245(3) and 242(3) of the 1971 Act.

40. Exceptionally a certificate may also be issued in respect of a pre-1964 use commenced pursuant to a planning permission, but where a condition was imposed which has not been complied with since the end of 1963: see section 94(1) (b).

17 Other Remedies for Planning Action

1. Introduction

Apart from that normal remedy of the landowner who has failed to get a favourable planning decision, to appeal to the Secretary of State, he will also have the possibility of questioning the validity of a planning authority's action (or non-action) by asking the High Court to quash the decision or to grant him a declaration defining the legal position (hopefully, of course, in his favour). There are also the less conclusive remedies provided by way of complaint to the Parliamentary Commissioner or a Local Commissioner, or even to the Council on Tribunals. These remedies are discussed in other passages in this book;[1] it remains to describe such other remedies as are provided by the 1971 Act, namely the power of the landowner to require the local planning authority (or some other public body) to take his land from him. The Act assists such a landowner who has been prevented by some form of planning action, to make any viable use of his land; he can then offload his *damnosa hereditas,* in return for compensation, although the latter may often be derisory. There are two separate procedures applying to different circumstances that may be available in this context. The 'purchase' notice (chronologically the older of the two) and the 'blight' notice will therefore be considered separately.

In addition, there is the remedy of compensation. As a general rule it has not been considered necessary to provide for the payment of compensation in a case where a landowner is refused planning permission, even if it means that he cannot make some profitable use of his land. The thinking behind the English legislation differs in principle from that of some countries. Those which have a written constitution often include a clause to the effect that private property may not 'be taken for public use without just compensation'.[2] In 1922 in *Pennsylvania Coal Co* v. *Mahon,*[3] Mr Justice Holmes in the United States Supreme Court held that a State statute infringed this principle of the Federal Constitution when it empowered the State to impose a total restriction on building on land under which coal mining was in progress, without any provision for compensation. Such a restriction amounted to 'taking'. The right to enjoy and use one's land was, in Mr Justice Holmes's view, a property right which could not be removed completely without provision for the payment of compensation.

However, the Town and Country Planning Act 1947 'nationalised' or vested in the State, the right to develop land; as from 1 July 1948 no one can develop land without obtaining permission from the agency of the State, the local planning authority. In England Parliament is supreme,[4] and, there being no written constitution, there can be no question of a statute being invalid, even if there is a 'taking' and no provision is made for compensation. In Northern Ireland in 1960 there was a written constitution, with a no-taking without compensation clause, similar to that in the US Constitution, and a system of land use control precisely similar to the English model was in force. In *O.D. Cars Ltd* v. *Belfast Corporation*,[5] the House of Lords (on appeal from the Court of Appeal in Northern Ireland) held that the planning legislation did not amount to a 'taking' of property; it was merely a restriction on the use of land similar to public health or housing restrictions.[6]

So no provision has been made generally in our law for compensation to be payable in respect of an unfavourable planning decision. Exceptionally, however some measure of compensation has been provided for in respect of land that was suitable ('ripe') for development in 1948, when the 1947 Act came into force, and there may still be a few cases where money can be claimed today. Certain other types of planning action may also give grounds for a compensation claim, but these are unusual in practice.

Claims for compensation will be considered later in ths chapter, and we will first describe the machinery governing purchase and blight notices, which may be considered as a modified form of compensation.

2. Purchase Notices

Sometimes a landowner may find that part or all of his land has become virtually unusable, because of the operation of the planning legislation. Perhaps he had laid out a housing estate and obtained planning permission for the development proposed, but he has been obliged by the planning authority as a condition attached to the permission, to leave vacant a corner plot so as to provide a visibility splay at the entrance to the estate from the main road. Perhaps, again, he has been required to leave a piece of land in the centre of the estate as a turning circle. Such a plot may be too small, or too inaccessible for agricultural or any other use, but the owner may have responsibilities, while it remains his property, to keep it in good order, free of weeds and rubbish. Again, there may be a large piece of scrub land on the outskirts of a town, outside the urban fence, for which development permission has been refused, and which is of too poor a quality to be usable for agriculture or grazing.

Section 180 of the 1971 Act allows a landowner to 'offload' useless plots of this kind. Where land has become incapable of reasonably beneficial use in its existing state, the owner may serve a 'purchase notice'. He must show that he has applied for planning permission and has been refused, or has been granted permission but this was subject to conditions, and as a consequence, taking account of what may lawfully be done on the land (including the effect of the GDO and the Use Classes Order, so far as may be relevant), the owner nevertheless cannot make any beneficial use of the land. If permission has been refused for residential use (for example) of a parcel of land, it may still be beneficial to continue to use that parcel for some agricultural purpose, as the section cannot be utilised so as to ensure that the owner can only make the *most* profitable use of his land.[7]

A purchase notice must be served on the district council, and it operates in effect as a notice of compulsory acquisition in *reverse;* in other words, instead of the owner being compelled to sell against his wishes, the authority are compelled to buy the land. Once the notice has become effective, the authority are deemed to have served a notice to treat[8] that cannot be withdrawn; the normal compulsory purchase procedure must then be followed, and the owner will be entitled to claim compensation. This will be assessed at the value of the land in its existing state, which is not likely, of course, to be a very substantial sum.

When a purchase notice has been served on the local authority they must within a period of three months reply to the landowner;[9] saying (i) that they accept the purchase notice, *or* (ii) that they have referred the notice to some other public body, *or* (iii) that they refuse to accept the purchase notice and have referred it to the Secretary of State.

In case (i) the notice becomes effective and the land is acquired by the authority and the owner will be entitled to his compensation as above stated, to be determined in case of dispute by the Lands Tribunal.[10] In case (ii) the notice will be referred to some other public body, such as the county council or perhaps the local electricity board (perhaps in the case of a small parcel on a housing estate (for use as a substation) where that body has agreed to acquire the land.

In case (iii) the notice will be referred to the Secretary of State, where neither the local authority nor any other public body are willing to agree to purchase the land. In such a case the authority must state their reasons for refusing to accept the notice, to the landowner and to the Secretary of State.

On receiving a purchase notice in case (iii) above, the Secretary of State must decide whether to confirm it (he must do so if he is satisfied that the conditions in section 180 are fulfilled).[11] Alternatively, 'if he considers it expedient to do so' he may grant planning permission for development of the land which is the subject matter of the purchase notice, if the land can thereby be put to some reasonably beneficial use. This he may do whether or not the landowner wants so to develop the land; the purchase notice is then discharged.

Before the Secretary of State takes a decision on the matter he must give at least 28 days notice to the landowner, the district council, the county council and to any public body which he may propose to substitute as the acquiring authority. If any of them object, he must give them an opportunity of being heard before one of his inspectors. If he then finally decides to confirm the notice, the acquisition of the land proceeds as before, unless there is an application to the High Court to quash the Secretary of State's order under section 242(3) and 245(3) of the 1971 Act.

A purchase notice may also be served in the following circumstances (not falling within section 180):

(a) if there has been an order revoking or modifying an existing planning permission or one requiring the discontinuance of an existing use;[12]
(b) where consent to fell has been refused in certain circumstances under a tree preservation order made in the terms of the model order, which applies section 180 *et seq.* (with modifications);
(c) on a refusal (or conditional approval) of listed building consent;
(d) under the Control of Advertisements Regulations where there is a refusal of consent (a case which will be extremely rare in practice);
(e) if planning permission is refused for development falling within Class I of Schedule 8 to the 1971 Act (see below, para. 4(vii).

3. Blight Notices

There are only comparatively few cases when a purchase notice may be served, and it was appreciated early in the 1960s that the value of land could often become 'blighted' or seriously depreciated as a consequence of threatened planning action, perhaps by the inclusion of a proposed motorway or airport in a development plan. This is the feature sometimes known as 'worsenment', the opposite of 'betterment', which will be more fully discussed later.[13] Section 192 *et seq.* of the 1971 Act attempts to deal with this situation, by enabling the 'blighted' landowner to serve a blight notice, which, as will be explained, has much the same effect as a purchase notice. However, a blight notice may be served only in a small number of precisely defined circumstances, and then only subject to prescribed conditions. Thus

(i) The land in question must fall within one of the nine classes listed in section 192(1). This includes land shown in a development plan as the site for a highway, or approved by a local authority resolution for that purpose, land in respect of which a compulsory purchase order is in force but where no notice to treat has yet been served, and also land shown as being subject to acquisition in a structure plan or local plan;
(ii) the interest in the land in respect of which the blight notice is served must be *either* the interest of an owner-occupier[14] of an agricultural unit or of land the annual value of which does not exceed a prescribed sum[15] *or* it must be the interest of a resident owner-occupier;
(iii) the person serving the blight notice must also prove that he has made reasonable endeavours to sell his interest, but in consequence of the land being subject as described in section 192(1), he has been unable to sell the interest, except at a price substantially lower than that for which it might reasonably have been expected to sell.

The owner of an interest who can overcome all these hurdles can serve a blight notice on the local authority requiring them to purchase the interest in the property, which will be a house, a small commercial property (perhaps a cornershop) or a farm, which has been seriously affected in value by a threatened new motorway or other major development.

Within a period of two months the authority may serve a counter-notice under section 194. This may state that the blight notice does not comply with the provisions described above (this amounts to a challenge on the facts and law put forward by the person serving the

notice), that the authority does not propose to acquire any part of the
land which is the subject of the blight notice, or that they propose to
acquire only part of that land. Within a further two months the person
who served the blight notice may object to the counter-notice and
require his objection to be determined by the Lands Tribunal.[16] The
Tribunal will then determine the validity of the notice or counter-
notice.

If the blight notice is found to be valid, or if no counter-notice had
been served under section 194, then the local authority is to be deemed
to have been authorised to acquire the interest compulsorily[17] and to
have served a notice to treat which cannot be withdrawn, unless the
blight notice itself is withdrawn.[18] The normal procedure on a
compulsory acquisition will then follow. Any order of the Lands
Tribunal, under this or any other provision, is subject to a right of
appeal to the Court of Appeal and eventually, perhaps, to the House of
Lords.

4. Rights to Compensation

A landowner will be entitled to claim compensation for general
planning restrictions only in exceptional cases; this topic will be
considered in the next chapter.[19]

There are also a number of special cases where the Act of 1971 makes
provision for claims for compensation by landowners. These may be
listed as follows:

(i) where an order has been made modifying or revoking an existing
planning permission;[20]
(ii) when an order has been made requiring the discontinuance of an
existing use;[21]
(iii) where alteration, etc., of a listed building has been refused, or
where an order has been made revoking or modifying a listed building
consent;[22]
(iv) where loss or damage has been sustained as a consequence of a
stop notice,[23] or a building preservation notice;[24]
(v) where a tree preservation order has been made, and consent to fell
is refused in circumstances specified in the order,[25] or where trees are
required to be replaced;[26]
(vi) where there has been a challenge to an existing advertisement;[27]

(vii) where planning permission is refused in respect of some development falling within Schedule 8.[28]

The last-mentioned case calls for further explanation. Compensation is payable under this provision when planning permission has been refused by the Secretary of State (either on an appeal to him or on a reference under section 35) for development of a class falling within Part II of Schedule 8 to the 1971 Act. The classes of development so listed in Part II are all comparatively minor matters, but perhaps the most important is the alteration or extension of any building by not more than one-tenth of its cubic capacity, if the building was erected after 1 July 1948. If permission for any such development is so refused, compensation may be claimed on the basis of the depreciation in the value of the claimant's interest in the land as a consequence of that refusal (section 169).

In all these cases compensation is to be assessed on the principles that apply to compensation for the compulsory acquisition of land,[29] and any dispute falls to be determined by the Lands Tribunal[30] (and an appeal from the Tribunal lies to the Court of Appeal). Claims for compensation must be made in due form as provided for in regulations,[31] and the claim (if established) must be met by the local planning authority, although in a few cases where a decision giving rise to the claim for compensation was made wholly or partly in the interests of a government department, the Minister responsible may make a contribution towards the compensation so payable.[32]

Compensation that may be claimed as a consequence of the introduction of planning legislation in 1948 is the subject of the next chapter.

Where a purchase notice is subsequently served and confirmed in respect of a parcel of land for which compensation had previously been paid under section 164 (orders modifying or revoking an existing planning permission) the compensation payable on the purchase notice will be reduced accordingly (section 187).

Notes

1. See Chapters 13 and 14, as to the Commissioners, see Chapter 4.
2. See the Fifth Amendment (part of the 'Bill of Rights') to the Constitution of the United States of America.
3. 260 US 393 (1922).
4. It can do anything, as we said in Chapter 1, p.11.

5. [1960] 1 All ER 65.

6. In the United States zoning restrictions on the use of land which amount to less than a total prohibition on any profitable use of the land, have been held to be not unconstitutional, as they amount to a use of the 'police power'; the leading case is *Village of Euclid* v. *Amble Realty Co* 272 US 365 (1926). On this subject see Bosselman, Callies and Banta *The Taking Issue* (Council of Environmental Quality, Washington D.C., 1973) and R.F. Babcock *The Zoning Game* (University of Wisconsin Press, 1966).

7. *R* v. *Ministry of Housing and Local Government, ex parte Chichester RDC* [1960] 1 WLR 597.

8. As to notices to treat, see Chapter 20, p.222.

9. Section 181 of the 1971 Act.

10. Chapter 20, p.224.

11. Section 183 of the 1971 Act.

12. See Chapter 15, p.164.

13. Chapter 18, p.201.

14. See definition in section 203.

15. At present this is £2,250: Town and Country Planning (Limit of Annual Value) Order (SI 1973 No. 425).

16. As to this Tribunal, see Chapter 20, p.224.

17. Section 196 and Chapter 20, p.221.

18. Under section 198 of the 1971 Act.

19. See Chapter 18, p.201.

20. Chapter 15, p.164, and section 164.

21. Chapter 15, p.164, and section 170.

22. Chapter 15, p.166, and sections 171 and 172.

23. Chapter 16, p.189, and section 177.

24. Chapter 15, p.169, and section 173.

25. Chapter 15, p.173, and section 174.

26. Ibid., and section 175.

27. Chapter 15, p.172, and section 176.

28. Section 169.

29. Section 178 of the 1971 Act applies the provisions of the Land Compensation Act 1961 (as subsequently amended by the Land Compensation Act 1973) and see Chapter 20, p.224.

30. Ibid., section 179.

31. Town and Country Planning General Regulations 1976 (SI 1976 No. 1410), Reg. 14.

32. 1971 Act, section 254.

18 Worsenment and Betterment

1. Introduction

We now turn to one of the most difficult problems of land use policy, and one which has given rise to political controversy. Basically, it concerns the effects that planning legislation and controls have on land values, and the extent to which those effects should be alleviated or reversed.

On the one hand planning restrictions on land use will frequently depreciate the value of land. Clearly a potential purchaser will pay more for land that he can use as he likes, than he will pay for land that he can use only for strictly limited purposes. Planning action by a State agency such as the construction of a motorway or an airport or even by the grant of planning permission for some objectionable use may similarly depress the values of residential or other land in the neighbourhood.

On the other hand, planning action may have the effect of increasing land values. When there is a strict regime of land use control, the landowner who is able to obtain permission to develop his land for, say, residential purposes, will be able to command a higher price for his land in the open market, than can his neighbour who has been refused a similar permission. If a pleasant amenity is provided by planned action, such as a national park, the value of land in the neighbourhood may rise. Better communications may have the same effect, as was demonstrated by the opening of the Metropolitan Railway into Middlesex in the 1930s which caused land prices in 'Metroland' to rise rapidly. Even a motorway may improve the value of some properties.

The problem then is, should these artificial decreases (worsenment) and increases (betterment) in land value, brought about by State action in the form of planning controls and development, be redressed or adjusted by State action? Should the legislature attempt to cream off the betterment, so that private individuals do not receive windfalls,[1] and compensate for the worsenment, so that the unfortunate landowners are redressed for their 'wipe-outs'?

The answers to these questions vary according to political party policies. The Conservatives favour compensation for worsenment; the

Socialists are anxious to take betterment for the benefit of the public, while not being so generous with compensation for worsenment. As a consequence, we have had changes in legislation each time there has been a swing in political party control of the legislature, with comparatively little stability. The whole problem has been further confused by the voracity of successive governments — of both political persuasions — for land acquisition at as low a price as practicable. We will now outline the history of the legislation. This aspect of the problem has already been discussed in Chapter 6, but for the sake of clarity, and at the risk of some repetition, it was thought desirable to outline the legislation afresh.

2. Town and Country Planning Act 1932

Between the two World Wars, at a time of rapid development, a half-baked attempt was made in the Act of 1932 to tax off betterment and to make some provision for the compensation of worsenment. It was provided in section 21 of that Act that where as a consequence of the coming into operation of a town planning scheme or of the execution of works by a public body, property was increased in value, the appropriate authority could recover not more than 75 per cent of the value of that increase, from the landowner. Similarly, section 18 provided for compensation to be paid in respect of any injurious affection to property caused by the coming into operation of a scheme or by 'any action' caused by a responsible authority. These sections in practice were barely used, by reason of a number of factors:

(a) very few schemes under the 1932 Act ever came into operation;
(b) the Act became virtually a dead letter on the outbreak of war in 1939; and
(c) in any event, it was extremely difficult to prove that an increase in value or injurious affection of land was 'by' [to use the wording of the sections] the coming into operation of the scheme or the execution of works or other action taken. It was for this latter reason no doubt that this particular statutory formula was not used in subsequent legislation.

3. The Act of 1947

1947 saw a revolution in land use control; the right to develop was for the first time fully nationalised and that particular common law right of the landowner was taken away and vested in the State. In consequence the Act made provision both for compensation and for a charge to be made (by way of a betterment tax) when a right to develop was recovered by the landowner, in the form of planning permission. These must be considered separately.

(a) Compensation

The owner of any land that was 'ripe' for development in 1947 (when the Bill that became the 1947 Act was published) was entitled to make a claim for compensation against a notional 'global' fund of £300 million, set aside for the purpose. The claim had to be made before 1 July 1949, and to be accepted by a government agency constituted under the Act, the Central Land Board. It was the original intention of the Labour legislators in 1947 that a percentage only of valid claims would eventually be met, and partly for this reason some landowners failed to register their claims; however a number of claims were made and accepted by the Board. Then in 1953 the Conservative Party were in power, and they enacted another Town and Country Planning Act, which provided that established claims on the £300 million should be paid in full:

(a) when planning permission for development was refused; *or*
(b) if the land was acquired compulsorily or by agreement by a public authority at existing use value (i.e. without taking into account the value of any planning permission for development).

The 1953 Act has long since been replaced, but a claim for compensation may still be made in respect of land that has an 'unexpended balance of established development value'. This means that the developer can claim compensation, even today, on the happening of (a) or (b) above, if he can prove:

(i) that the land in question was the subject of an established claim in 1949, *and*
(ii) that the whole of that claim has not already been paid.

Further, as the law now stands, in Part VII of the 1971 Act, the refusal of planning permission referred to in (a), above, must not be of a type excluded by the Act; in particular, permission must not have been refused on the ground that the development in question was premature or in respect of a material change of use (see section 147). Any compensation so paid is recoverable from the landowner if planning permission is subsequently given for development for which it had formerly been refused.

(b) Development Charges

The 1947 Act also provided that a developer should pay for any planning permission[2] in the form of a development charge. This was based on the difference in value of the land in its existing state, without the benefit of any planning permission ('existing use value') and the value of the land with the benefit of the planning permission in question ('development value'). This difference determined the amount of the 'development charge', fixed at 100 per cent and payable to the Central Land Board. Because this charge was made in respect of any kind of development,[3] with but few trivial exceptions, and also because local and other public authorities could acquire land at existing use value, and they did not have to pay a development charge, the system was very unpopular. It had been assumed that land would change hands between private individuals at existing use value, and the Central Land Board had statutory powers to intervene and acquire at that value land suitable for development. In practice, however, potential developers were held to ransom by landowners who refused to sell at existing use value. The Town and Country Planning Act 1952, passed by the Conservative Government of the time, therefore abolished development charges, while the 1953 Act, as explained above, made provision for limited payments from the £300 million global fund.

4. The Town and Country Planning Act 1959

The legislation of 1952 and 1953 retained the favourable position of public authorities; they were still able to acquire land at existing use value, leaving their vendors to such claims as they might be able to establish against the £300 million. In 1959 the Conservatives changed this, and in effect[4] provided that after that date public authorities should pay compensation on compulsory acquisition based on the full market value of the land, and the Land Compensation Act 1961 extended this principle to include the value of various 'planning assumptions', to be explained in Chapter 20.

5. The Land Commission Act 1967

The Labour Government which returned to power in 1964 and 1965, changed the law once more, and established a new public agency, the Land Commission, charged with the duty of collecting 'betterment levy' on all 'chargeable acts and events', the most important of which were sales and leases of land. This levy was charged at 60 per cent of 'betterment value', the difference in value of the land at its existing use, and the value of the land with the benefit of any planning permission for development. The Land Commission was also given wide powers to acquire at existing use value any land which was suitable for development.

This Act also was unpopular, partly because of the complexity of its drafting, but also because many local authorities were jealous of the land acquisition powers of the Land Commission. When political power changed again in 1970, the Conservatives lost no time in repealing the Act of 1967 and abolishing the Land Commission.

6. The Community Land Act 1975

Once the Labour Party returned to power in 1974, the pendulum swung back again. This time there was a fresh start, and the Act of 1975 eschewed the notion of a separate agency to administer the scheme (except in Wales).

The Act of 1975 had two basic principles:[5]

(a) to ensure that the 'community' (ie. presumably, the public) should be able to control and encourage the development of land in accordance with its needs and priorities; *and*
(b) to restore to the community the increase in value of land arising from the efforts of the community, principally through the planning legislation.

The first objective was to be achieved by providing that as from a specified date,[6] development could take place only on land that was in, or had passed through, public ownership. All land suitable for development (with a few minor exceptions) would be acquired by the local authority at existing use value, and they would then *either* develop it themselves, *or* dispose of it for development by private or public enterprise at development value.

By this means, the second objective also would have been achieved, as the local authority would be able to keep, as profit, the difference between development value and existing use value, although they would under the Act have had to pass on some proportion of that profit to the Central Government. In the meantime, before all development land had been so acquired, the Development Land Tax Act 1976 provided that any developer would have to pay a development land tax based on 66 per cent of the increase in value of his land caused by the grant of planning permission for development (again subject to exceptions in favour of changes of use and minor forms of development).

7. The Land Compensation Act 1973

In the meantime, the Conservative Government of 1970-4 had turned its mind to the compensation or worsenment side of the main problem. The Act of 1973 provides that any owner whose land has been depreciated in value to an extent in excess of £50, as a consequence of 'physical factors', can claim compensation in respect of public works resulting in that depreciation. Public works here are confined to the construction of a new highway ('new' means after 1971) or aerodrome, and 'physical features' are confined to such matters as noise, fumes, vibration and the escape of liquids. In certain circumstances also a house owner can have his house sound-proofed at the expense of a public authority (section 20).

This Act survived the Labour Governments of 1974-9 and remains good law today.

8. The Modern Position

By the Local Government, Land and Planning Act 1980, the Conservative Government that came to power in 1979, has repealed the Community Land Act 1975, which had not in fact been at all vigorously implemented.[7] The Development Land Tax Act 1976, however, has not yet been repealed, and so the present position may be summarised as follows:

(i) in the case of major development, 66 per cent of any betterment is creamed off in the form of development land tax;

(ii) some small amount of compensation for worsenment may still be recoverable in respect of the introduction of the planning restrictions of 1947, if an unexpended balance of established development value can still be shown to exist;

(iii) compensation may also be recoverable in respect of worsenment caused by physical factors under the 1973 Act, as amended in minor details by the 1980 Act;

(iv) the 1980 Act preserves in some measure the wide land acquisition powers of local authorities (but not at existing use values) given by the 1975 Act,[8] and the Land Authority for Wales is left in being;[9]

(v) agreements under section 52 of the 1971 Act may be so operated as to secure for local authorities and the public advantages at the expense of the developer;[10]

(vi) specific types of planning restrictions are expressly made the subject of compensation claims under the 1971 Act, as explained in the last chapter;

(vii) there is still no compensation for the worsenment of land which has not been acquired,[11] but the value of which has been injuriously affected by some State action. Even where there has been no grant of planning permission, betterment in a corresponding situation may be taxable, either under the Development Land Tax Act or as a 'capital gain'.

Notes

1. 'Windfalls and Wipeouts' are terms coined by several American writers to describe this double situation.

2. Not in the sense of a fee for the administrative work as has been provided for under the 1980 Act, but it was envisaged rather as a purchase back from the State of the rights to develop.

3. The Reports of the Utthwait and Barlow Committees published during the Second World War had recommended that a development charge should be imposed only in respect of development of vacant land; development charges under the 1947 Act were levied even in respect of minor extensions of buildings and changes of use.

4. See Chapter 20, p.224.

5. See the White Paper, *Land,* dated 12 September 1974 (Cmnd. 5730).

6. 'The second appointed day', to be fixed by the Secretary of State.

7. Because of the economic recession of the late 1970s, local authorities had

insufficient staff and financial resources to utilise the extensive land acquisition powers given them by the 1975 Act.

8.   1980 Act, Part XIV.
9.   Ibid., Part XII and Sched. 18.
10.   See Chapter 12, p.139.
11.   Unless some property right has been infringed; see Chapter 20, p.229.

19 Other Land Use Controls

1. Introduction

Historically, the most important of all statutory land use controls was the public health legislation, which was itself founded in the common law of nuisance. The great Public Health Acts of 1848 and 1875 dealt effectively with the nineteenth-century cholera epidemics, and this was followed by the movement for better housing, exemplified by the Housing of the Working Classes Act 1890, which itself led to the planning legislation of 1909 and later years. Meanwhile, the common law had elaborated a system of highway law, which did not need much addition from the legislature until the age of the motor car in the early and middle years of our own century. In this chapter, therefore, we shall attempt an outline of the modern law of public health and the control of pollution, explain the land use provisions of housing law, and outline the nature of a highway and the principal functions of highway authorities, especially where these latter overlap with land use control.

There are of course other, minor statutory controls over land use, such as the rights of the National Coal Board to undertake open cast coalmining, and the rights of the Ministry of Civil Aviation to control the use of land in the neighbourhood of a civil airport, etc, but we do not have the space to make a complete catalogue of these minor controls.

2. Public Health

It is impossible to describe the whole of public health law in this chapter; we shall confine ourselves to a brief account of the principal land use controls. The statutory mechanism here tends to be much more rigid and precise than that governing the planning controls; local authorities are again responsible for its administration[1] but they have only a few discretionary powers, and they are more commonly subject to duties to enforce the law, which they are frequently required to do by serving a notice, followed by prosecution or default action if their notice is not complied with. The principal controls may be listed as follows:

(i) premises that have been allowed to get into a condition that is prejudicial to health or a nuisance[2] may be made the subject of abatement action, by service of a notice followed by proceedings before the magistrates.[3] This is the commonest form of statutory nuisance, but there are other forms of such nuisances provided for in the Public Health Acts.[4]

(ii) There is also a considerable body of law dealing with the use and maintenance of sewers, drains and sanitary appliances generally. A sewer is a conduit for waste water (surface water and foul water) from more than one building; a drain deals with the effluent from a single building.

(iii) The Clean Air Acts 1956 and 1968 prohibit[6] the emission of black smoke into the atmosphere, and make provision for the establishment of smoke control areas within which only authorised fuels[7] may be used for heating purposes. The emission of chemical and other noxious fumes from industrial premises is regulated by the Alkali Works, etc. Regulation Act 1906, under which 'scheduled processes' are required to be registered, and are subjected to the supervision of the Alkali Inspectorate,[8] who have the duty to ensure that the 'best practicable means' are employed to avoid atmospheric pollution.

(iv) The pollution of watercourses is regulated by Part II of the Control of Pollution Act 1974;[9] a licence from the water authority is required for the discharge of effluent into rivers and a separate licence for discharges of industrial effluent into public sewers, in the latter case under the Public Health (Drainage of Trade Premises) Act 1937.

(v) Pollution by noise is controlled by Part IV of the Control of Pollution Act 1974;[10] noise amounting to a nuisance may be dealt with as a statutory nuisance, and the local authority may declare an area to be a noise abatement zone, within which noise levels may not be increased; there is also a special control over noise emitted from construction sites.

3. Building Regulations

Under the Public Health Acts of 1936 and 1961, the Secretary of State has power to make regulations controlling the construction of new buildings, and of extensions and alterations to existing buildings (and in respect of certain changes of use), in the interests of public health and safety. The Regulations currently in force apply to the whole country[11] and are administered and enforced by the district councils.

Any person proposing to undertake building work to which the Regulations apply, must first submit plans and details of his proposal to the district council, which will normally (but not necessarily) be done at the same time and on the same application form as the application for planning permission.[12] The appropriate fee must be paid before the application will be considered. The application will have to demonstrate that the proposed works will, when completed, comply with the requirements of the Regulations, and with certain sections of the Public Health Acts of 1936 and 1961.

The current Regulations of 1976[13] deal with the following main topics: the materials to be used; preparation of the site and resistance to moisture; the structural stability of the building; fire safety (a very elaborate section); thermal insulation of dwellings; sound insulation (of all buildings); provisions regulating stairways, balustrades, and vehicle barriers; open space about buildings; their ventilation and the height of rooms; chimneys, flues, hearths and fireplaces; works and fittings (including heat-producing appliances, private drains, sewers and cesspools, and sanitary conveniences).

In administering the Regulations, the district councils have much less discretion than they have as planning authorities. In principle, if the plans show that the work will comply with the Regulations they must pass the plans; if the work would contravene the Regulations (or if the plans are not sufficiently detailed) the plans must be rejected; and if the plans are not rejected within five weeks of submission, the building owner is entitled to assume that the plans have been passed.

However, the council have some measure of discretion in the following respects:

(a) they may agree to dispense with or modify a particular Regulation in a specific case if, for example, some new form of construction or materials is to be used which they are satisfied will meet the objectives of the Regulations. There is a right of appeal to the Secretary of State if the council refuse to dispense with or to modify a Regulation in any particular case, under the Public Health Act 1961;

(b) the plans must comply with a number of sections of the Public Health Acts (e.g. there must be satisfactory provision for access for refuse removal; if the building is being erected on a site filled with

offensive material, etc., satisfactory precautions must be taken); the authority must be satisfied that these provisions will be met;
(c) in some instances a Regulation provides that if a specified method of construction is followed, the requirements of a particular Regulation will be deemed to have been satisfied, but in these cases the authority may agree that those requirements will in fact be satisfied if some other method of construction is followed.

If building work is constructed without prior approval of plans, or if the work eventually proves to contravene the Regulations, the building owner can be prosecuted for an offence. The local authority also has power to pull down offending work and to recover their costs in so doing from the building owner, unless they have (wrongly) approved the plans and the work has been constructed in accordance with approved plans. Even in the latter case, however, the authority may be able to obtain an injunction from the High Court to prevent the owner from proceeding with the work (Public Health Act 1936, s.65(5)).

If the building owner is aggrieved by a refusal of approval of his plans, he may appeal to the local magistrates; there is no right of appeal to the Secretary of State, except in cases (as above mentioned) where there has been a refusal to dispense with or modify a Regulation in a particular case.

4. Housing

By the end of the nineteenth century it was realised that there was little point in endeavouring to clean up living conditions in the crowded urban areas of Victorian England, if new slums were being built every year. Stringent building byelaws, to be replaced as we have said by the modern Building Regulations, achieved this objective to some extent, but the Housing of the Working Classes Act 1890 introduced a new concept. From that date it was accepted that local authorities should themselves be entrusted with the task of providing satisfactory housing accommodation 'for the working classes'. After the courts had interpreted the expression 'working classes' to include school teachers and police inspectors,[14] the expression disappeared from modern legislation, and district councils are now under a general duty to review housing conditions in their area and to make provision for those in need of accommodation.[15] Wide powers to acquire land for housing and to build houses on land so acquired, are conferred on district councils by Part V of the Housing Act 1957, and later legislation. Obviously the development of extensive Council housing estates involves questions of land use planning, and there should be close liaison in any district council between the housing committee and the planning committee (and the two departments), but the two functions of housing and planning are kept separate in the legislation.[16]

In spite of the Public Health controls and the extensive Council housing of the present century, the problem of unsatisfactory housing has not been solved. It has been tackled by the legislature in three separate ways:

(i) the improvement of single 'fit' but unsatisfactory houses;
(ii) the repair or demolition of individual 'unfit' houses; and
(iii) clearance or rehabilitation of 'slum' areas.

(i) Improvement

The individual house which is structurally sound, but unsatisfactory, perhaps because it lacks a bathroom and interior toilet accommodation or a kitchen, may be dealt with by means of a grant from the district council (who are assisted in this matter by Exchequer contributions) towards the cost of providing 'standard amenities' (a sink, wash-basin with hot and cold water, a bath, and a water closet within the house, etc.)[17] These grants, for approved works, may be claimed as a matter of right, and the authority cannot refuse to pay. At the discretion of the authority, grants may also be available towards the cost of providing other improvements (such as a new kitchen) or towards the cost of converting a building (such as a barn or a disused commercial building) to a dwelling or dwellings.[18]

(ii) The Single Unfit House

Section 4 of the Housing Act 1957 (as amended in 1969) defines what is meant by a house being 'unfit for human habitation'. The section sets out a list of items (e.g. structural stability, facilities for cooking, etc.) and provides that the house will be unfit if with regard to those items it is so far defective as to be unsuitable for occupation in that condition.

If a house is unfit as so defined, the district council may require the 'person having control' of the house (the owner or the landlord, normally) to carry out necessary repairs to make it fit, provided this can be done at reasonable expense (1957 Act, section 9). If the house cannot be repaired at reasonable expense, the district council have a duty either to make a demolition order or (if, for example, the house is in a row, and demolition would cause neighbouring houses to become unfit) a closing order (1957 Act, sections 16 and 17). A demolition order requires the house to be demolished, either by the owner or by the council at his expense: when the house has been so demolished the owner retains the site and a tenant or the owner who is displaced from the house may be entitled to a 'home loss' payment and to be re-housed by the district council.[19]

A closing order requires that the house may not be used for human habitation until (if ever!) it has been rendered fit. Again, any person displaced may be entitled to a home loss payment and to be re-housed.

(iii) Clearance and Rehabilitation

The problem of the slum area — the 'twilight' area of an inner city or the decaying suburbs of an industrial town — has been the subject of almost continuous legislative activity in the present century, especially since the Second World War.

Under the Housing Acts of 1930, 1936 and 1957, the principal procedure has been to declare a *clearance area* for any area of unfit houses or where the houses and other buildings are badly arranged.[20] The district council formerly followed this with a *clearance order*, requiring the owners to clear all the buildings in the area but leaving the sites in private ownership. Alternatively, the council could acquire all the land and buildings in the area (if necessary, by compulsory purchase) and they were then under a duty to demolish the buildings and redevelop the area with satisfactory housing. Since 1974, the power to make clearance orders has been removed, and *compulsory purchase orders* (or acquisition by agreement) must follow the declaration of a clearance area.

However, new concepts have been introduced in recent years. Under the Housing Act 1969, a district council may define an area of 'twilight' housing to be a *general improvement area*. The authority will then have power to acquire land in the area, to encourage house improvement, provide garages and other necessary buildings, make traffic orders and improve the street furniture, etc. The Housing Act 1974 followed this with the concept of the *housing action area*, where social conditions as well as the physical conditions of the houses are required to be taken into account. Further powers of land acquisition are conferred on the district council and there are also powers to make grants for environmental improvements, and the council have a right of pre-emption in respect of any house that is offered for sale or letting within the area. *Priority neighbourhoods* are areas adjoining a housing action area, and much the same powers exist in relation to them, but whereas the council must take remedial action in relation to a housing action area within a period of five years, there is not the same degree of urgency in relation to a priority neighbourhood.

Then the Inner Urban Areas Act 1978 enabled local authorities to declare areas to be specially designated, which then attracted central exchequer grants towards their rehabilitation. This Act was virtually overtaken by the Act of 1980, providing for urban development corporations and 'enterprise zones', which have already been described in Chapter 6.

4. Highways

Something has already been said, in Chapter 6, about the extensive powers of highway authorities (i.e. county councils, and for trunk roads, including the motorways, the Secretary of State for Transport) to acquire land and construct new highways, and also the duties of county councils to record and preserve footpaths and bridleways in their areas.

It is now necessary to explain what is meant by a 'highway'. A highway is a way, leading from one precise point to another by a defined route[21] over which all members of the public have a right to pass and re-pass on their lawful occasions. This right is confined to passing and re-passing, and does not include, for example, frightening grouse off the adjoining landowner's moor,[22] walking up and down recording the form of racehorses on the adjoining land,[23] sitting on a pile of stones on a roadside verge and talking about bees,[24] or parking a car while the occupants trespass in an adjoining field.[25]

There are now four types of highway known to the law:

(i) footpaths, open to members of the public on foot only;
(ii) bridleways, open to members of the public on foot or on horseback and with or without cattle, and a bridleway may also be used by a pedal cyclist provided he gives way to pedestrians;[26]
(iii) carriageways, open to all traffic;
(iv) motorways, on which certain classes of traffic, including pedestrians, may be prohibited by order made by the Secretary of State.

Footpaths and bridleways, or 'rights of way', have to be recorded on county 'definitive maps'[27] and new footpaths or bridleways may be created by agreement with landowners or by means of public path creation orders. These rights of way may be diverted or closed by use of a special statutory process.[28] Apart from statute, however, the rule at common law has been 'once a highway always a highway'. A right of way may come into existence by long use by the public over a period of at least 20 years without interruption.[29]

It is also possible under section 210 of the 1971 Town and Country Planning Act for the local authority to make an order diverting or closing a right of way across that land, under section 3 of the Acquisition of Land (Authorisation Procedure) Act 1946.

Access roads and means of access from private premises to trunk or classified roads may be stopped up by order made by the Secretary of State, and in any such case alternative means of access to a highway must be provided, and compensation may be payable.[30]

In all these cases of diversion or stopping up, there are rights for persons affected to object, and inquiries must be held before any orders become operative.

Highway authorities own the fee simple of the surface of the highway and as much below[31] and above[32] the surface as is necessary for the traffic that may be expected there. They are under a duty to maintain the condition of all highways that have been adopted or are 'maintainable at the public expense', by them, in a fit condition for that traffic.[33] If a new street is laid out by a developer, this is not maintainable by the highway authority unless and until it has been adopted by them, and they will adopt it (normally) only when it has been made up to an acceptable standard. The making up of a private street may be carried out by the highway authority at the expense of the frontagers, after following a complicated procedure laid down in Part X of the Highways Act 1980, which may involve proceedings before the local magistrates if there are objections.

The highway authority have extensive powers under the Highways Act 1980 to protect highways vested in them, including such matters as controls over the making of a carriage crossing over a footpath[34] the placing of builders' scaffolding in the highway[35] and the discharge of water and soil from adjoining premises onto the highway.[36]

Notes

1. Some of the functions relating to public health, and to sewers and drains in particular, are conferred on the ten water authorities which together cover the whole of England and Wales (Water Act 1973). Nevertheless in most cases those functions are administered by the district councils as agents for the water authorities. The water authorities are public corporations, whose members are appointed by the Secretary of State, and they draw their income from special rates levied on the occupiers of premises served by them.

2. 'Nuisance' as used here, in section 92 of the Public Health Act, 1936, is to be understood in the common law sense of some act causing serious inconvenience or annoyance to the normal enjoyment of a neighbour's premises: see *National Coal Board* v. *Neath BC* [1976] 2 All ER 478.

3. Public Health Act 1936, ss.92-100.

4. See, for example, 1936 Act, s.259, dealing with stagnant village ponds and water-courses.

5. Public sewers are vested in the water authorities. Unsatisfactory drains, sanitary appliances, etc., can be delt with by the district councils under various sections of the 1936 Act, especially under section 39 thereof.

6. Subject to minor exemptions to cover periods of lighting up a furnace.

7. Fuels specified for the purpose by the Secretary of State, including gas, electricity, and certain forms of smokeless solid fuels.

8. A sub-department of the Health and Safety Executive consisting of some 45 inspectors.

9. Not all of these provisions are yet in force, although the Act was passed by Parliament in 1974. The earlier provisions of the Rivers (Prevention of Pollution) Acts 1951 and 1961 have therefore not yet been repealed; they are similar in effect to some of the sections of the 1974 Act, but the latter will be more stringent when brought into operation (by order made by the Secretary of State).

10. Now fully in force; this Act replaced and considerably strengthened the Noise Abatement Act 1960, which was the first statute to deal with the subject.

11. For nearly a century before 1965, district councils and their predecessors were empowered to make building by-laws with a similar objective. Each council made its own by-laws, and there were a number of local variations, although as all by-laws were subject to Ministry confirmation, they tended to keep very closely to the Models published from time to time by the central authorities.

12. Chapter 9, p.108.

13. SI 1976 No. 1676.

14. *Green* v. *Minister of Health* [1946] KB 608.

15. Housing Act 1957, section 91, as amended by the Housing Act 1969, and see also the duties under the Housing (Homeless Persons) Act 1977.

16. The 'social mix' of persons to live on a private or Council housing estate is not a planning matter, and therefore is not apt for control by planning conditions: *R* v. *Hillingdon LBC, ex parte Royco Homes Ltd* [1974] QB 720.

17. The amounts that may be claimed are prescribed in the Acts and Regulations and a claim must normally be made before the work is undertaken.

18. In some cases grants may also be payable towards the cost of repairs to dwellings; see Housing Act 1974, as amended by the Housing Act 1980.

19. Land Compensation Act 1973, sections 29 and 39, as amended by the 1980 Act, and see Chapter 20, p.225.

20. See now Housing Act 1957, section 43 *et seq.*

21. There can be no public right to wander at will about an open space: *Att.-Gen.* v. *Antrobus* [1905] 2 Ch. 188.

22. *Harrison* v. *Duke of Rutland* [1893] 1 QB 142.

23. *Hickman* v. *Macey* [1900] 1 QB 752.

24. *Liddle* v. *North Riding CC* [1934] 2 KB 101.

25. *Randall* v. *Tarrant* [1955] 1 All ER 600.

26. Countryside Act 1968, section 30.

27. National Parks and Access to the Countryside Act 1949, ss.29 *et seq.* recently replaced by the Wildlife and Countryside Act 1981, and see Chapter 6, p.73.

28. Highways Act 1980, ss.119-125.

29. Ibid., section 31.

30. Ibid., ss.126-131.

31. *Tithe Redemption Commission* v. *Runcorn UDC* [1954] 1 All ER 653.

32. *New Towns Commission* v. *Hemel Hempstead Corpn* [1962] 3 All ER 183.

33. Highways Act 1980, section 58.

34. Ibid., section 186.

35. Ibid., section 171.

36. Ibid., section 165.

20 Compulsory Purchase and Compensation

1. Introduction

English law uses the expression 'compulsory purchase' for the process whereby a public authority (usually, but not necessarily, a local authority) possessing the appropriate statutory powers, compels a private landowner to transfer ownership of his interest in the land to the acquiring authority. 'Purchase' is a mis-nomer, as this connotes some measure of agreement; nor is the acquiring authority compelled to acquire but the owner is compelled to transfer. Other countries are more accurate; 'eminent domain' in the United States, 'resumption' in Australia, and 'expropriation' in most European countries. As Parliament is supreme and England has no written constitution,[1] the legislature in this country could lawfully authorise a taking without providing for compensation, but the courts will presume that any statutory provision authorising compulsory purchase was intended by Parliament (unless the contrary was expressly stated, which has never yet occurred), involves a liability to pay compensation.[2] The amount of compensation is to be assessed in all cases in accordance with the rules laid down in the Land Compensation Acts of 1961 and 1973, and the same rules apply also to the assessment of compensation for planning restrictions where applicable.[3] There is also a common code of procedure for the procedure of compulsory purchase, and all disputed compensation claims fall to be determined by the Lands Tribunal.

Compulsory purchase procedure falls into the following four stages:

(i) the power to acquire;
(ii) the application of the power to acquire to particular parcels of land;
(iii) the acquisition of interests in those parcels of land; and
(iv) the determination of compensation claims.

We will now consider these stages in turn, and conclude with some discussion of the principal rules governing the assessment of compensation.

2. The Power to Acquire

There must be power conferred by Parliament for the purpose or purposes for which the particular land is to be acquired. Thus, Sydney Corporation attempted to use a statute which conferred a power to acquire land for town centre redevelopment, to acquire land (which would have appreciated in value once the central redevelopment had been carried out) outside the redevelopment area. The Privy Council (on appeal from the Australian courts) held that the purported acquisition was *ultra vires* the Corporation. Although the acquisition was intended to ensure that the appreciation in value would accrue for the public benefit, this was not a purpose authorised by the statute, and the proposal was unlawful.[4] On the other hand, when some part of a large portion of land acquired under the Housing Act 1957, was to be used as an open space and for access roads, the court refused to strike down the compulsory purchase order on the ground that this was a 'planning', not a 'housing' purpose. The use of land for an open space and for roads was a perfectly acceptable ancillary use of land acquired for housing purposes.[5]

In the context of section 112 of the Act of 1971, as amended by section 91 of the 1980 Act, it would be extremely difficult to persuade a court that a proposed compulsory acquisition of land was *ultra vires* the planning authority, when the land was expressed to be acquired for the 'proper planning' of the area. How can a court be a better judge than the local planning authority themselves as to what is 'proper planning'?[6]

3. The Application of the Power

Having power to acquire, and it must be a power to acquire land compulsorily,[7] the authority must, if it proposes to use that power, first make a compulsory purchase order. This part of the process is governed by the Acquisition of Land (Authorisation Procedure) Act 1946, which, with one solitary exception,[8] applies to all compulsory acquisitions by public authorities.[9] The order (and notices required to be served by the Act) must be drafted substantially in the form specified in regulations.[10] The order must be duly sealed by the authority, and notification of the making of the order must be served on the owners of interests in the land to be acquired, scheduled to the order.[11] Notice of the making of the order must also be duly advertised locally and an opportunity given for objections to be sent to the confirming Minister (usually[12] the Secretary of State) within a time stated in the notice, not less than 28 days. The order itself must be available in the offices of the acquiring authority for public inspection free of charge.

If any objections are lodged with the confirming Minister, and these are not withdrawn, and do not relate exclusively to the question of compensation, the Minister will convene a public inquiry before a person appointed by him. Procedure at the inquiry is governed by regulations,[13] and will be very similar to that at an inquiry into a planning appeal,[14] except that the acquiring authority's representatives will speak first and consequently have the right to make a final reply.

After conclusion of the inquiry the inspector will report to the Secretary of State or other confirming Minister, who must consider[15] the inspector's report, and decide whether or not to confirm the compulsory purchase order, with or without any modifications. The Minister's decision must be advertised and an appropriate notice must be sent to all the owners concerned; if he confirms the order, it will come into effect on the expiration of six weeks from the date of the first publication of the advertisement.[16] However, within that six weeks, and no later,[17] any person aggrieved may apply to the High Court for an order to quash the compulsory purchase order or to suspend its operation temporarily on the ground that

(a) the order was not within the powers of the enabling Act conferring powers on the acquiring authority; *or*
(b) that there has been some error of procedure[18] whereby the applicant has been substantially prejudiced.[19]

Such an application will in any event delay the coming into operation of the compulsory purchase order until such time as the application has been finally determined by the High Court and any subsequent appeal to the higher courts disposed of.

4. The Acquisition of Interests

The above stage in the process is as far as the Act of 1946 goes; from this point the acquiring authority must for the most part use the Compulsory Purchase Act 1965, and this statute also applies to all cases of compulsory purchase (in this case without any exception). Within a period of three years from the coming into operation of the

compulsory purchase order, the acquiring authority must serve on all
the owners in fee simple or holding a tenancy greater than one from
year to year, of the land to be acquired, a 'notice to treat'.[20] This notice
will require the recipients to 'treat', or negotiate with the authority for
the acquisition of their interests in the land.

Persons served with a notice to treat should respond with a formal
claim for compensation, stating the nature of their interest in the land,
and saying how much compensation they want. Naturally, the sum is
not always agreed forthwith, and there may be protracted negotiations
over the amount of compensation; if those negotiations break down,
either the acquiring authority or the claimant may refer the claim to the
Land Tribunal[21] for determination. Under the law of compulsory
purchase as it was formulated in the canal and railway age of Victorian
times,[22] the usual practice was for no further steps to be taken until the
amount of compensation had been settled. Once this had been done,
the matter became a normal conveyancing transaction, the acquiring
authority paying over the agreed compensation in return for the deeds
transferring the legal interests to them, and the authority were then
entitled to take possession of the land.

Today, however, this is rarely followed completely, and there are
several variants on the procedure, in the interests of speeding up the
acquisition. Thus,

(i) At any time after service of the notice to treat, the acquiring
authority may serve a notice of their intention to enter on the property
on a specified date, not less than 14 days after the date of service.[23] The
authority, after expiry of that period, may then enter on the land, but
will be liable to pay a high prescribed rate of interest[24] on the
compensation, when this is eventually paid, as from that date of entry.
(ii) Under the Act of 1968,[25] if the compulsory purchase order
included a notice of the acquiring authority's intention to use the
procedure, the authority may, not less than two months after the date
on which the compulsory purchase order comes into operation as
above described, pass by way of resolution a 'general vesting
declaration' (GVD). This will have the effect of vesting automatically
in the acquiring authority, on a date specified in the GVD, *all* the
interests of all other persons in the land to be acquired under the
compulsory purchase order, without any deeds of transfer. The former
owners of the interests so transferred are left to pursue their claims for
compensation, which can be settled without holding up the acquiring
authority in their desire to use their newly acquired land.[26]

(iii) Even under the old law of 1845,[27] provision was made for dealing with the obdurate landowner who refuses to co-operate in any way with the acquiring authority, and the procedure has been continued in the Act of 1965. If a landowner refuses to agree or even to claim the compensation, refuses to execute a deed of transfer, and finally fails to surrender possession of his land, the acquiring authority may pay into the High Court such sum by way of compensation as may have been determined on an *ex parte* application to the Lands Tribunal, and they may then execute a deed poll[28] vesting the obdurate owner's interest in themselves.[29] If the owner still refuses to surrender possession of the land, the acquiring authority may obtain a warrant from the court, and with the assistance of a court bailiff (and such police officers as may be necessary) make forceable entry on the land, eject the owner and take possession. In such a case the owner will be left to make out a claim to the satisfaction of the court that he is the person entitled, and then the compensation money in court will be paid out to him.

(iv) Sometimes the delay, or reluctance to proceed with the acquisition, may be on the part of the acquiring authority. Delay in the service of a notice to treat after the compulsory purchase order has been confirmed cannot be too long, as such a notice must be served within three years,[30] and once land has been made the subject of an order, it may be possible to serve a blight notice.[31] However, there may be further delay, even after service of the notice to treat. Once the amount of the compensation has been agreed or determined, the parties are in the position of a purchaser and vendor under a binding contract for sale, and the owner will be able to obtain a decree of specific performance against the acquiring authority.[32] Alternatively he may be able to treat the proposal to acquire his land as having been abandoned, and obtain a declaration from the court to that effect.[33] In a case where abandonment has been established, the acquiring authority would have to start again and make a fresh order (leading to the possibility of a new public inquiry) if it eventually proposed to proceed with the acquisition.

5. Special Property

If the land that is to be acquired has been reserved as an open space, is part of a common, or belongs to a local authority, to the National Trust or to a statutory undertakers, an additional step in the acquisition procedure has to be followed. After the coming into operation of the compulsory purchase order, but before any notice to treat has been served, the order has to be further confirmed by resolution of both Houses of Parliament under the Statutory Orders (Special Procedure) Acts 1945 and 1965. The order will be referred to a joint committee of both Houses, and an opportunity will be given for a hearing of objectors. If the order is not then confirmed, it ceases to have any effect (Acquisition of Land (Authorisation Procedure) Act 1946, 1st Schedule, Part III).

6. Determination of the Compensation

On receipt of a compensation claim from the owner of an interest in land to be acquired, the acquiring authority will normally open negotiations with the object of reaching agreement as to the amount of the compensation. If the acquiring authority is a local authority the negotiations on their side will normally be conducted by the District Valuer (an officer of the Board of Inland Revenue). This is because the authority will in most cases need to raise a loan for the project of which the land acquisition forms part, and the Secretary of State will not give his sanction to the raising of the loan unless the District Valuer has certified that the amount of the compensation proposed to be paid is reasonable.

If agreement cannot be reached between the parties (and failure to reach a settlement is in practice comparatively rare), either party can refer the matter for determination by the Lands Tribunal. This is a special administrative tribunal established by the Lands Tribunal Act 1949, staffed by a lawyer chairman and a number of full-time members having professional qualifications, as surveyors, planners, etc. Proceedings before the Tribunal, which is based in London but which holds sittings in the provinces as may be convenient, are similar to those before a court, and an appeal lies from a decision of the Tribunal direct to the Court of Appeal, on a question of law or of valuation. There is then a further right of appeal (by leave of the Court or of the Lords) to the House of Lords.

The Tribunal has jurisdiction to order interest to be paid on the compensation, and the assessment of the compensation, based on a valuation of the land to be acquired, will be made usually as at the date of notice to treat, or as at the date when the acquiring authority actually took possession of the land, whichever is the *later;*[34] a very important point in times of inflation. Fees are payable on a hearing before the tribunal.

7. Assessment of Compensation: the Six Rules

Compensation is assessed primarily in accordance with six rules set out in section 5 of the Land Compensation Act 1961, but as will appear, there are also a number of subsidiary rules to be taken into account. These six rules are as follows:

Rule 1

No allowance is to be made for the fact that the acquisition is made contrary to the wishes of the owners; there is to be no *solatium* to smooth the ruffled feelings of the owner. This rule, first formulated in 1919[35] makes it clear that the practice of nineteenth-century courts to add a 10 per cent 'sweetener', is no longer to be followed. However, the Land Compensation Act 1973 (the 'Act of 1973') has made two exceptions to the rule, the 'home loss payment', and the 'farm loss payment'. The owner who is losing the dwelling that has been his sole or principal residence for at least five years, can claim a sum in addition to any compensation otherwise due, equivalent to three times the current rateable value of the dwelling, being a sum not less than £150 nor more than £1500.[36] Similarly, if an occupier is displaced from an agricultural unit in which he has a freehold interest or a tenancy of which at least three years are unexpired, he will be entitled, in addition to any other compensation, to a farm-loss payment equivalent to one year's profits on the farm, averaged over the previous three years.[37]

Rule 2

Compensation is to be based on the assumption that the acquisition was as between a willing vendor and a willing purchaser; in other words, the interest[38] to be acquired is to be assumed to have changed hands at 'market value'.

This means that every potential purchaser must be taken into account; if there is a neighbour (for example) who would have been particularly anxious to buy the property, the fact that he would have been prepared to pay more than other purchasers, will increase the amount of the compensation accordingly.

As Swinfen Eady, LJ, said in *R* v. *Clay*,[39]

A value ascertained by reference to the amount obtainable in an open market shows an intention to include every purchaser. The market is to be the open market as distinguished from an offer to a limited class only, such as the members of the family. The market is not necessarily an auction sale. The section [corresponding to Rule 2] means such amount as the land might be expected to realise if offered under conditions enabling every person desirous of purchasing to come in and make an offer, and if proper steps were taken to advertise the property and let all likely purchasers know that the land is in the market for sale.

Nevertheless, 'market value' does not mean that the vendor is entitled to make a profit out of the transaction. When land was acquired compulsorily from a builder, he claimed compensation, not only in respect of the value of the land, but also for the profit that he would have gained had he been able to build houses on that land and sell them to purchasers. The court would not allow him compensation for the profit; he was being paid for the land, and he could use that sum to buy more land and make his profit by building on the new land.[40] In another case, land was acquired from a farmer. He claimed compensation in respect of the loss of his farm as a going concern, and also in respect of the value of gravel, sand and lime in the subsoil under the farm. The latter claim was disallowed, for the gravel, etc, could not have been extracted if the farmer had continued to operate the farm.[41]

Rule 3

The special suitability or adaptability of the land to be acquired for the purpose of the acquisition is not to be taken into account by way of increasing the compensation if the purpose is one which can be realised only by an authority possessing special statutory powers, or for which there would be no market. This is a difficult rule to apply in practice, but it may be explained by saying that the 'vendor' is not to get inflated compensation just because his land is peculiarly attractive to the acquiring authority, when it would not be readily saleable to ordinary purchasers.

Therefore an owner of land on the outskirts of a town being expanded under the Town Development Act 1952, was not entitled to compensation on the basis of an increase in the value of his land caused by the very scheme of development for which his land was being acquired.[42] Nevertheless, the use or 'purpose' in Rule 3 refers to the land itself, and not to some special characteristic of the *interest* being acquired in that land; a sitting tenant is likely to pay more for land being acquired from his landlord, and that consequent increase in the compensation is not to be excluded under Rule 3.[43] Nor is an additional value accruing by virtue of materials on the land which, by virtue of their location, are particularly attractive to the acquiring authority. This latter point is illustrated by the *Pointe Gourde case*[44] decided in 1947, where a harbour authority in Trinidad was asked to pay a higher rate of compensation because there were minerals on the land acquired, which were particularly useful for the construction of the harbour extensions to be built on the land acquired. This heading of compensation was eventually disallowed, because it was caused by the scheme itself; the existence of the attrctive minerals did not, however, justify excluding that further compensation was payable for the minerals themselves.

Rule 4

This rule is much simpler to apply; it merely provides that in assessing the compensation, any value accruing to the land, as a consequence of some illegal use, is to be disregarded. This would exclude value accruing from a use in breach of a restrictive convenant or a clause in a lease, a use which contravened planning control, or one which was for an illegal or immoral purpose, such as use as a brothel, or one which involved overcrowding of a dwelling.

Rule 5

If there is no market for the land and it is devoted to a special purpose, the Lands Tribunal (on application by the landowner) may agree that compensation should be assessed on the basis of the cost of equivalent reinstatement of the premises, provided the Tribunal is satisfied that there was (at the time of the acquisition) a genuine intention to continue the purpose to which the land was then devoted.

So, in order that the Lands Tribunal may exercise its discretion in favour of this very high rate of compensation, there must be:

(a) Devotion to a special purpose, as in the case[45] where a non-conformist chapel in the East End of London was acquired soon after the end of the Second World War. During the war, as most of the congregation had moved away due to enemy action, the church was used for the storage of organ parts, but a room was still used for meetings of the church trustees. It was held that the premises were devoted to use as a church, *and* there was evidence that

(b) the trustees intended to build a new church which would be used by the same congregation.

Therefore compensation on an equivalent reinstatement basis was granted. However, when a private railway company lost a section of their line, but intended to continue operations on a new route at a cost of £150,000, the Lands Tribunal exercised their discretion to refuse to allow equivalent reinstatement, as the Tribunal considered the cost was out of all proportion to the value of the land acquired[46] (in spite of losing their case the Festiniogg Railway are still operating!). Compensation on this basis is essentially discretionary.

Rule 6

These rules take effect without prejudice to the law on severance and disturbance.

These two elements, which are not separate items of compensation, but are to be taken into account when assessing the total sum due,[47] have been developed by the courts. *Severence* is concerned with the case where part only of a claimant's land is taken; his compensation is then to be increased by any depreciation in the value of the land he retains as a consequence of that severance.[48] *Disturbance* includes any expense caused to the claimant as a consequence of the acquisition. Consequently, when Mrs Harvey's house was acquired by the Crawley New Town Development Corporation, the compensation was based on the value of the house to *her,* which meant that in addition to the actual value she could add in her claim, the surveyor's and solicitor's costs of finding and buying a new home, her necessary travel, and the cost of altering her curtains and carpets to fit the new house. She was not, however, entitled to a further £2,000, representing the higher price that she had to pay for her new house in excess of the value of the old house. That £2,000 was still in effect held by her; she had not lost that sum, because it could be realised by a sale of the new house.[49]

8. Assessment of Compensation: the Assumptions

These six rules (and Rule 2 in particular) must be applied to the particular interest to be acquired. This refers not only to the legal status of the interest — be it a fee simple or a long or short-term tenancy — but also to its planning status. The interest may be valued according to the existing use to which it may lawfully be put in accordance with current planning law.

However, in ascertaining what is the existing use in this sense, the claimant for compensation is entitled to choose the benefit of several 'planning assumptions' set out in the 1961 Act, and to select the one that suits him best and gives him the most compensation, provided this is justified under the Act.

These assumptions are:

(a) it is to be assumed in assessing the value that development may lawfully be carried out if authorised by the GDO, or any special development order that is relevant, and also any existing planning permission may be taken into account, whether or not that development has been actually carried out;

(b) it is to be presumed that planning permission would be given for any development contemplated in an operative development plan;

(c) it is also to be presumed that planning permission would be granted for any development necessary for the acquiring authority to enable them to achieve the purpose of the land acquisition in question;

(d) it may also be presumed that planning permission would be given for any development covered by a 'certificate of appropriate alternative development'. Such a certificate may be the subject of an application to the local planning authority, and the procedure will be similar to that governing an application for planning permission, including a right of appeal to the Secretary of State.[50] On such an application the authority must make the philosophically difficult decision as to whether, if the land were not being acquired (perhaps by themselves) for a specified purpose, the land would be suitable for some alternative type of development. Thus, if a 100-acre field (for example) that is being acquired for a school, were not to be acquired for education purposes, would it be suitable for residential purposes? If the answer is in the affirmative, a certificate must be given. The claimant for compensation would then have the choice of claiming compensation on the basis of educational purposes (under paragraph (b) or (c) above, as the case may be) or on the basis of residential purposes, whichever would give him the larger sum.

9. Assessment of Compensation: Land Not Taken

There is also the question of injurious affection as the consequence of the acquisition of land, caused to the value of some other land that is *not* being taken by the acquiring authority. Compensation for this special kind of 'worsenment' is payable in limited circumstances, as provided for in section 68 of the Lands Clauses Consolidation Act 1845, preserved in modern law by section 10(2) of the Compulsory Purchase Act 1965.

Compensation is payable for any depreciation in value that can be proved, subject to the following rules that have been worked out by the courts:

(i) the damage or loss must have been actionable at common law had there not been the defence in such proceedings that the acquiring authority were acting under statutory authority. In other words, there must have been some infringement of a property right that had caused the depreciation in value, such as an interference with an easement, or some act that would have amounted to an actionable nuisance;[51]

(ii) if the injury results from some improper use of the statutory power, such as negligence, the remedy is not for compensation, but by way of a common law action for damages, for the acquiring authority cannot plead a statutory power to act unlawfully or negligently (in the absence of express words to that effect);[52]

(iii) the injury or loss must result from the actual acquisition, not from the use made of the property when so acquired. Injury caused by the construction works is compensatable, but not (for example) injury caused by vibrations from traffic using the railway or motorway when constructed;[53]

(iv) the injury or loss must be caused to the property or land of the claimant, and not to the business carried out there.[54]

It will be appreciated from these four principles that compensation for injurious affection to land that is not itself the subject of a compulsory acquisition is not easy to establish.

10. Compensation — a Summary

We have been able here only to state the basic principles of a very complex branch of the law, and it may clarify matters somewhat if we give a summary of the principal matters to be taken into account when formulating a compensation claim, whether this be in a case of compulsory acquisition, or whether the claim is made out in respect of planning restrictions.[55]

The land in respect of which the claim is being submitted must be assessed for the purposes of valuation:

(i) on the basis of the most favourable of the planning assumptions;
(ii) the nature of the claimant's legal interest in the land must be established;
(iii) this planning status and legal interest must then be assessed in accordance with the six rules of section 5 of the 1961 Act, including (if appropriate) allowances for severance and disturbance;
(iv) this must be done as at the correct *date,* namely, the date when notice to treat was served, or when the authority actually took possession;
(v) the claimant will also be entitled to his proper legal and other professional costs and, if the matter is determined by the Lands Tribunal, the Tribunal may award him interest on the capital sum;
(vi) the claimant may also be entitled to a home-loss or farm-loss payment, and, if he has lost his home, to be provided with suitable alternative accommodation by the local authority;[56]
(vii) in the special case where the premises acquired is a house that is unfit for human habitation, the claimant will be entitled to compensation based on site value only;[57]
(viii) if the authority have taken possession before the amount of the compensation has been determined, the claimant may be entitled to payment of a limited amount in advance,[58] and to interest on the compensation money at a special rate.

Notes

1. Cf. the 'taking issue' in (for example) the United States; Chapter 17, p.193.
2. See, for example, *Sisters of Charity* v. *The King* [1922] AC 315.
3. Chapter 17, p.198.
4. *Sydney Corporation* v. *Campbell* [1925] AC 338. The Privy Council is a special court, consisting principally of the Lords of Appeal in Ordinary and therefore having virtually the status of the House of Lords, which hears appeals from the higher courts in the British Commonwealth. Many Commonwealth countries have now abolished this right of appeal, by their own statutes passed this century.
5. *Hanks* v. *Minister of Housing and Local Government* [1963] 1 All ER 47.
6. 1971 Act, section 112(1) (b), as amended.
7. And not only by agreement, as in the Housing Act 1957, section 96 (powers to buy houses, as distinct from open land).
8. Part III of the Housing Act 1957, providing for slum clearance; the procedure

there laid down is almost identical with that under the 1946 Act, but different forms must be used.

9. Whether those authorities are district or county councils, new town or urban development corporations, gas or electricity boards, etc., or government departments. In the text the procedure is explained in the context of a local authority making the order; *mutatis mutandis,* a similar procedure applies to other public bodies, except that a Minister has to confirm (or otherwise) his own order.

10. Compulsory Purchase of Land Regulations 1976 (SI 1976 No. 307).

11. One of the first administrative tasks that has to be undertaken on behalf of the acquiring authority is to prepare a terrier, or schedule of all the interests in land that will need to be acquired for the proposed scheme.

12. Particularly where the acquiring authority is a local authority or development corporation.

13. Compulsory Purchase by Public Authorities (Inquiries Procedure) Rules 1976 (SI 1976 No. 746).

14. Chapter 13, p.144.

15. *Nelsovill* v. *Minister of Housing and Local Government* [1962] 1 All ER 423; he may not 'rubber stamp' the report, but must give his mind to the decision.

16. 1946 Act, First Schedule, para. 15.

17. *Smith* v. *East Elloe RDC* [1956] 1 All ER 855, confirmed in *R* v. *Secretary of State, ex parte Ostler* [1976] 3 All ER 90, in spite of *Anisminic* v. *Foreign Compensation Commission* [1969] 2 AC 147.

18. Either by failing to comply with the regulations (or the Acts) or because there has been some breach of the rules of natural justice, perhaps because the inspector in his report has taken into account some factor that was not open for comment at the inquiry: *Fairmont Investments Ltd* v. *Secretary of State* [1976] 2 All ER 865.

19. Act of 1946, First Schedule, para. 16.

20. Compulsory Purchase Act 1965, section 5.

21. See below, para. 5.

22. The law was then contained in the Lands Clauses Consolidation Act 1845, which even now has not been completely replaced by the Act of 1965 (see the comment on 'injurious affection', para. 9, below).

23. Acquisition of Land (Authorisation Procedure) Act 1946, section 11(1).

24. Ibid. The rate varies from time to time, but is always in excess of bank rate.

25. Town and Country Planning Act 1968, Schedule 3 (not repealed by the Act of 1971).

26. This procedure obviates a great deal of administrative work in ascertaining exactly who owns what interests in the land concerned.

27. Lands Clauses Consolidation Act 1845, sections 76-78.

28. I.e. a deed executed by a single party.

29. Act of 1965, section 9(3).

30. Ibid., section 4.

31. Chapter 17, p.197.

32. *Cardiff Corpn* v. *Cook* [1923] 2 Ch 115.

33. *Grice* v. *Dudley Corpn* [1958] 1 Ch 329.

34. *Birmingham Corpn* v. *West Midlands Baptist Assn* [1969] 3 All ER 172.

35. Acquisition of Land (Assessment of Compensation) Act 1919, replaced by the 1961 Act.

36. Land Compensation Act 1973, sections 29 and 30, as amended by section 114 of the Act of 1980.

37. Ibid., sections 34 and 35.

38. But note what is the nature of the interest: see below, para. 8.

39. [1914] 3 KB 466; the actual decision in this case has since been modified by Rule 3, below.

40. *Collins* v. *Feltham UDC* [1937] 4 All ER 189.
41. *Horn* v. *Sunderland Corpn* [1941] 1 All ER 480.
42. *Viscount Camrose* v. *Basingstoke Corpn* [1966] 3 All ER 161; and see section 6 of the 1961 Act.
43. *Lambe* v. *Secretary of State for War* [1955] 2 QB 612, and *Rugby Water Board* v. *Foottit* [1972] 1 All ER 1057.
44. *Pointe Gourde Transport Co Ltd* v. *Sub-Intendent of Crown Lands* [1947] AC 565.
45. *Aston Charities Trust* v. *Stepney Corpn* [1952] 2 QB 642.
46. *Festiniogg Railway Co* v. *Central Electricity Generating Board* (1962) 60 LGR 167.
47. *Horn* v. *Sunderland Corpn,* note 41 above.
48. Perhaps a motorway has been cut through farm land, separating some of the pasture land from the farm. Unless the authority provide the farmer with an underpass or bridge over the motorway, he will have a substantial severance claim. Such a claim is not confined to the depreciation in value caused by the use made of the land actually taken but includes harm caused by the scheme: 1973 Act, section 44, reversing the effect of *Edwards* v. *Minister of Transport* [1964] 2 QB 134.
49. *Harvey* v. *Crawley New Town Development Corpn* [1957] 1 QB 485.
50. 1961 Act, section 17.
51. Consequently, where a railway was constructed that cut across the main road (but not the only access) to the 'Pickled Egg' Public House, as the proprietor was not entitled to a right of way, he had not lost any property right and could not claim compensation: *Rickett* v. *Metropolitan Rlwy Co* (1867) LR 2 HL 175.
52. *Metropolitan Asylums Board* v. *Hill* (1881) 6 App Cas 193.
53. *Hammersmsith Rlwy Co* v. *Brand* (1869) LR 4 HL 171. This rule is now subject to the right to claim compensation caused by physical factors, under the Land Compensation Act 1973 (Chapter 18, para. 7), *ante,* p.206.
54. This is another ground for the decision in *Rickett's case* (note 51 above). See also *Joliffe* v. *Exeter Corpn* [1967] 2 All ER 109.
55. Chapter 17, p.198.
56. Only if the claimant does not have any other accommodation available: 1973 Act, section 39.
57. Housing Act 1957, Second Schedule, but the principle is subject to exceptions in favour of an owner-occupier.
58. Land Compensation Act 1973, section 53.

Appendix I

Some Definitions

'Advertisement'

This is defined in section 290(1) of the Act of 1971 in very wide terms to *mean* [not 'include'] 'any word, letter, model, sign, placard, board, notice, device or representation, whether illuminated or not, in the nature of, and employed wholly or in part for the purpose of advertisement, announcement or direction and (without prejudice to the preceding provisions of this definition) includes any hoarding or similar structure used, or adapted for use, for the display of advertisements', but in the Town and Country Planning (Control of Advertisements) Regulations 1969, while repeating this definition, there is an express exclusion therefrom of 'any such thing employed wholly as a memorial or as a railway signal'.

'Amenity'

This is not defined in any legislation, but it was long ago explained by Scrutton LJ (a very eminent authority in his time), as 'pleasant circumstances, features, advantages'; see *re Ellis and Ruislip and Northwood UDC* [1920] 1 KB 34.

'Cause or permit'

Causing involves some direct action by the offender; permitting means that he must know all the circumstances, and yet he refrains from taking any action to prevent the matter (e.g. the felling of a tree subject to a tree preservation order) complained of.

'Common Law'

This means the law developed by the courts over the ages by the doctrine of precedent, and is used in contrast to statute law *(q.v.)*.

'County matter'

This was a matter of planning policy declared by the appropriate county council to be a matter of concern to them and so a county matter, or one which the district council recognises as such; if a county matter is involved in an application for planning permission, the district council will forward it, with their observations to the county council for a decision. Since 1980 these matters are confined in practice to matters concerning minerals and the disposal of waste material 1980 Act, s.86 and SI, 1980, No. 2010.

'Development'

This key word is defined in section 22(1) of the 1971 Act, to *mean,* 'the carrying out of building, engineering, mining or other operations in, on, over or under land, or the making of any material change in the use of any building or other land'. This definition is qualified by the extensions and exceptions provided for in the remainder of section 22; for further comment, see Chapter 8, page 101. 'New development' is specially defined in section 22(5) and Schedule 8, but this is of consequence only in connection with the circumstances in which compensation may be claimed under that Schedule (as to which, see Chapter 17, page 199).

'Easement'

This is a property right recognised by the common law, whereby the owner of the freehold in property A can, for the benefit of such property, exercise a specified right (such as a right of way or a right to run water through a pipe or drain) over property B. This right is then exercisable by any subsequent owner of A against any subsequent owner of B. (See Chapter 3, page 36).

'Fee Simple'; 'Freehold'

These two expressions are synonymous, as indicating the most considerable estate in land known to English law, being of uncertain, and possibly infinite duration. It will last for as long as the holder or 'tenant' of the fee for the time being has heirs or descendants.

'Functions'

Generally in a statute law context (see 1971 Act, section 290(1)); this includes powers and duties.

'Highway'

This is a way over which all of Her Majesty's subjects have a right at common law to pass and re-pass on their lawful occasions. A highway may be a footpath, a bridleway or a carriageway, and the rights of pedestrians have been excluded by statute in the case of a 'special road' or motorway.

'Land'

This is defined by the Interpretation Act 1978, to include 'buildings and other structures, land covered with water, and any estate, interest, easement, servitude or right in or over land'.

'Leasehold'

This is a limited property-interest in land, limited, that is, in point of time to a precise period of years (or less). It is granted by a landlord having a greater interest, perhaps a freehold or a longer leasehold, than the interest he is granting.

'Listed Building'

This is a building of special architectural or historic interest included in a list made or approved by the Secretary of State under section 54 of the 1971 Act.

'Local Planning Authority'

This is the district council in all cases of development control and enforcement, unless a 'county matter' is concerned (see above). The county council are the planning authority for the preparation of the structure plan, but the district council is responsible for the local plans.

'Material Considerations'

These are matters that must be taken into account when the planning authorities are considering an application for planning permission, or whether to serve an enforcement notice, or take certain other action under the 1971 Act, such as to revoke or modify an existing planning permission. See Chapter 11, page 129.

'Operations'

These are contrasted with 'material change of use' in the definition of development in section 22(1) of the 1971 Act. 'Building operations' and 'engineering operations' are defined below; 'other operations' apparently refers to any operations of a planning nature: see the *Coleshill case,* Chapter 8, page 97. 'Building operations' is defined in section 290(1) as including 'rebuilding operations, structural alterations of or additions to buildings, and other operations normally undertaken by a person carrying on business as a builder', while 'engineering operations' is defined in the same subsection to include, 'the formation or laying out of means of access to highways'. For the purposes of a stop notice (q.v.) 'activities' probably includes both 'operations' *and* 'changes of use'.

'Owner'

This is defined in section 290(1) of the 1971 Act to mean, in relation to any land, 'a person, other than a mortgagee not in possession, who, whether in his own right or as trustee for any other person, is entitled to receive the rack rent of the land, or where the land is not let at a rack rent, would be so entitled if it were so let'. Rack rent is not itself defined, but it commonly means the rent of not less than two-thirds of the rent at which the property could reasonably be expected to be let from year to year. In sections 27 and 29 of the 1971 Act, 'owner' has a special meaning so as to include a freeholder and any person holding under a lease of which the unexpired term is not less than seven years.

'Statute'

This is an Act of Parliament, which may overrule or amend the common law, or may amend or repeal an existing statute, but is itself subject to interpretation by the courts in accordance with the ordinary rules of statutory interpretation. 'Subordinate' or 'delegated' legislation (rules, orders, regulations) made by Ministers of the Crown under statutory authority may be regarded as part of statute law, as may regulations (but *not* directives) of the European Community, by virtue of the European Communities Act 1972.

'Stop Notice'

This is a notice issued under s.90 of the 1971 Act supplementary to an enforcement notice (see p.187).

WARNING

The statutory definitions apply in particular context only in so far as the contrary intention is not expressed in the statute or may be inferred by the court when determining a particular issue.

Key to a Few Sections of the 1971 Act

Item	Principal Section of 1971 Act
Advertisements, control of	63
Blight notices	193
Certificate of established use	94
Completion notice	44
Conservation areas	277, 277A
Default powers, of Secretary of State	276
Development, meaning of	22
Enforcement notice	87, 88
Information notice	284
Inquiry Commission	47
Listed buildings	54-56
Non-conforming uses	45, 51
Trees, conservation of	59, 60
Service of notices	283
Stop notices	90
Waste land, control of	65

Appendix II

A Select Bibliograpy

Reference

Heap, Sir Desmond (ed.) *The Encyclopaedia of Planning Law and Practice,* 4 volumes loose-leaf with periodic supplements, (Sweet & Maxwell Ltd, London)
J.F. Garner (ed.) *The Control of Pollution Encyclopaedia,* loose-leaf with periodic supplements, (Butterworths, London)

Case Books

[Reproducing verbatim a selection of leading cases and sections of relevant statutes]
McAuslan, Patrick, *Law, Land and Planning,* (Weidenfeld & Nicolson, London, 1975)
Purdue, M, *Cases and Materials in Planning Law,* (Sweet & Maxwell, London, 1977)

Textbooks

Hamilton, R.N.D., *A Guide to Development and Planning,* 6th edn. (Oyez, London, 1975)
Heap, Sir Desmond, *An Outline of Planning Law,* 7th edn. (Sweet & Maxwell, London, 1978)
Telling, A.E., *Planning Law and Practice* 5th edn. (Butterworths, London, 1977)

American and Australian Books

Babcock, R.F., *The Zoning Game,* (University of Wisconsin Press, 1969)
Bosselman, F., *et al. The Taking Issue,* (Council of Environmental Quality, Washington, D.C., 1973)
Fogg, A.C., *Australian Town Planning Law,* (University of Queensland Press, 1974)
Reilly, W.K. (ed.), *The Use of Land,* (Thos. Y. Crowell Co., N.Y., 1973)

Miscellaneous

Garner, J.F. (ed.) *Compensation for Compulsory Purchase, A Comparative Study,* (UK National Committee of Comparative Law, 1975)

Garner, J.F. (ed.) *Planning Law in Western Europe,* (North Holland, Amsterdam, 1975)

McAuslan, Patrick, *The Ideologies of Planning Law,* (Pergamon Press, Oxford, 1980)

Roberts, N.A., *The Reform of Planning Law,* (Macmillan, London, 1976)

Periodicals

The Journal of Planning and Environment Law, monthly, (Sweet & Maxwell, London)

The Urban Lawyer, quarterly, (Local Government Section of the American Bar Association, Washington, D.C.)

The Town Planning Review, quarterly, (The University of Liverpool)

Index

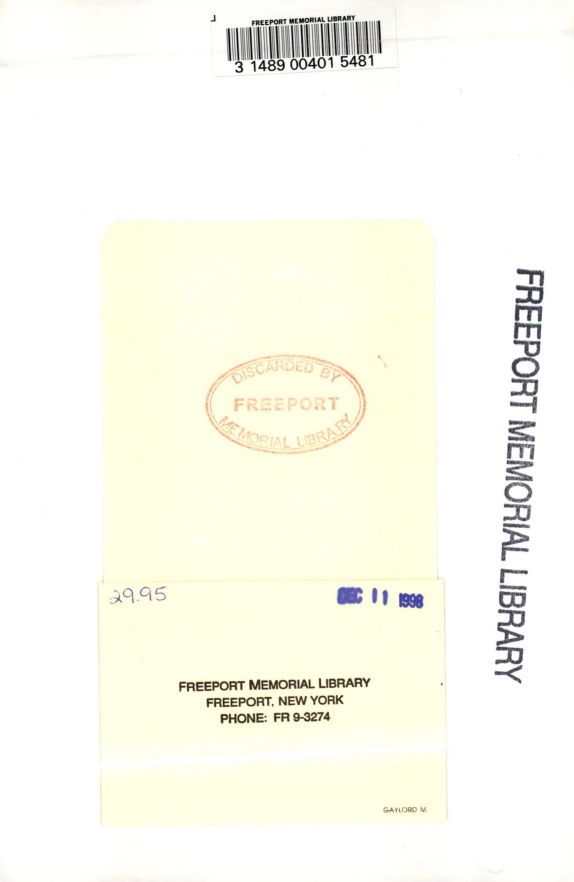